SCHOOL LIBRARY MEDIA SERIES
Edited by Diane de Cordova Biesel

1. *Chalk Talk Stories*, written and illustrated by Arden Druce, 1993.
2. *Toddler Storytime Programs*, by Diane Briggs, 1993.
3. *Alphabet: A Handbook of ABC Books and Book Extensions for the Elementary Classroom,* 2nd ed., by Patricia L. Roberts, 1994.
4. *Cultural Cobblestones: Teaching Cultural Diversity*, by Lynda Miller, Theresa Steinlage, and Mike Printz, 1994.
5. *ABC Books and Activities: From Preschool to High School*, by Cathie Hilterbran Cooper, 1996.
6. *Zoolutions: A Mathematical Expedition with Topics for Grades 4 through 8*, by Anne Burgunder and Vaunda Nelson, 1996.
7. *Library Lessons for Grades 7–9,* by Arden Druce, 1997.
8. *Counting Your Way through 1–2–3 Books and Activities,* by Cathie Hilterbran Cooper, 1997.
9. *Art and Children: Using Literature to Expand Creativity,* by Robin W. Davis, 1996.
10. *Story Programs: A Source Book of Materials,* 2nd ed., by Carolyn Sue Peterson and Ann Fenton, 2000.
11. *Taking Humor Seriously in Children's Literature: Literature-Based Mini-Units and Humorous Books for Children Ages 5–12,* by Patricia L. Roberts, 1997.
12. *Multicultural Friendship Stories and Activities for Children, Ages 5–14,* by Patricia L. Roberts, 1997.
13. *Side by Side: Twelve Multicultural Puppet Plays,* by Jean M. Pollock, 1997.
14. *Reading Fun: Quick and Easy Activities for the School Library Media Center,* by Mona Kerby, 1997.
15. *Paper Bag Puppets,* by Arden Druce with illustrations by Geraldine Hulbert, Cynthia Johnson, Harvey H. Lively, and Carol Ditter Waters, 1999.
16. *Once upon a Childhood: Fingerplays, Action Rhymes, and Fun Times for the Very Young,* by Dolores C. Chupela, 1998.
17. *Bulletin Bored? or Bulletin Boards!: K–12,* by Patricia Sivak and Mary Anne Passatore, 1998.
18. *Color and Shape Books for All Ages,* by Cathie Hilterbran Cooper, 1998.
19. *Big Books for Little Readers,* by Robin W. Davis, 1999.
20. *Family Values Through Children's Literature, Grades K-3,* by Patricia L. Roberts, 2000.

Story Programs

A Source Book of Materials,
Second Edition

Carolyn Sue Peterson
and Ann D. Fenton

Revised and Edited by
Stefani Koorey

School Library Media Series, No. 10

The Scarecrow Press, Inc.
Lanham, Maryland, and London
2000

SCARECROW PRESS, INC.

Published in the United States of America
by Scarecrow Press, Inc.
4720 Boston Way, Lanham, Maryland 20706
http://www.scarecrowpress.com

4 Pleydell Gardens, Folkestone
Kent CT20 2DN, England

British Library Cataloguing in Publication Information Available

Library of Congress Cataloging-in-Publication Data

Peterson, Carolyn Sue, 1930–
    Story programs : a source book of school materials / Carolyn Sue Peterson
and Ann D. Fenton ; revised and edited by Stefani Koorey. —2nd ed.
        p.   cm. —(School library media series ; 10)
    Includes bibliographical references and index.
    ISBN 0-8108-3207-0 (pbk. : alk. paper)
    1. Storytelling. 2. Activity programs in education. I. Fenton, Ann D.
II. Koorey, Stefani, 1959– . III. Title. IV. School library media series ;
no. 10.

LB 1042.P47 2000
372.67'7—dc21
                                                    99–058989

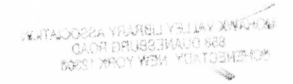

*This book is dedicated to the staff of the
Children's Library at the Orange County Library System,
without whom this revision could not have
been conceived or attempted:*

*Marlene Gawron, Sally Hardy,
Margaret Wells, Dana Oscarson,
Margaret Jennings, Charlie Hoeck,
Crystal Sullivan, Patti Aman, Richard Peeples,
Rosemary Breithaupt, and Ron Anselowitz.*

CONTENTS

INTRODUCTION

How to Use this Book

When *Story Programs: A Source Book of Materials* by Carolyn Sue Peterson and Brenny Hall was first published twenty years ago in 1980, most of the storytelling in this country was heard in public libraries and performed by children's librarians whose sole purpose in this endeavor was to gently lead children into books.

Since that time, storytelling has emerged as its own true art form, taught at both the Disney Institute in Orlando, Florida, for vacationing tourists and offered as a graduate degree at several major universities in the United States. Supported by both local and regional storytelling guilds and a national association, and celebrated at international, national, regional, and local festivals, storytelling has since become a lucrative full-time career for those many talented individuals who delight in the joy of entertaining and enlightening others through this ancient and important oral tradition.

Interestingly, what has not changed much in the past several decades is the fact that story programs continue to be the mainstay of public libraries and their children's departments—in many instances offered and presented in precisely the same manner as they had been decades ago. Literally generations of family members have been introduced to quality literature through library story programs. Patrons who first heard stories as children at their local library are now bringing their children, and their grandchildren, for similarly rewarding experiences.

As was true for their ancient counterparts, today's storytellers keep alive the rich literature of multicultural traditions. The modern storyteller serves yet another significant function in our society—that of foreshortening time itself. The act of listening to story transports its listeners to a time when the pace of life was slower and people gathered to hear the local wise person weave tales of beauty, humor, and wonder.

The root of modern society's deep-seated paranoia has been linked to the architectural changes of our homes and communities in the past fifty or so years—changes which have resulted in this unfortunate cultural distrust of strangers. Yet this was not always the case. Not too long ago, houses were designed with front porches. People sat out on them in the evenings, knew their neighbors by name, watched out for one another, believed they were part of the space in which they lived, and felt connected. People trusted one another more because *they knew their stories*—and in some smaller communities this is still true.

Story has proven to possess the magical power to heal and entertain as well as inspire and educate. Almost all human beings innately enjoy connecting with others once the offer is made through story. Storytelling works, then, to unite us all by literally bringing back the front porch.

The importance of continuing the tradition of presenting story programs to children in any story setting must not be devalued. Children, especially, benefit from hearing stories, from hearing the use and flow of words and the variety, quality, and flavor of language. These elements make tales come alive, entertaining both adults and children, while awakening and encouraging an interest in stories, books, and reading.

In *Story Programs: A Source Book of Materials, 2nd edition,* we have again attempted to provide you with a handbook of information designed to aid you in conducting story programs for young children. While created with the needs of public children's librarians in mind, this extensive work will also appeal to day care workers, public and private elementary school teachers, professional and amateur storytellers, parents interested in hands-on ideas for creating story fun in the home, and anyone in need of story ideas and copyright free patterns for personal use of flannel board stories and puppets. Moreover, in some instances, this guide will be helpful to anyone who is teaching the childcare giver to prepare for their most important work.

Unlike the first edition of *Story Programs,* which included story program sources and materials for toddlers, preschoolers, and primary level children only, this book contains programming sources and sample program materials developmentally suitable for *five* age groups: infants (ages birth to eighteen months), toddlers (ages eighteen to thirty-six months), preschoolers (ages three to five years), primary level children (ages six to eleven years), and families (all ages). This change reflects the ever-growing diversity of children's story programming in public libraries, school media centers, and professional storytelling venues.

By far, the most significant additions to the second edition are two sections that deal with the before and after aspects of story programming. The first section, entitled "Preparing for Your Story Program," includes information on planning a program, age appropriate material selection and child development, length and timing of story programs, indexing and record keeping techniques, tips on advertising your program, story program elements and variety, and information and ideas regarding the physical location of your program, including program set up and book displays.

The second additional section, "Appraisal and Problem Solving," offers guidelines on judging your programming success and information on program evaluation. To better prepare you for those unexpected moments, this section also includes a menu of choices for answering those tricky questions that you'll encounter during your story programs, as well as time-tested advice on dealing with crowd control issues.

Story Programs, 2nd ed., contains the text of complete story programs, including fingerplays, songs, flannel board stories with fully traceable patterns, puppet scripts with patterns accompanied by complete detailed instructions for making eleven different types of puppets, physical activities, creative dramatics, ideas for themed story programs, and an annotated listing of great picture books that work well in story programs. New to this edition is a detailed section on selecting, learning, and performing told stories without props. This chapter includes many tried and tested stories for both preschool and primary level children.

The book is arranged into six major parts—"Preparing for Your Story Program"; "Targeting Your Story Program"; "Storytelling / Storysharing"; "Participation Activities and Wigglebreaks"; "Appraisal and Problem Solving"; and "Story Program Sources." This approach will enable this all-encompassing tool to be useful not only to those who wish to gain access to particular sources, but to anyone searching for an easy-to-learn quality story program for *any age.*

Story Programs, 2nd ed., is a book designed for the modern teller of tales. Be they an amateur or professional storyteller, parent, children's librarian, childcare giver, educator, camp counselor, or home-schooler, this work will prove meaningful for anyone who is interested in bringing back that front porch.

PART ONE

PREPARING FOR YOUR STORY PROGRAM

CHAPTER ONE

Story Program Planning

Why have a story program? *Every* child needs to hear stories, and the story program offers a unique setting in which children can hear stories and share them and related experiences with others.

The story program can do all of the following:

- ✧ Stir a child's imagination
- ✧ Stimulate creative thinking
- ✧ Create life-long readers
- ✧ Help a child develop new interests
- ✧ Improve a child's self-concept
- ✧ Introduce story structure and a sense of cause and effect
- ✧ Arouse a child's curiosity about the world around them
- ✧ Help a child develop sensitivity to others
- ✧ Provide a child with an array of vicarious experiences
- ✧ Increase a child's vocabulary
- ✧ Help a child develop valuable listening skills
- ✧ Increase attention span
- ✧ Offer a child an escape from their everyday activities
- ✧ Introduce word sounds and patterns of language
- ✧ Help a child to associate the printed page with spoken words
- ✧ Expand a child's awareness of world cultures and traditions
- ✧ Extend the enjoyment of a sharing, social experience
- ✧ Provide literary experiences before a child can read on their own
- ✧ Provide a child practice in visualization
- ✧ Introduce word sounds and the rhythm of language
- ✧ Help a child to understand and express their own emotions
- ✧ Provide insight into human behavior
- ✧ Entertain, delight, and inspire
- ✧ Help build a child's confidence in his or her abilities

You, the storyteller, can provide children with all of these things, plus endow them with memorable opportunities for sharing intellectual and emotional experiences. By carefully planning the story program, by selecting and presenting the best in children's literature, and by choosing material appropriate for a specific age group, you can help children to not only explore new worlds but gain a better understanding of their own familiar environments.

A story program can take place almost anywhere—at a library, at a school, around the campfire, at a childcare center, at Sunday school, on a playground, or in a home. For some children, the story program may be their first introduction to stories. For others, it may be their first encounter with a group experience. For still others, it may be their first time to share stories with their peers. For all, it should be an occasion so special that it creates a level of eagerness and anticipation for the next storytime session.

In planning a story program, you ask yourself several questions. What are the ages of the children? How many children will be involved in the program? How much experience will they have had with literature or with listening activities such as a story program? How much involvement will they have had with other children or groups of children? What selections will the children relate to and understand? What selections might children that age enjoy? The content, format, and length of your program should reflect the answers to these questions.

Planning an Infant Program

If you are preparing a story program for infants (ages birth to eighteen months), often referred to as a "Mother Goose" or "Tiny Tales" program, you will want a very short session—no longer than fifteen minutes in length. These programs should be simple, repetitive, calming, and aimed toward introducing, or reintroducing as the case might be, nursery rhymes, songs, and infant literature (board books, lap-sit books, nursery rhyme books, lullaby books, etc.) to the parents of babies up to the age of a year and a half.

It is of the utmost importance that the parents or adult childcare givers in your program understand that they must participate with their infants, mirroring the storyteller with their actions and repeating each song and rhyme with their baby.

If you have the resources, provide a handout of some sort which includes the text of the rhymes and songs, along with suggestions for hand or body movements. In this way, the adults will have the opportunity to practice the program at home between visits, thereby, hopefully, improving the quality of the time they might spend in your program.

Planning a Toddler Program

Likewise, if you are preparing a story program for toddlers (ages eighteen to thirty-six months), you will want your session to be no longer than twenty minutes. These programs should be fast-paced, snappy, and packed with a wider variety of selections. Since these children are just now learning language, you will need to use many clear, realistic visuals. Study prints, pictures, flannel board pieces, and simple puppets are useful in this regard.

Because the toddler group programs are quite short, you will probably find it helpful to develop them around themes, such as animals, transportation, family, weather, etc. The themes should be selected from the children's own limited experiences with their environment, for these youngsters are too busy assimilating familiar experiences to try to deal with vicarious ones.

Picture books should be included in the toddler story program, but only those with the vaguest thread of a plot. Most toddlers have difficulty following a plot, especially in a group situation. For this reason, simple songs, fingerplays, and short poems can all prove effective and should become integral parts of the program. Remember also to include a variety of group movement activities for this is the age of first walking.

Planning a Preschool Program

Story programs for preschoolers (ages three to five years) can be longer—up to thirty minutes in length—and more sophisticated than for toddlers. For this age group, picture books should form the basis of the program. Stories with rather detailed plots are suitable, with subjects ranging from home and family to fairy tales.

At this age, children are avid explorers, delving deeply into their own environments as well as dealing vicariously with the experiences of others. They are still in the process of developing their listening skills and can enjoy short selections without the use of visuals. They do, however, love variety and relish fingerplays, songs, big books, flannel board stories, creative dramatics, and puppet stories.

Preschoolers are more adept at expressing themselves verbally and like to contribute to the program by formal participation and informal conversations. Treat their contributions seriously, but also let them know at which time in the program their comments are welcome and at which times they are interruptions. By including several participation activities in your story program, you can help direct the preschoolers responses into constructive and enjoyable channels.

Planning a Primary Level Program

Working with primary level children is a satisfying and rewarding experience. At this age, and with few exceptions, the children are generally interested and eager to please. They thoroughly enjoy all types of stories and eagerly respond with enthusiasm to every part of the story program, whether it be picture book, activity, song, or puppet play.

The content of the program for the younger primary level children (ages six to eight years) should become increasingly more involving and intriguing. The stories you present can be considerably longer with more complicated plots than those you have used for preschoolers. Picture book art can be more abstract and interpretive as primary level children enjoy comparing and analyzing the books' varied illustrations and techniques.

Be sure to have several transitional story activities up your sleeve for variety, to be used between the longer program elements. Youngsters at this age participate thoughtfully and spontaneously, but want their comments to be appreciated.

Primary level children ages nine to eleven years are even more adept at listening and do not require stories to be presented with props, but rather prefer those told without them. The stories presented to this age group may be the most ad-

vanced in your repertoire, including scary stories, long folk tales, complicated participation activities such as games and call-and-response songs, sign language stories that they can mimic, advanced humorous stories involving irony and word play, multicultural tales that may require some explanatory remarks, and story poems.

Planning a Family Story Program

Because of their wide range of ages and developmental levels, family story programs, by their very nature, must be diverse in form and content. The program itself may be thirty minutes to one hour in length, and could include as many as three or four major story components in addition to mixed media (videos, filmstrips, or film) and shorter participation activities.

Expect the unexpected with this type of program as each family story time will be made up of a different combination of ages, from infants to senior citizens. While some programs may contain mostly toddler age children, others may be primarily school age in composition. Additionally, as this may be your first encounter with young adults as audience members, don't forget to prepare a little something special for this age group as well.

Since small children can only actively listen for a brief amount of time to stories above their level of comprehension, it is recommended that you focus at least half of your stories to the younger ones in your program, regardless as to whether they are in the majority. In this way, you will eliminate a lot of fast exits by parents with disinterested and possibly disruptive children who are bored by long and complicated tales meant for a much older crowd.

The family story program may be the only evening program you offer, so it could be fun to make this a "sleepy time" or "bedtime story" type of session. Invite your audience to wear their favorite slippers and permit their children to attend in pajamas, bringing along blankets and pillows. By creating a comfortable, homey feel in your family programs, you will inspire a unique and memorable story experience.

Indexing and Record Keeping

It is not only a smart idea but an important one to remember to keep track of the various stories, rhymes, songs, and activities that you have learned, their sources, the dates and times of your performances, and the story elements which you presented in them. This record keeping can take the form of a program log, which might also include attendance figures, or a simple index card file, divided by developmental level and subdivided by type (song, story, resource, pattern, etc.). In this way, you will make available all of your resources at your fingertips, ready to be recalled at a moment's notice should the need arise.

If the thought of "record keeping" is unappealing to you, think of this component of your programming as an artistic project akin to creating a journal, scrapbook, or memory book. You might even elect to include photographs taken during your programs, drawings given to you by the children, or a sampling of the many thank-you notes and letters that you have received from appreciative patrons. Not only are you recording pertinent statistical information, but assembling a history of your programs and their development.

You should also include any notations that may assist you in remembering an inspirational moment or a problem you might have encountered during your program. For example, while your group was waiting for the program to begin, you might have overheard a teacher, parent, or caregiver do a little rhyme or activity that kept their children occupied and seated. You may have never heard it before, but you did notice that it had the desired effect on the children and you might want to learn it yourself later and add it to your repertoire. Or perhaps a child in your program responded in an unusual or creative way to a question or made a suggestion out of the blue which you would like to incorporate into your program routine. Keep some

sort of note pad handy with your program materials so you can jot these things down as they come to you.

Likewise, you might have used a song or a story in your program that garnered a negative response from a child or an adult, thereby making you hesitant to use it again until you have further thought out the problem. If you don't write these program notes down, you might not remember the incident and accidentally repeat the same or a similar mistake in another setting. For this one reason alone, it becomes clear why indexing and record keeping should be an integral part of your programming routine.

Advertising Your Program

There are many avenues available to advertise your story programs, including your own library's newsletter, local newspapers, radio and television public service commercials, flyers, the Internet (both listservs and web pages), press releases, telephone calls, personal invitations, community contacts, posters, and word-of-mouth.

You may elect to try to tackle every possible route, which takes lots of time and money, or focus your energies and limited financial resources on one or two of the most promising. If this is your first experience in promotions, instead of reinventing the wheel, consider making a few calls (by email or telephone) to other children's librarians and professional storytellers and inquire as to their best bets. Most of these professionals are only too happy to share their own success and horror stories with you.

The community in which you live will contain more than enough organizations, social groups, and interested parties that are dedicated to children's services and educational interests to meet your needs. Your public library will have a listing of such organizations on file. Your program could be target marketed through press releases or fliers to those agencies and adults that work primarily with children, including:

✧ Public and private schools, including private kindergartens
✧ Teachers and library aides
✧ Red Cross chapters
✧ County or city recreational departments
✧ Pediatricians and obstetricians
✧ Baby super stores
✧ La Leche Leagues
✧ Head Start centers
✧ Day Care centers
✧ Other children's librarians
✧ School media specialists
✧ Parent-teacher organizations
✧ Sunday School teachers
✧ Foster grandparents clubs
✧ Playground directors
✧ Children's hospitals
✧ Midwife associations
✧ Service and civic groups, including high school, college, and adult
✧ Social clubs, including college and adult
✧ Housing projects
✧ Public assistance agencies
✧ 4-H Clubs
✧ Home schooling groups
✧ Food cooperatives
✧ Boy and girl scouts groups
✧ Public health centers
✧ YMCA and YWCA clubs
✧ Boys' and Girls' Clubs
✧ Coalitions for the homeless
✧ Juvenile homes, orphanages, etc.

Sample Programs for Each Age Group

To help you get started, part two ("Targeting Your Story Program") contains a number of sample program outlines for five distinct types of audiences—infants, toddlers, preschoolers, primary level, and families. These outlines incorporate a variety of stories and story activities, including creative dramatics, puppetry, flannel board materials, fingerplays, action songs and stories, and picture books. Each of these types of activities will be described and elaborated on in succeeding chapters of this book.

The suggested programs include more material than you will need for the recommended time frames. In this way, you can choose your favorites from among those provided. The exact length of your program will be determined by several factors: the attention spans, developmental level, and story program experiences of the participating children. The quality of the program, on the other hand, is entirely up to you.

CHAPTER TWO

Story Program Considerations

If there is a watchword for presenting story programs it would have to be *balance*—both between the program elements themselves and between the storyteller and his or her audience. Care must be taken in your planning stage to ensure that you meet not only the time frame requirements of your program but the developmental level of your audience. A balanced presentation will include elements from a number of sources that are a variety of lengths and satisfy an expansive scope of interests. The balance that you seek will not mystically reveal itself to you, but will naturally evolve over time as you develop your repertoire and encounter situations in which your expertise and common sense are tried and tested.

Since your audiences will consist of children and adults from a broad range of social, economic, cultural, and ethnic backgrounds, there is, unfortunately, no magical programming formula that will help you to please all of the people all of the time. Fortunately, with a little basic information regarding group dynamics, you will easily be able to delight, inform, enlighten, inspire, and entertain like the experienced storyteller you are becoming.

Crafting a program to suit the developmental needs and entertainment expectations of any group may appear to be a daunting endeavor. However, this needn't prove to be a stressful part of your planning. No matter how much you prepare, or how many times you practice your program in front of the mirror or a loved one or a group of co-workers, it still requires a few live presentations to a group of strangers to feel your way around your material.

Trust those who have been doing story programs for decades when they say that until you jump into the water and do your first few story programs, you will never know just how easy and fun it is to swim. In fact, after only a few days of presenting programs, you will have gained the much needed confidence to actually enjoy yourself while telling.

Telling Stories

There are countless methods by which one might tell a story. You might try a combination of ways for your story program, or decide that you are most comfortable with one particular technique. Either way, experiment with other systems, when you have the time or inclination, in order to get the feel of the alternate choices available to you. You never know when this kind of experience will come in handy.

The short list of ways to tell a story includes: cut and tell (which uses paper plates or construction paper), flannel board, traditional storytelling without props, paper folding, puppetry, tangrams, creative dramatics, draw and tell, reading aloud, magic, shadow puppetry, and singing. There are also stories written to be told with lengths of string, expressed through sign language, or performed in pantomime.

This book offers sample program material and details on presenting flannel board stories, puppet theater, told stories, creative dramatics, and stories read aloud. For information on presenting the other types of stories, there is a resource list included in section six that will lead you to some great recommended reads.

As stated previously, any story program you present, for whatever age or developmental level, must include a variety of program elements with a mixture of lengths for optimal success. In addition to the various ways of telling stories, these program elements include, but are not limited to, songs, attention grabbers, wigglebreaks, transitions, fingerplays, and games. A general overview of these elements is included below.

Songs and Attention Grabbers

One of the best ways to bring a group together is to have your audience participate in some meaningful way in your program, and one of the easiest and most enjoyable means to do this is to have a singalong. Even if your singing voice is uneven and you are literally tone deaf, you should still try to include some sort of singing activity in your program. If you possess a fear of singing in public, take heart and remember that in a singalong you are not the only one in the room with your mouth open; in fact, everyone is expected to participate. In addition, if you pick a well-known song for this portion of your program (like "B-I-N-G-O" or "If You're Happy and You Know It"), you won't even have to teach the words or tune to the audience before you begin, thereby eliminating any solo vocalization on your part.

Once you have gained some self-assurance in using your singing voice, introduce more song into your program by adding an opening or closing tune or activity. Opening and closing songs work to perfectly frame your program, like "once upon a time" and "the end" do for story, and gently in-

vites your audience to become the attentive group that you know and hope they can be.

Now that you have incorporated the singalong and the opening and closing song, select some humorous songs, such as "On Top of Spaghetti," "Nobody Likes Me," "Spider on the Floor," and "Do Your Ears Hang Low?" for the next addition to your singing bag of tricks. Fred Penner, Raffi, Tom Glazer, Tom Chapin, Kathy Fink, Woody Guthrie, and Barry Louis Polisar all have written numerous sure-fire winners from which you may choose. There are many fine sources of humorous children's songs available, almost all with sheet music or chords charts, some on tape and CD, and they are included in a resource list in section six.

If you find your audience mentally wandering during your program, there are several positive and productive things you can do about it instead of losing your patience. Attention grabbers are a fantastic method by which you can easily get everybody on the same page without ordering them to do so. If your audience starts to chat amongst themselves, a few adults break away to discuss personal problems, or the children appear restless, hit them with a clap rhyme, knock-knock joke, riddle, short anecdote, or call-and-response chant and you will have them back, attentive and smiling.

You can also use attention grabbers as a start to your program and avoid the unremarkable and deadly dull "Now I'm Going to Start the Program" speech. Almost any nursery rhyme will work as a clap rhyme, but there are also jump rope rhymes that will work well in this regard. Remember "Mary Mack" and "Dr. Knickerbocker"? Once you try out a few of these at the appropriate moment, you will fall in love with the effect they have on restless youth and adults.

Wigglebreaks and Transitions

A wigglebreak is an attention grabber on steroids. Wigglebreaks involve the entire group standing and participating in some sort of full-body activity (like "Head, Shoulders, Knees, and Toes,"

"Hokey Pokey," and "Shake My Sillies Out"). Wigglebreaks are perfect for that ants-in-the-pants group of children who just can't seem to sit still. Use them sparingly in your program, however, and only when you have the room for the successful completion of the routine. Part four of this book offers three chapters that contain sample wigglebreaks for all developmental levels, from infants to primary level children.

Transitions are one of the most important elements in your story program, second only to the stories themselves. It has been said that transitions are the glue that holds your entire session together. The difference between a transition and a story is that transitions do not require a set up. You simply drop them into the program, between the longer program elements, without announcement, thereby surprising your audience and shifting their listening gears.

Many different types of material can be used for transitional purposes, including:

✧ Fingerplays
✧ Songs
✧ Rhymes
✧ Questions
✧ Jokes
✧ Anecdotes
✧ Jump rope rhymes
✧ Personal observations
✧ Short physical activities
✧ Conversational banter
✧ Riddles
✧ Mouth sounds
✧ Tongue twisters
✧ Puppetry
✧ Introductions to longer stories
✧ Tall tales
✧ Poetry
✧ Factoids and trivia
✧ Short games
✧ Clap rhymes

Transitions serve several purposes. They allow your audience a break from being quiet and still, offer a fun segue into the next program element, provide an opportunity for you to rest your feet and mind, and are a fun and easy way to keep your audience attentive to your program.

Fingerplays and Games

Fingerplays, like stories themselves, are a vital mode of presenting language to young children. For the infant who is not yet able to use their digits to make a hopping rabbit or a crawling turtle, fingerplays have little use except as a clap rhyme. Toddlers and preschool age children, on the other hand, are an excellent group for fingerplays, and you should include many of them in your story programs. There are also more sophisticated fingerplays for primary level children.

Sources for fingerplays are plentiful and simple to use. Some offer detailed drawings on exact hand and finger movement to accompany the poem. Others let you improvise your own motions. Fingerplays are usually brief with a rhyming pattern, so they are quite easy to learn. Chapter fourteen contains sample fingerplays for all age groups and the bibliography in section six offers many outstanding sources for you to use.

The idea of using games in your program may seem, on first glance, to be contrary to your mission of introducing language and good literature to children. It is not recommended that you use playground type games such as "Red Rover" or "Musical Chairs" in story programs, but simple word games and amusements that work to focus your audience at the task at hand are all appropriate.

For instance, you could use "Open, Shut Them" not only as a clap rhyme for infants, but as a listening game for preschoolers (details in chapter sixteen). Make a game out of the more simple tongue twisters, allowing smaller groups of children to actually stand and try some themselves. Games involving the names of the children in the group are a particularly popular choice.

Games can also be used as an opportunity for cooperative learning in which no child's suggestion is considered wrong and everyone shares in the outcome. Children love the idea of game playing, and when you introduce this program element with the question "who wants to play a game?" everyone's hand will shoot up into the air.

Attention Spans and Learning to Listen

As studies show, and any good children's librarian, preschool teacher, or professional storyteller will tell you, children are not born with listening skills but, rather, must be trained to develop them. Story programs are one of the best and most enjoyable ways to master these skills. In fact, parents should be encouraged to introduce their children to story from birth as story has the magical ability to enthrall even the most difficult to reach or to teach individual.

You will meet children in your programs, however, who seem to possess little in the way of attention spans and have some really atrocious listening skills. Do not be disheartened. Understand that this particular child is starting late on the path to being able to pay attention, but still deserves the opportunity to develop into a listening person.

If possible, have a little one-on-one with the parent of such a child and let them know that they are indeed welcome in your programs, but that junior might need some guidance from them as to appropriate and inappropriate behavior in a group setting. Suggest to them that it would not disrupt the program if they were to choose to remove their child from the program "when he has had enough fun" for the day. They can always try again another time. Let the adult know that, in this way, their child will not only learn to like the programs but will eventually develop those important listening skills through shorter doses of exposure.

CHAPTER THREE

Story Program Space

The ideal space in which to present story programs, for any developmental level of child, is an enclosed, well-ventilated room without chairs or furniture. It is equally important that this space be free of disruptive elements, such as ringing telephones, people traffic, and windows to the outside world. If you are lucky enough to have such a space in which to work, your job is immediately made much easier. If, however, you do not find yourself with such an optimal environment, there are a few things you can do to replicate the effect.

Try to find a space less traveled, perhaps a corner, as far away as possible from any entrance or exit. You can use chairs or tables for your program boundaries, but be sure to turn the chairs so that the seats are facing away from the space or you will end up having them filled. This way, if there is an adult who cannot join the group on the floor, they may turn a chair around for their use.

Children are easily distracted at any age, so your mission in deciding where to place your program should be directed at finding the least possible distracting location. Always place the storyteller facing the opening to the space so that the audience will have their backs to the entrance. Then, if you have latecomers, your group will not all stop and look at the new member and divert their attention away from your program.

The setting you create should have a relaxed, intimate, and informal quality about it. This will allow your group a feeling of comfort that is vital for a successful story program. A row of chairs or a preset seating arrangement will create unease on the part of your audience, especially when they find they must cross in front of already seated people and disrupt the program with their entrance. In addition, an informal seating arrangement will allow for a faster exit for the parent with a disruptive child—a consideration you must prepare for in any program setting.

For the infant program, you might want to offer brightly colored carpet or felt squares for your audience to place and sit upon, or pre-place the squares into the semicircle you wish the adults to form. Oftentimes, parents of infants will bring in a small quilt or blanket for their baby's space. As these can take up a great deal of precious space, offering the carpet squares will alleviate any awkward requests for their removal that you might have to make.

It is an ingenious idea to also have some type of table in the space on which your audience can place their belongings, books, bags, and purses. Keeping the floor space clear of obstacles is your primary goal. This can be especially important in the toddler and preschool programs in which full-body activities are an integral part. You don't want to have to circumvent a pile of belongings or worry that a child or adult is going to trip or fall when the group rises for the activity. It is your duty and legal responsibility to make sure that you have created as safe a space for your audience that you possibly can.

Book Displays

The table that holds patron belongings would also be an excellent location for your book display, an important and often neglected component to your program. Typically, book displays contain copies of the stories you are presenting, several developmentally appropriate sources of further interest to parents and children, and any handouts, brochures, or giveaways you wish to distribute after the program.

Creating a book display needn't be a complicated or time-consuming event. In your program planning phase, as you are selecting read-aloud books and sources, simply pull a few extra copies of each and set them aside. As long as your planning does not take place too long before the presentation, it is not inappropriate to save a small pile of sources for your future audience.

If your program takes place many weeks or months following your planning stage, or there proves to be no copies of your particular choices on the shelves, pull those books that are similar in theme and content and supplement them with nonfiction titles relating to the activity level of the group. For instance, if you are presenting an infant program, select some lap-sit, Mother Goose, and lullaby books. Or, if toddlers are your target audience, grab some fingerplay and poetry sources. Parents and caregivers often don't think of the nonfiction sources available for their younger children and these books might be their first exposure to them as a primary collection of information and activities.

If your library offers book displays by age group or developmental level, select a few of these recommendations and supplement them with some parenting sources, audio-visual material, or magazines. Again, this display of mixed media might prove to inspire an adult into thinking beyond the book paradigm to other avenues of information and entertainment for their children.

PART TWO

TARGETING YOUR STORY PROGRAM

CHAPTER FOUR

Infant Story Programs

The infant program, for children age birth to eighteen months, should take place in a clean, well-lighted, uncluttered, enclosed room with lots of open floor space. It is essential that the program be conducted in a circle or semicircle and, if at all possible, include several developmentally appropriate elements, each repeated at least once for best effect and retention. These elements include:

- ❖ an opening song or activity of some kind
- ❖ two or three clap rhymes
- ❖ activity songs
- ❖ two or three rhymes which include the movement of a major muscle group, such as the legs or arms
- ❖ several flying activities
- ❖ several transition songs or activities
- ❖ several riding games
- ❖ one infant story book
- ❖ a lullaby or soothing song
- ❖ a closing song or activity

Nursery rhymes should already be a significant part of an infant's young life. Encourage parents and childcare givers in your programs to use nursery rhymes throughout their day, as rhymes not only introduce language, but song, rhythm, simple story lines, poetry, and humor. Remind the adults that birth to eighteen months is the age of rhyme, rhythm, and repetition, and while they as grown-ups might grow weary of using nursery rhymes, their infants, on the other hand, are nourished by them and do not have a similar saturation point.

Mother Goose or nursery rhymes are important for a number of reasons, not the least of which concerns the richness of the language contained within them. From the simple (tub, rub, shoe, baby, cake, dog, pig, etc.) to the sophisticated (doth, nimble, betwixt, knaves, soundly, tinker, etc.), with phrases just plain fun to say (peas porridge, cockle shells, misty-moisty, dainty dish, fiddlers three), Mother Goose rhymes delight infants, toddlers, preschoolers, and adults with their wealth of wonderful words. As an important source in children's programming in libraries states, "A child who hears a lot of words will learn a lot of words. And a child who learns a lot of words will speak well, think clearly, and grow to be a good listener. All of this will add up to a child's becoming a good reader" (*First Steps to Literacy*, ALA, 1990, p. 2).

In addition, Mother Goose rhymes contain subjects of special interest to the infant, such as getting dressed, taking a bath, eating, playing, nap time, and going to bed. Parents can say these rhymes during the corresponding daily activity to help make going to the store, visiting the doctor, going to sleep, taking a ride, or eating breakfast a game instead of a chore.

Luckily, since infants crave repetition and routine, it is not at all inappropriate for you to conduct the same or a similar program at each meeting. With very little variation, your infant program can become one of the most relaxing sessions you offer, allowing the parent, infant, and storyteller a calm and soothing experience.

As an introduction, ask each adult in your infant program to share the name and age of their baby. This is a great way to alleviate any discomfort or uncertainty about participation in the program to follow. It also solves the rather sticky problem of determining the gender of the infants in the room and avoids the embarrassment of having the innocent question "and what is your little boy's name" answered with the blunt reply "it's a *girl*." Since every parent likes to show off their new baby, these introductions are also an excellent tool for creating a group atmosphere in which everyone in the room responds and, in turn, fully participates in the program.

During your program, consider incorporating a soft "yeah" while clapping approval for baby after each little rhyme or song you do. This will not only serve as a unification activity but will double as much needed transitions between the various parts or elements of your program. Have several transitions in reserve for those moments when your group becomes restless. It will refocus them and you back onto the task at hand.

Aiming Your Infant Program

There has been a great deal of debate among children's librarians as to whether the infant program should be specifically directed toward the parent/caregiver or the infant child. One school of thought holds that since an infant cannot participate in any meaningful way at this extremely early developmental level, one should aim "the message" directly at the adults and use this time together as an opportunity for an informational/instructional type workshop. Other children's professionals, just as well meaning, support the notion that adults do not attend infant programs for informational purposes as much as for the sake of their infant's enjoyment and their own opportunity to meet other new moms and dads and perhaps share some personal moments with similarly blessed adults.

It is not unwise to craft your infant program to accomplish the needs and desires of both the adults and the infants in the room. By repeating each rhyme several times, for instance, you are "teaching" the adults the words and accompanying motions that they, in turn, may do at home. By using the book-sharing portion of the program as a way of introducing the adults to various, and perhaps never before seen, infant story books, you are guiding them to good sources and recommended literature. And by fashioning the program with the needs of the infants in mind, focusing on developmentally appropriate songs, rhymes, and activities, you are also delighting the infants. In this very subtle way, the adults in your programs will come to understand and truly feel the importance of your message that one is never too old or too young to enjoy story.

Sample Infant Programs

Following, is an extensive collection of nursery rhymes, songs, transitions, and activities that you may use to create your own infant programs, each divided into their recommended program elements. As always, feel free to incorporate your own favorites among those provided. As you practice a few, you will soon come to understand the reasoning behind the decision to include a certain rhyme in a particular category.

Opening Songs

Good Day

Good day, good day,
Good day and how are you?
I'm fine,
I'm fine.
And I hope that you are too.

Hello Everybody

Hello everybody and how are you?
How are you? How are you?
Hello everybody and how are you?
How are you today?

I Love You

I love you. You love me.
We're a happy family.
With a great big hug and a kiss from me to you.
Won't you say you love me too?

The More We Get Together

The more we get together, together, together,
The more we get together, the happier we'll be.
For your friends are my friends,
and my friends are your friends.
The more we get together the happier we'll be.

Clap Rhymes

Peas Porridge Hot

Peas porridge hot, peas porridge cold.
Peas porridge in the pot, nine days old.
Some like it hot,
Some like it cold.
Some like it in the pot, nine days old.

There Was a Crooked Man

There was a crooked man
Who walked a crooked mile.
He found a crooked sixpence
Against a crooked stile.
He bought a crooked cat
Which caught a cooked mouse,
And they all lived together
In a crooked little house.

Polly, Put the Kettle On

Polly, put the kettle on,
Polly, put the kettle on,
Polly, put the kettle on,
We'll all have tea.

Suky, take it off again,
Suky, take it off again,
Suky, take it off again,
They've all gone away.

Georgie Porgie

Georgie Porgie, pudding and pie,
Kissed the girls and made them cry.
When the girls when out to play,
Georgie Porgie ran away.

Pat-a-Cake

Pat-a-cake, pat-a-cake, baker's man,
Bake me a cake as fast as you can.
Roll it, and pat it, and mark it with a "B"
And put it in the oven for baby and me.

Old King Cole

Old King Cole
Was a merry old soul,
And a merry old soul was he.
He called for his pipe,
And he called for his bowl,
And he called for his fiddlers three.

One Misty, Moisty Morning

One misty, moisty morning,
When cloudy was the weather,
I chanced to meet an old man
Clothed all in leather.
He began to compliment,
And I began to grin,
How do you do?
And how do you do?
And how do you do again?

Jack Sprat

Jack Sprat could eat no fat,
His wife could eat no lean.
And so betwixt them both, you see,
They licked the platter clean.

See-Saw, Marjorie Daw

See-saw, Marjorie Daw,
Jack shall have a new master.
He shall have but a penny a day,
Because he can't work any faster.

Hark! Hark!

Hark! Hark! The dogs do bark,
The beggars are coming to town.
Some in rags, some in tags,
And one in a velvet gown.

Barber, Barber, Shave a Pig

Barber, barber, shave a pig!
How many hairs to make a wig?
Four and twenty, that's enough.
Give the barber a pinch of snuff.

Birds of a Feather

Birds of a feather flock together
And so will pigs and swine;
Rats and mice will have their choice,
And so will I have mine.

Bobbie Shaftoe

Bobbie Shaftoe went to sea,
Silver buckles on his knee.
He'll come back to marry me;
Pretty Bobbie Shaftoe.

Rub-a-Dub-Dub

Rub-a-dub-dub, three men in a tub,
And who do you think they be?
The butcher, the baker, the candlestick maker,
Turn 'em out, knaves all three.

Tom, Tom, the Piper's Son

Tom, Tom, the piper's son,
Stole a pig and away did run!
The pig was eat, and Tom was beat,
And Tom went crying down the street.

Green Cheese

Green cheese, yellow laces,
Up and down, the market places

Jack and Jill

Jack and Jill went up the hill,
To fetch a pail of water.
Jack fell down and broke his crown,
And Jill came tumbling after.

Up Jack got and home did trot
As fast as he could caper.
Went to bed and plastered his head
With vinegar and brown paper.

Little Bo-Peep

Little Bo-Peep has lost her sheep,
And can't tell where to find them.
Leave them alone,
And they'll come home,
Wagging their tails behind them.

Doctor Foster

Doctor Foster went to Gloucester
In a shower of rain.
He stepped in a puddle,
Right up to his middle,
And never went there again.

Monday's Child

Monday's child is fair of face,
Tuesday's child is full of grace,
Wednesday's child is full of woe,
Thursday's child has far to go,
Friday's child is loving and giving,
Saturday's child works hard for a living,
But the child that's born on the Sabbath day,
Is fair and wise and good and gay.

Peter, Peter, Pumpkin Eater

Peter, Peter, pumpkin eater,
Had a wife and couldn't keep her.
He put her in a pumpkin shell
And there he kept her, very well.

Sing a Song of Sixpence

Sing a song of sixpence,
A pocket full of rye,
Four and twenty blackbirds
Baked in a pie.
When the pie was opened,
They all began to sing.
Now wasn't that a dainty dish
To set before the King?

The King was in his counting house,
Counting out his money;
The Queen was in the parlor
Eating bread and honey.
The maid was in the garden,
Hanging out the clothes.
Along came a big black bird
And snipped off her nose!

Higglety Pigglety

Higglety pigglety, my black hen.
She lays eggs for gentlemen.
Gentlemen come every day
To see what my black hen doth lay.
Sometimes nine,
Sometimes ten,
Higglety, pigglety, my black hen.

If All the World Were Paper

If all the world were paper,
And all the sea were ink,
If all the trees were bread and cheese,
What should we have to drink?

The Queen of Hearts

The Queen of Hearts,
She made some tarts
All on a summer's day.

The Knave of Hearts,
He stole the tarts
And took them clean away.

The King of Hearts,
Called for the tarts
And beat the Knave full sore.

The Knave of Hearts,
Brought back the tarts
And vowed he'd steal no more.

There Was an Old Woman

There was an old woman who lived in a shoe,
She had so many children,
She didn't know what to do,
She made them some broth
Without any bread,
And whipped them all soundly,
and sent them to bed.

If Wishes Were Horses

If wishes were horses,
Then beggars would ride.
If turnips were watches,
I'd wear one by my side.
And if "ifs" and "ands" were pots and pans,
There'd be no work for tinkers.

Pussycat, Pussycat, Where Have You Been?

Pussycat, pussycat,
Where have you been?
"I've been to London to visit the Queen."
Pussycat, pussycat,
What you did there?
"I frightened a little mouse under a chair."

To Bed, To Bed

"To bed, to bed,"
Says Sleepy-head.
"Tarry a while,"
Says Slow.
"Put on the pan,"
Says greedy Nan,
"We'll sup before we go."

Activity Songs

Open, Shut Them

Open, shut them, open, shut them,
Give a little clap, clap, clap.
Open, shut them, open, shut them,
Put them in your lap, lap, lap.
Creep them, creep them,
Creep them, creep them,
Right up to your chin, chin, chin.
Open up your little mouth,
But do not let them in.

Eensie Weensie Spider

The eensie weensie spider,
Went up the water spout,
Down came the rain
And washed the spider out.
Up came the sun
To dry up all the rain,
And the eensie weensie spider,
Went up the spout again.

I'm Growing

I'm growing, I'm growing,
I'm growing up all over.
I'm growing here, I'm growing there,
I'm just growing everywhere.

Row, Row, Row Your Boat

Row, row, row your boat,
Gently down the stream.
Merrily, merrily, merrily, merrily,
Life is but a dream.

Major Muscle Group
(while babies are lying on their backs with their feet closest to their parents)

These Are Baby's Fingers

These are baby's fingers,
These are baby's toes,
This is baby's belly button,
Round and round it goes.

Diddle Diddle Dumpling

Diddle diddle dumpling, my son John,
Went to bed with his stockings on.
One shoe off and one shoe on.
Diddle diddle dumpling, my son John.

One, Two, Three, Four, Five

One, two, three, four, five,
Once I caught a fish alive.
Six, seven, eight, nine, ten,
Then I let it go again.

Why did you let it go?
Because it bit my finger so.
Which finger did it bite?
The little one upon the right.

One Potato, Two Potato

One potato, two potato,
Three potato, four,
Five potato, six potato,
Seven potato, more.

Round and Round the Garden

Round and round the garden,
Goes the teddy bear.
One step, two step, tickle them under there.

Hot Cross Buns

Hot cross buns! Hot cross buns!
One a penny, two a penny,
Hot cross buns!
Hot cross buns! Hot cross buns!
If you have no daughters, give them to your sons!

Cross Patch, Draw the Latch

Cross patch, draw the latch
Sit by the fire and spin;
Take a cup, and drink it up,
Then call the neighbors in.

Flying Activities

Flying Man

Flying man, flying man, up in the sky,
Where are you going to, flying so high?
Over the mountain, and over the seas,
Flying man, flying man, won't you take me?

Jack Be Nimble

Jack be nimble,
Jack be quick.
Jack jumped over
The candlestick.

Hickory Dickory Dock

Hickory dickory dock.
The mouse ran up the clock.
The clock struck one, the mouse ran down.
Hickory dickory dock.

Here We Go

Here we go up, up, up.
Here we go down, down, down.
Here we go up, up, up.
Here we go down, down, down.

Hey, Diddle Diddle

Hey, diddle diddle, the cat and the fiddle,
The cow jumped over the moon.
The little dog laughed to see such sport,
And the dish ran away with the spoon.

Humpty Dumpty

Humpty Dumpty sat on the wall.
Humpty Dumpty had a great fall.
All the king's horses and all the king's men,
Couldn't put Humpty back together again.

Transition Songs

Twinkle, Twinkle

Twinkle, twinkle, little star,
How I wonder what you are.
Up above the world so high,
Like a diamond in the sky.
Twinkle, twinkle, little star,
How I wonder what you are.

It's Raining, It's Pouring

It's raining, it's pouring,
The old man is snoring.
Went to bed with a bump on his head,
And he couldn't get up in the morning.

Baa, Baa Black Sheep

Baa, baa black sheep, have you any wool?
Yes, sir. Yes, sir, three bags full.
One for my master, one for the dame,
One for the little boy who lives down the lane.
Baa, baa black sheep, have you any wool?
Yes, sir. Yes, sir, three bags full.

Mary, Mary, Quite Contrary

Mary, Mary, quite contrary,
How does your garden grow?
With silver bells, and cockle shells,
And pretty maids all in a row.

Wee Willy Winkie

Wee Willie Winkie, runs through the town,
Upstairs and downstairs, in his nightgown.
Rapping at the windows,
Crying through the locks,
"Are the children in their beds,
For now it's eight o'clock?"

My Bonnie Lies Over the Ocean

My Bonnie lies over the ocean,
My Bonnie lies over the sea,
My Bonnie lies over the ocean,
Please bring back my Bonnie to me.

Bring back, bring back,
Oh, bring back my Bonnie to me, to me.
Bring back, bring back,
Oh, bring back my Bonnie to me.

To Market, To Market

To market, to market, to buy a fat pig,
Home again, home again, jiggety jig.
To market, to market, to buy a fat hog,
Home again, home again, jiggety jog.
To market, to market, to buy a plum bun,
Home again, home again, market is done.

Muffin Man

Do you know the muffin man,
The muffin man, the muffin man?
Do you know the muffin man
Who lives in Drury Lane?

Yes, I know the muffin man,
The muffin man, the muffin man.
Yes, I know the muffin man,
Who lives in Drury Lane.

Riding Games

This Is the Way the Farmer Rides

This is the way the farmer rides:
a-jiggety-jog, a-jiggety-jog.
This is the way the lady rides:
a-prance, a-prance.
This is the way the gentleman rides:
a-gallop, a-gallop, a-gallop, a-gallop.

Trot, Trot, to Boston

Trot, trot, to Boston; Trot, trot, to Lynn;
Trot, trot, to Salem; Home, home, again.

Mother and Father and Uncle John

Mother and Father and Uncle John,
Went to town one by one.
Mother fell off. Father fell off.
But Uncle John went on and on.

Ride a Cock Horse

Ride a cock horse to Banbury Cross
To see a fine lady upon a white horse.
Rings on her fingers and bells on her toes,
She shall have music wherever she goes.

Infant Story Books

I Like it When by Mary Murphy
Hush Little Baby by Aliki
Once: a Lullaby by Anita Lobel and bp Nichol
Read to Your Bunny by Rosemary Wells
Little Donkey Close Your Eyes by Margaret Wise Brown
All the Pretty Horses by Susan Jeffers
Farm Noises by Jane Miller
Mother Goose by Tasha Tudor
The Ball Bounced by Nancy Tafuri

Clap Hands by Helen Oxenbury
Where Does the Brown Bear Go? by Nicki Weiss
Good Night, Baby Bear by Frank Asch
The Very Hungry Caterpillar (board book) by Eric Carle
Goodnight Moon by Margaret Wise Brown
Book of Nursery and Mother Goose Rhymes by Marguerite DeAngeli
I Am a Little Rabbit (board book) by Francois Cruzat

Lullaby Songs

All the Pretty Little Horses

Hush-a-bye,
Don't you cry.
Go to sleepy, little baby.
When you wake,
You shall have,
All the pretty little horses.
Blacks and bays,
Dapples and grays,
All the pretty little horses.
Hush-a-bye,
Don't you cry.
Go to sleepy little baby.

Lavender's Blue

Lavender's blue, dilly, dilly,
Lavender's green;
When I am king, dilly, dilly,
You shall be queen.
Call up your men, dilly, dilly,
Set them to work,
Some to the plough, dilly, dilly,
Some to the cart.
Some to make hay, dilly, dilly,
Some to thresh corn,
While you and I, dilly, dilly,
Keep ourselves warm.

Rock a Bye Baby

Rock a bye baby
On the treetops,
When the wind blows,
The cradle will rock.
When the bough breaks,
The cradle will fall,
And down will come baby,
Cradle and all.

Toora, Loora, Loora

Toora, loora, loora,
Toora, loora, la,
Toora, loora, loora,
Hush now, don't you cry.
Toora, lorra, loora,
Toora, loora, la,
Toora, loora, loora,
That's an Irish lullaby.

Hush Little Baby

Hush, little baby, don't say a word,
Mama's going to buy you a mockingbird.
And if that mockingbird don't sing,
Mama's going to buy you a diamond ring.
And if that diamond ring turns brass,
Mama's going to buy you a looking glass.
And if that looking glass gets broke,
Mama's going to buy you a billy goat.
And if that billy goat won't pull,
Mama's going to buy you a cart and bull.
And if that cart and bull turns over,
Mama's going to buy you a dog named Rover.
And if that dog named Rover won't bark,
Mama's going to buy you a horse and cart.
And if that horse and cart fall down,
You'll still be the sweetest little baby in town.

Brahms' Lullaby

Lullaby, and good night,
With pink roses bedight,
With lilies o'erspread,
Is my baby's sweet head.
Lay you down now, and rest,
May your slumber be blessed!
Lay you down now, and rest,
May thy slumber be blessed!

Closing Songs

The More We Get Together

The more we get together,
Together, together,
The more we get together,
The happier we'll be.
For your friends are my friends,
And my friends are your friends.
The more we get together,
The happier we'll be.

Good Day, Everybody

Good day, everybody,
Good day, everybody,
Good day, good day, good day.
Let's hope, everybody,
Let's hope, everybody,
To meet again real soon.

I Love You

I love you,
You love me,
We're a happy family.
With a great big hug
And a kiss from me to you,
Won't you say you love me too?

Happy Trails to You
(words and music by Dale Evans)

Happy trails to you,
Until we meet again.
Happy trails to you,
Keep smilin' until then.
Who cares about the clouds when we're together,
Just sing a song and bring the sunny weather.
Happy trails to you, til we meet again.

CHAPTER FIVE

Toddler Story Programs

As with the infant programs, the toddler program should also take place in an uncluttered room with lots of open floor space for movement. Additionally, the room should be devoid of any chairs, boxes, or furniture that might appeal to the climbing or hiding instincts of the toddler child, age eighteen to thirty-six months. In other words, don't take it personally if the bench or stool in your program room suddenly becomes much more appealing to a beginning walker than your story or your song.

To insure a safe environment, remember to make certain that your wall decorations, program materials, and book displays are out of the reach of the toddler and that all electrical outlets are capped with child-proof plugs. Do a thorough once-over of the room before the public is allowed into the space for errant tacks, staples, or bits of thread or string that may eventually and unpredictably interfere with the group's comfort or end up in a child's mouth.

As in all story programs, parents and caregivers of this age group should participate in all aspects of the toddler session, thus serving as models for their children. Toddler time is the age of imitation, and the adults must assist their children in acting out the fingerplays and activities for greatest retention and enjoyment. Between the ages of one and two, toddlers are also developing their senses of humor and will begin to laugh at stories, songs, and rhymes if their parents do.

At this very active age, you may find that toddlers will decide to explore the story space, empty though it may be, instead of remaining with their parents. If they are not loudly disturbing the group or in any danger of accident or injury, try to ignore the child as best you can. Even when they are not directly observing you, a child that is quiet is usually listening still. If you feel the group as a whole getting fussy or irritable, try singing "Twinkle, Twinkle, Little Star" in your most soothing voice. You will be surprised by the magical calming effect this simple song has on young children.

Toddler Program Elements

As with all types of programs, it is advisable to have some sort of standard opening and closing routine that you repeat at each session exactly the same way. This may be a song, a poem, or a special greeting. This will provide your session with a frame of sorts while signaling to your audience both when the program is beginning and ending. A good opening will also catch the toddlers' attention and beckon them to settle down and begin to listen.

As this is the age of motion, it is a good idea to include several full-body movement activities in each toddler program to cut down on normal wandering and disinterest. "Here We Go Round the Mulberry Bush," "Down by the Station," "I'm a Little Teapot," and "Ring Around the Rosie" all work well to provide circle-time stretches. "Ring Around the Rosie" is a smart way to end the movement portion of your program as it perfectly positions the toddlers where you want them—on the floor and in the mood to stay there for a while.

A recommended order of presentation for the toddler program is:

✧ Opening song or activity
✧ Fingerplay
✧ Song
✧ Fingerplay
✧ Clap rhyme
✧ Song
✧ Story book
✧ Transition activity
✧ Full-body activities
✧ Transition song for calming down
✧ Story book
✧ Clap rhyme
✧ Fingerplay
✧ Closing song or activity

Many of the same nursery rhymes used in the infant program can easily be adapted for use with toddlers. Since toddlers are too big for flying games, and would probably enjoy more jumping and walking activities, you can elect to use those rhymes for a full-body activity. For instance, in "Jack Be Nimble" have the toddlers literally jump over their candlesticks. Or for "Flying Man," inspire the toddlers to pretend to be airplanes and zoom around the room to the words (another good reason not to have much furniture in the story space).

Since there will be a good deal of movement in your toddler program, it is highly advisable to set up a table in the room for adults to drop off their books and bags. This will keep the floor area clear of hazards and insure a safer toddler play space. This table can also double as your toddler book display.

Toddler Story Books

Since the toddler has a greater attention span than the infant, now is the perfect opportunity to introduce a second book during the program, separated by some other activity. This second book should be mainly participatory, and include the ability to repeat a line or allow for animal sounds. Two- to three-year-olds have a literary need to hear any kind of language, especially words that are rhythmic, rhyming, sung, or chanted. At this age, with a vocabulary of over 300 words, they respond to simple questions and can remember what comes next in familiar stories.

Studies show that toddlers enjoy books in which the main characters are in charge or in control of their situation, books that involve guessing what comes next, stories of toddler accomplishments, books with bold illustrations, and books with rhymes that can be acted out. In addition, toddlers enjoy stories and books which reflect the child's own world, such as dressing, bath time, family, and pets. They especially respond to simple stories that feature families and interesting characters.

Sample Themed Programs for Toddlers

Animals

Story Books

The Three Little Pigs	Paul Galdone
I Am a Little Rabbit	Francois Crozat
Where's Spot?	Eric Hill
Little Gorilla	Ruth Bornstein
All the Pretty Horses	Susan Jeffers

Activities, Songs, and Fingerplays

Hey Diddle Diddle	clap rhyme
I Went to the Animal Fair	song
Hickory Dickory Dock	nursery rhyme
Five Little Ducks	activity song
To Market, To Market	song
Three Little Monkeys	fingerplay
Three Blind Mice	song

Birds

Story Books

The Chick and the Duckling	Mirra Ginsburg
Have You Seen My Duckling?	Nancy Tafuri
Feathers for Lunch	Lois Ehlert
Who Took the Farmer's Hat?	Joan L. Nodset

Activities, Songs, and Fingerplays

Two Little Blackbirds	fingerplay
Sing a Song of Sixpence	nursery song
Little Robin Redbreast	creative dramatics
Birds of a Feather	clap rhyme
Five Little Ducks	song/activity
Little White Duck	song

Bears

Story Books

One Bear All Alone	Caroline Bucknall
Happy Birthday, Moon	Frank Asch
Brown Bear, Brown Bear, What Do You See?	Bill Martin
The Three Bears	Byron Barton
Where Does the Brown Bear Go?	Nicki Weiss

Activities, Songs, and Fingerplays

Bear Went Over the Mountain	song
Fuzzy Wuzzy	poem
Five Little Bears	fingerplay
Bear Hunt	activity
Teddy Bear, Teddy Bear	activity/song

Bugs

Story Books

In the Tall, Tall Grass	Denise Fleming
Fireflies, Fireflies, Light My Way	Jonathan London
The Very Quiet Cricket	Eric Carle
The Very Busy Spider	Eric Carle
The Very Lonely Firefly	Eric Carle

Activities, Songs, and Fingerplays

I'm Bringing Home a Baby Bumble Bee	song
Lady Bug, Lady Bug, Fly Away Home	poem
Ants Go Marching	counting song
Eensie Weensie Spider	activity song
The Beehive	fingerplay

Cats

Story Books

Tom and Pippo in the Garden	Helen Oxenbury
He Wakes Me	Betsy James
Angus and the Cat	Marjorie Flack
Cat's Colors	Jane Cabrera

Activities, Songs, and Fingerplays

Five Little Kittens	fingerplay
I Love Little Kitty by Jane Taylor	poem/puppet
Three Little Kittens	flannel board
Pussy Cat, Pussy Cat, Where Have You Been?	nursery rhyme

Family

Story Books

Little Gorilla	Ruth Bornstein
I Like it When	Mary Murphy
My Mom Is Excellent	Nick Butterworth
Dads Are Such Fun	Jakki Wood
Just Like Daddy	Frank Asch

Activities, Songs, and Fingerplays

There Was an Old Woman	rhyme
Mother and Father and Uncle John	activity
Are You Sleeping?	song
He's Got the Whole World in His Hands	naming song

Dogs

Story Books

No, No, Titus!	Claire Masurel
Hello, Biscuit!	Alyssa S. Capucilli
Where's Spot?	Eric Hill
Tom and Pippo and the Dog	Helen Oxenbury

Activities, Songs, and Fingerplays

The Puppy	fingerplay
My Puppy	poem/puppet
Hark, Hark, the Dogs Do Bark	nursery rhyme
Old Mother Hubbard	flannel board rhyme
Where Has My Little Dog Gone?	song
B-I-N-G-O	action song
How Much Is That Doggie in the Window?	action song

Farms

Story Books

Barnyard Banter	Denise Fleming
Farm Noises	Jane Miller
When the Rooster Crowed	Patricia Lillie
Spots, Feathers and Curly Tails	Nancy Tafuri
One Duck, Another Duck	Charlotte Pomerantz
Cock-a-Doodle-Do!	Jill Runcie

Activities, Songs, and Fingerplays

Old MacDonald Had a Farm	flannel board
Mary Had a Little Lamb	song with puppet
Baa, Baa Black Sheep	song
Little Bo-Peep	poem
The Farmer in the Dell	flannel board song
This Is the Way the Farmer Rides	activity
Ride a Cock Horse	clap rhyme

Food

Story Books

The Very Hungry Caterpillar	Eric Carle
Blue Bug's Vegetable Garden	Virginia Poulet
It Looked Like Spilt Milk	Charles Shaw
Benny Bakes a Cake	Eve Rice

Activities, Songs, and Fingerplays

Peanut Butter and Jelly	chant rhyme
Jack Sprat	rhyme
Pat-a-Cake	action rhyme
Do You Know the Muffin Man?	song
Peter, Peter, Pumpkin Eater	rhyme
Hot Cross Buns	rhyme
One Potato, Two Potato	counting rhyme

Me

Story Books

Hello Toes! Hello Feet!	Ann W. Paul
Here Are My Hands	Bill Martin
From Head to Toe	Eric Carle
The Carrot Seed	Ruth Krauss
No, David!	David Shannon
Dancing Feet	Charlotte Agell
My Hands Can	Nancy Tafuri
I See	Rachel Isadora

Activities, Songs, and Fingerplays

Five Fingers	fingerplay
Parts of the Body	flannel board
Open, Shut Them	participation song
Where is Thumbkin?	song/fingerplay
I'm a Little Teapot	activity song
I'm Growing	activity song

Frogs, Fishes, and Turtles

Story Books

Jump, Frog, Jump!	Robert Kalan
Fish Eyes	Lois Ehlert
Farm Noises	Jane Miller
Franklin in the Dark	Paulette Bourgeois
Turtle Tale	Frank Asch
The Frog	Pat Paris

Activities, Songs, and Fingerplays

Once I Caught a Fish Alive	fingerplay
Five Green and Speckled Frogs	song
Little Turtle	fingerplay
Five Little Froggies	fingerplay
Glack Goon	song

Nature

Story Books

The Very Hungry Caterpillar	Eric Carle
The Carrot Seed	Ruth Kraus
Vegetable Garden	Douglas Florian
Planting a Rainbow	Lois Ehlert
It Looked Like Spilt Milk	Charles Shaw
My Spring Robin	Anne Rockwell

Activities, Songs, and Fingerplays

Twinkle, Twinkle	song
Mr. Sun	song/activity
Zip-A-Dee-Doo-Dah	song
Eensie Weensie Spider	activity
Mary, Mary Quite Contrary	clap rhyme

═══ Transportation ═══

Story Books

The Big Red Bus	Ethel and Leonard Kessler
1, 2, 3 to the Zoo	Eric Carle
I Went Walking	Sue Williams
Miffy Goes Flying	Dick Bruna
Freight Train	Donald Crews
Trains	Byron Barton

Activities, Songs, and Fingerplays

Choo, Choo, Choo	fingerplay
The Train	flannel board
Down by the Station	activity/song
Wheels on the Bus	song
Row, Row, Row Your Boat	activity/song

═══ Weather ═══

Story Books

Listen to the Rain	Bill Martin
Rainsong/Snowsong	Philemon Sturges
In the Rain with Baby Duck	Amy Hest
It Looked Like Spilt Milk	Charles Shaw

Activities, Songs, and Fingerplays

It's Raining, It's Pouring	song
Eensy Weensy Spider	fingerplay
Mr. Sun	song
Rain, Rain Go Away	poem
It Ain't Gonna Rain No More	song
Doctor Foster	poem
One Misty Moisty Morning	clap rhyme

CHAPTER SIX

Preschooler Story Programs

Unlike infants and toddlers, preschool age children, ages three to five years, can, and often do, fully enjoy a story program without a parent or caregiver at their side. Some preschoolers, in fact, prefer it. Regardless of the makeup of your audience in the preschool program, it is now the time for you, the storyteller, to direct your attention wholly on the children in the room to ensure their optimal enjoyment.

If you have the inclination, suggest to parents beforehand that they allow their preschool children to attend story programs without them, as this is the perfect age for peer-group play. As independent and confident children, most preschoolers enjoy the temporary separation from their parents and feel grown up that they have accomplished the program on their own.

While you should direct the program to the preschooler, do not allow the adults in the room to get away with not participating in your program. It is vital that the children see their parents and teachers following the storyteller's instructions and paying attention. There is nothing more distracting than an adult just sitting, unaffected, in your best-effort story program.

A simple, safe, and nonconfrontational way to involve reluctant adults is to make some sort of general group-wide announcement that everyone in the room is expected to participate in all parts of the program. Jim May, a professional storyteller,

was once heard telling a group of adults who were not partaking of his participation story that while he understood that they didn't want to play along, later, in the car driving home, they were going to say to themselves, "Now, why didn't I just do like the man said and have a good time?" So, May instructs, save time on the regrets later, and play along now.

Preschool Program Elements

Preschool children enjoy a combination of variety and routine. To meet this developmental need, you might contemplate structuring your sessions similarly while switching out the major stories told from meeting to meeting.

The following is program format that is particularly effective:

✧ Opening routine or song
✧ Fingerplay, action rhyme, song or poem
✧ Shorter story
✧ Fingerplay, action rhyme, song or poem
✧ Longer story
✧ Creative dramatics/puppetry
✧ Shorter story
✧ Fingerplay, action rhyme, song or poem
✧ Closing routine or song

Preschool age children are independent and outgoing, have an increasing interest span, and thankfully, can sit listening for a longer period of time.

Preschool Story Books

Three to fives delight in a variety of books of different types and lengths. A child's vocabulary by the age of five ranges from 1,200 to 2,500 words and they can average 4+ words per sentence. Preschoolers can clap and march to music, respond to rhythm, and especially enjoy group activities.

Preschoolers sit well for stories containing complex plots with themes that move beyond the everyday into the silly and adventurous. For this age range, choose a wide range of programming materials: participation activities, cumulative tales, humorous and nonsense stories, stories with repetition, folk tales, riddles, poetry, puppetry, and creative dramatics.

A preschooler has reached the age of make-believe, imaginary friends, dramatic play, and fantasy. While fingerplays and movement games are still suitable, three- to five-year-olds will insist that these elements be either funny or complicated in order to hold their attention. Books that contain superheros, dinosaurs, monsters, dragons, and silly stories are well received.

If you have the wonderful good luck to be able to perform preschool programs for the same group of children over a period of time, you will soon notice that you may slowly introduce more and more sophisticated stories into your program, thereby gradually increasing both their literary tastes and listening abilities.

Emotionally, the preschool child can be stubborn, argumentative, and questioning of authority. They have a definite sense of right and wrong and will not tolerate unfairness when they see it. The preschooler's strong sense of curiosity may often manifest itself in inappropriate interruptions while others are speaking. In other words, you will have your hands full when presenting preschool programs.

On the other hand, preschool age children are some of the best and most appreciative audiences you will find. Three- to five-year-olds crave hearing stories and already have favorites which they know by heart. This is the group that will warm your soul when they blurt out "tell it again!" after your story is finished. Consider this as highest praise, similar in form and feel to "encore!" or "bravo!"

Sample Themed Programs for Preschoolers

══ Animals ══

Story Books

Walking Through the Jungle	Debbie Harter
Goodnight, Owl!	Pat Hutchins
Old Black Fly	Jim Aylesworth
Leo the Late Bloomer	Robert Kraus
Frederick	Leo Lionni
Baby Duck and the Bad	
Eyeglasses	Amy Hest
The Camel Took a Walk	Jack Tworkov
If You Give a Mouse a	
Cookie	Laura Numeroff

Activities, Songs, and Fingerplays

Five Little Squirrels	fingerplay
Over in the Meadow	flannel board
The Lion and the Mouse	puppet play
A Secret (poem)	flannel board
Little Robin Redbreast	fingerplay
Three Billy Goats Gruff	told story
Three Blind Mice	song
Bear Hunt	activity

══ Cats ══

Story Books

Six-Dinner Sid	Inga Moore
Pretend You're a Cat	Jean Marzollo
This and That	Julie Sykes
The Barn Cat	Carol P. Saul
The Cat Barked?	Lydia Monks
Marmalade's Nap	Cindy Wheeler
The Gingham Dog and the	
Calico Cat	Eugene Field
Angus and the Cats	Marjorie Flack
Cat Kong	Dav Pilkey

Activities, Songs, and Fingerplays

Pepper	action story
Cats Sleep Anywhere	poem
The Cat Came Back	song
The Owl and the Pussy-Cat	poem
Cat Goes Fiddle-I-Fee	song
Siamese Cat Song	song
Don't Dress Your Cat in	
an Apron	poem

Dogs

Story Books

Martha Speaks	Susan Meddaugh
I Swapped My Dog	Harriet Zieffert
Dog Breath	Dav Pilkey
The Gingham Dog and the	
Calico Cat	Eugene Field
Whistle for Willy	Ezra Jack Keats
Harry the Dirty Dog	Eugene Zion
Clifford's Puppy Days	Norman Bridwell

Activities, Songs, and Fingerplays

How Much Is That Doggie in the Window?	song
B-I-N-G-O	song
Hark, Hark the Dogs Do Bark	clap rhyme
Hey, Diddle Diddle	flannel board

Family

Story Books

Runaway Bunny	Margaret Wise Brown
Gone Fishing	Earlene Long
Emma's Pet	David McPhail
Is Your Mama a Llama?	Deborah Guarino
Jafta's Father	Hugh Lewin
Mommy, Buy Me a China Doll	Harve and Margot Zemach

Activities, Songs, and Fingerplays

Yellow Submarine	song
Hi, My Name is Joe	activity
Frog Went a-Courtin'	song
The Three Bears	creative dramatics
My Aunt Came Back	activity
Grandma's Spectacles	fingerplay

Elephants

Story Books

Elmer	David McKee
"Stand Back," Said the Elephant, "I'm Going to Sneeze"	Patricia Thomas
Seven Blind Mice	Ed Young
The Right Number of Elephants	Jeff Sheppard
17 Kings and 42 Elephants	Margaret Mahy

Activities, Songs, and Fingerplays

The Box with Red Wheels	flannel board
The Elephant Goes Like This and That	action rhyme
Elephant Jokes	game
Going on an Elephant Hunt	activity

Farms

Story Books

Sitting on the Farm	Bob King
The Day the Goose Got Loose	Reeve Lindbergh
Rosie's Walk	Pat Hutchins
This Is the Farmer	Nancy Tafuri
When the Rooster Crowed	Patricia Lillie
Who Took the Farmer's Hat?	Joan L. Nodest

Activities, Songs, and Fingerplays

Little Red Hen	flannel board
Old MacDonald Had a Farm	puppet/song
Aunt Jean's Farm	creative dramatics
I Had a Rooster	flannel board/song
Did You Feed My Cow?	call/response song
Great Big Enormous Turnip	told story

Feelings

Story Books

Peter's Chair	Ezra Jack Keats
The Ant Bully	John Nickle
Alexander and the Terrible, Horrible, No Good, Very Bad Day	Judith Viorst
I Like Me	Nancy Carlson

Activities, Songs, and Fingerplays

Faces	creative dramatics
Little Miss Muffet	puppets
Jennie Jenkins	song/flannel board
If You're Happy and You Know It	song
Tony Chestnut	activity

Monkeys

Story Books

Good Night Gorilla	Peggy Rathmann
Why Can't I Fly?	Rita Golden Gelman
Caps for Sale	Esphyr Slobodkina
So Say the Little Monkeys	Nancy Van Laan
The Camel Took a Walk	Jack Tworkov
Curious George	H. A. Rey
Little Gorilla	Ruth Bornstein

Activities, Songs, and Fingerplays

Three Little Monkeys	fingerplay
Five Little Monkeys Jumping on the Bed	fingerplay
I Went to the Animal Fair	song
Monkey See, Monkey Do	activity

Food

Story Books

My Sister Ate One Hare	Bill Grossman
Jake Baked a Cake	B. G. Hennessy
Stop That Pickle!	Peter Armour
Carrot Seed	Ruth Krauss
Chicken Soup with Rice	Maurice Sendak

Activities, Songs, and Fingerplays

Apples and Bananas	song
Beans in My Ears	song
The Gingerbread Boy	told story
Sandwiches Are Beautiful	song
Sipping Cider Through a Straw	song
Peanut Butter and Jelly	activity

Outer Space

Story Books

It Came from Outer Space	Tony Bradman
UFO Diary	Satoshi Kitamura
Zoom, Zoom, Zoom, I'm Off to the Moon	Dan Yaccarino
Here Come the Aliens	Caroline Naughton
Happy Birthday, Moon	Frank Asch
Moongame	Frank Asch
Mooncake	Frank Asch

Activities, Songs, and Fingerplays

Aiken Drum	song
1, 2, 3, Zoom	activity
Mr. Sun	song
The Man in the Moon	poem

Rhinos, Hippos, and Crocs

Story Books

Lyle, Lyle Crocodile	Bernard Waber
The Happy Hippopotami	Bill Martin
Hot Hippo	Mwenye Hadithi
George and Martha	James Marshall

Activities, Songs, and Fingerplays

Never Smile at a Crocodile	song
The Crocodile's Toothache by Shel Silverstein	poem
Rhinoceros Stew by Mildred Lutton	poem
Recipe for a Hippopotamus Sandwich by Shel Silverstein	poem
Three Little Monkeys	fingerplay

Poetry

Story Books

Life Doesn't Frighten Me	Maya Angelou
The Sneeches and Other Stories	Dr. Seuss
Where the Sidewalk Ends	Shel Silverstein
Something Big Has Been Here	Jack Prelutsky

Activities, Songs, and Fingerplays

Hector the Collector	Shel Silverstein
Be Glad Your Nose Is On Your Face	Jack Prelutsky
Sneaky Bill	William Cole
Tree Toad	tongue twister
Smart	Shel Silverstein
Puppy and I	A. A. Milne

Pigs

Story Books

Geraldine's Blanket	Holly Keller
Louella Mae, She's Run Away	Karen Alarcón
Tommy at the Grocery Store	Bill Grossman
Pig Pig Rides	David McPhail
Cow That Went Oink!	Bernard Most

Activities, Songs, and Fingerplays

Three Little Pigs	flannel board
Pig Limericks by Arnold Lobel	poetry
The Old Woman and Her Pig	chant
Five Little Pigs	flannel board
Old Woman and Her Pig	flannel board

Silly Time Number One

Story Books

The Foolish Frog	Pete Seeger
Tackey the Penguin	Helen Lester
Down by the Bay	Raffi
The Day Jimmy's Boa Ate the Wash	Trinka Hakes Noble
The Doorbell Rang	Pat Hutchins

Activities, Songs, and Fingerplays

Hokey Pokey	song
Little Skunk Hole	fingerplay
Spider on the Floor	song
I'm Being Swallowed by a Boa Constrictor	poem
There's a Hole in the Bottom of the Sea	song

Silly Time Number Two

Story Books

There's a Nightmare in My Closet	Mercer Mayer
King Bidgood's in the Bathtub	Audrey Wood
Tikki Tikki Tembo	Arlene Mosel
The Funny Old Man and the Funny Old Woman	Martha Barber
There's an Alligator Under My Bed	Mercer Mayer

Activities, Songs, and Fingerplays

Do Your Ears Hang Low?	song
Roll Over	fingerplay/song
Willoughby Wallaby Woo	song
The Cat Came Back	song
John Jacob Jingleheimer Schmidt	song
Mary Mack	chant rhyme
On Top of Spaghetti	song
Head, Shoulders, Knees, and Toes	activity

Weather

Story Books

Wind	Ron Bacon
What Will the Weather Be Like Today?	Paul Rogers
Rain Talk	Mary Serfozo
It Looked Like Spilt Milk	Charles Shaw
Rainbow of My Own	Don Freeman
Bringing the Rain to Kapiti Plain	Verna Aardema
Greetings, Sun	Phillis and David Gershater

Activities, Songs, and Fingerplays

Eensie Weensie Spider	song with puppet
Who Has Seen the Wind? by Christina Rossetti	poem
The North Wind Doth Blow	creative dramatics
Fox Went Out on a Chilly Night	song
One Misty Moisty Morning	clap rhyme
Mr. Sun	song

CHAPTER SEVEN

Primary Level Story Programs

The primary level story program is your first opportunity to introduce stories with complicated plots and sophisticated language. Appropriate types of stories for six- to eleven-year-olds include folktales, trickster tales, myths, legends, hero tales, animal fables, scary stories, *pourquoi* (why) stories, tall tales, and story poems. In addition, transitional elements such as knock knock jokes, riddles, games, tongue twisters, and songs work amazingly well with this age group.

Primary level children's attention spans, while still developing, are quite advanced, and this age level will accept stories of significant length—up to fifteen minutes or so—and complexity. Older children in this group (the nine- to eleven-year-old crowd) especially enjoy told stories without props. Puppetry, if used well, can still delight and entertain even the oldest of the group, even though the magical quality associated with this form of entertainment has somewhat waned.

Developmentally, the primary level child age six to eight is a highly active, assertive (sometimes to the point of stubbornness), competitive, and self-confident individual. At this age, there is a tendency to crave attention and question authority, so care must be taken not to let the primary level child "run" your show. Disinterest in this age group can manifest as a rude interruption and refusal to participate with the group. If you can include a great deal of variety in your program —length, subject matter, and complexity—you will at least have covered some probable attention span challenges that this age group faces.

Primary Level Program Elements

The format of a primary level story program is not much different than that of the preschooler, with one obvious difference—the school age child is less interested in learning new things or concepts as they are in being entertained. Your challenge then becomes one of subliminally introducing quality literature into their steady diets of computer games and television.

Your story program for the school age group might look something like this:

- ✧ Opening routine or attention grabber
- ✧ Shortest story
- ✧ Activity/riddle/game
- ✧ Longest story
- ✧ Activity/riddle/joke
- ✧ Song
- ✧ Story
- ✧ Closing routine

Try not to patronize the primary level child by talking down to them or presenting material well below their developmental level. If you do either, you might never see them in your program again. On the other hand, this age group is also highly enthusiastic if properly approached. Think back to yourself and your interests at this age, the books and stories you enjoyed, to get your best handle on just what makes a six- or nine-year-old tick.

As mentioned above, this is the age that loves, no make that *adores*, scary stories—the grosser and scarier the better. If you have the capability, consider turning off the lights for your more frightening tales to really set the mood. In fact, it is an excellent idea to begin the primary level story program, not with a song or activity, but with a good ghost story. You will not only gain their attention, but their respect, primarily because you have given them something that they want, not something "educational" or "librarian-like."

If your group is small enough, no more than twenty, go around the room and ask each audience member to introduce themselves by their first name. As with adults, the act of naming oneself in a public setting works to bond the group together and dispel any unease they might be feeling. You can even turn this part of the program into a game as you boastfully announce that you are able to remember their names after one introduction. Of course, when they make you prove it, you will fail miserably, but this is your plan as you are actually creating a very humorous bit in the process.

Picture Books for Primary Level

While younger children need bold and uncomplicated illustrations in their picture books, the primary level child can appreciate differences in artistic styles and enjoy more complex illustrations. Stories that contain humor, word play, puns, suspense, irony, and adventure are ideal for this sophisticated crowd. Refer to both the list of recommended picture books in chapter nine and the list of suggested stories to tell in this chapter as a guide.

Sample Themed Programs for Primary Level
Ages Six to Eight

At the Beach

Story Books

Lottie's New Beach Towel	Petra Mathers
The Happy Hippopotami	Bill Martin
Rhinos Who Surf	Julie Mammano
Harry by the Sea	Gene Zion

Activities, Songs, and Fingerplays

Surfin' USA	
by The Beach Boys	song
It's All the Same to a Clam	
by Shel Silverstein	poem

Food, Glorious Food

Story Books

The Stinky Cheese Man	Jon Sciezka
Stop That Pickle	Peter Armour
My Sister Ate One Hare	Bill Grossman

Activities, Songs, and Fingerplays

Nobody Likes Me	song
On Top of Spaghetti	song
Eyeballs for Sale	
by Jack Prelutsky	poem
Take Me Out to the	
Ball Game	song
If the World Was Crazy	
by Shel Silverstein	poem

Laughter is the Best Medicine #1

Story Books

What Do You Do With a Kangaroo?	Mercer Mayer
The Stinky Cheese Man	Jon Scieszka

Activities, Songs, and Fingerplays

My Aunt Came Back	call/response song
Hi, My Name Is Joe	activity
Mama Mama	call/response song
That's Good. That's Bad	told story
Never Smile at a Crocodile	song

Laughter is the Best Medicine #2

Story Books

Dogzilla	Dav Pilkey
An Octopus Followed Me Home	Dan Yaccarino

Activities, Songs, and Fingerplays

Eddie Coocha Catcha Camma	song
Ladies First	
by Shel Silverstein	told story
Little Rabbit Foo Foo	song
Ordinary Red Beans	told story
Old Woman Who Swallowed a Fly	song

Little Folk

Story Books

*Clever Tom and the
    Leprechaun*   Linda Shute
*The Woman Who
    Flummoxed the Fairies* Heather Forest
The Blueberry Pie Elf   Jane Thayer

Activities, Songs, and Fingerplays

Little Elf's Adventure   action story
The Shoemaker and the
    Elves   puppet play
The Three Wishes   told story

Royalty

Story Books

17 Kings and 42 Elephants   Margaret Mahy
Ashpet   Joanne Compton
*King Bidgood's in the
    Bathtub*   Audrey Wood

Activities, Songs, and Fingerplays

The King's Breakfast
    by A. A. Milne   flannel board
The Noble Duke of York   action song
King's Prized Possession   told story
The Frog Prince   puppet play

Suggested Stories to Tell to Primary Level
Ages Nine to Eleven

"Anansi Drinks Boiling Water" (Jamaica). Sharon Creech. *Fair Is Fair: World Folktales of Justice*. August House, 1994. 122-123.

Tricky, lazy Spider-man figures out a way to stock his storehouse full of yams without once tending to his garden. Then he tricks the King into believing his innocence in stealing the yams.

"Anansi Returns" (Jamaica). Josepha Sherman. *Trickster Tales: Forty Tales from Around the World*. August House, 1996. 140-143.

Anansi tricks Tiger into allowing all stories to be named after him.

Ants Can't Dance. Ellen Jackson. Macmillan, 1991.

No one will believe Johnathan when he tells them he has an ant that can dance, a peanut that can talk, and a stone that whistles.

"The Big-Mouth Frog." Margaret Read MacDonald. *The Parent's Guide to Storytelling: How to Make Up New Stories and Retell Old Favorites*. HarperCollins Juvenile Books, 1995. 83-85.

Humorous story of a loud and annoying big-mouthed frog who drives everybody crazy.

"The Big Toe" (Appalachian). Richard Chase. *American Folk Tales and Songs and Other Examples of English-American Tradition As Presented in the Appalachian Mountains and Elsewhere in the United States*. Dover, 1971. 57-59.

Jump tale involving a boy who, while hoeing, hacks off something's big toe. He is so hungry for meat in his dinner that he adds the toe to the pot of beans. Later, he is haunted by The Something who demands his toe back.

The Dancing Skeleton. Cynthia C. DeFelice. Macmillan, 1989.

Scary story with a touch of humor. It seems that while Aaron Kelly is dead, he doesn't want to stay that way and he is ruining his wife's chances of finding a new suitor.

"A Dispute in Sign Language" (Israel). Jane Yolen. *Favorite Folktales from Around the World*. Pantheon, 1986. 42-44.

A wicked priest who hates Jews challenges the chief rabbi to find someone to have a dispute with him in sign language or he will kill them. A lowly poultry dealer saves the day in this ingenious tale.

"The Freedom Bird" (Thailand). David Holt. *Ready-to-Tell Tales: Sure-Fire Stories from America's Favorite Storytellers*. Ed., David Holt and Bill Mooney. August House, 1994. 220-222.

Hunter tries to kill a beautiful golden bird in various ways, only to have it come back to life and multiply.

"The Goat and the Rock" (Tibet). Pleasant DeSpain. *Thirty-Three Multicultural Tales to Tell*. August House, 1993. 117-119.

A dispute arises between a milk-seller and a goat who breaks his milk jug. A judge determines each should be arrested. When the crowd gathers to hear his decision, the judge fines each person one penny for their "improper thoughts" and donates the funds to the milk-seller.

"The Great Tug-O-War" (African-American). Judy Sierra and Robert Kaminski. *Multicultural Folktales: Stories to Tell Young Children*. Oryx, 1991. 73-75.

Tale of Brother Rabbit who arranges a tug-of-war between Brother Elephant and Sister Whale, only to make fools of them both.

The Green Gourd (North Carolina). C. W. Hunter. Putnam, 1991.

Very funny mountain tale of an old woman in need of a water-dipper who defies the caution not to pick green gourds. She soon regrets her decision.

"The Haunted House" (Virginia). Richard Chase. *American Folk Tales and Songs and Other Examples of English-American Tradition as Presented in the Appalachian Mountains and Elsewhere in the United States*. Dover, 1971. 60-62.

Jump tale concerning a preacher who visits a settlement to "lay a ha'nt" in a house that has been haunted for ten years.

"How Anansi Got the Stories" (Ghana). Barbara Reed. *Joining In: An Anthology of Audience Participation Stories and How to Tell Them*. Ed., Teresa Miller. Yellow Moon, 1988. 75-88.

Recounts how most African folk tales came to be known as "spider stories."

"How to Count Crocodiles." Margaret Mayo. *Tortoise's Flying Lesson*. Harcourt, 1995. 11-16.

Tricky monkey devises a way to cross the river to the side with the delicious mango tree.

"Ladies First." Shel Silverstein. *Free to Be You and Me* by Marlo Thomas. McGraw, 1974. 39-45.

"Did you ever hear the one about the little girl who was a 'tender sweet young thing?'" Well, she gets her comeuppance in a very humorous and tasty way.

"Lazy Jack" (England). Tana Reiff. *Timeless Tales: Folktales*. New Readers Press, 1991. 10-15.

Classic humorous tale of lazy boy whose mother insists he get a job. Of course, in the end, Jack saves the day.

The Leopard's Drum: An Asante Tale from West Africa. Jessica Souhami. Little, Brown, 1995.

Osebo the leopard has a magnificent drum that he won't share with anyone. Nayme, the Sky-God, offers a reward for the animal who will bring him the drum.

"The Lion and the Rabbit" (India). Heather Forest. *Joining In: An Anthology of Audience Participation Stories and How to Tell Them*. Ed., Teresa Miller. Yellow Moon, 1988. 5-7.

In order to relieve the fear caused by a ferocious lion who roams the jungle and kills for pleasure, the animals decide to send him one animal each day for his supper. Wise rabbit eventually tricks the lion into a well by convincing him the reflection in the water is a rival lion.

"Little Crab and His Magic Eyes." Margaret Read MacDonald. *Twenty Tellable Tales: Audience Participation Folktales for the Beginning Storyteller*. Wilson, 1986. 24-34.

Engaging tale that, in a roundabout way, offers an explanation as to why jaguars kill their prey and leave the carcasses for the vulture family.

The Little Old Lady Who Was Not Afraid of Anything. Linda Williams. Crowell, 1986.

Not-so-scary story for younger ages of an old woman who meets various pieces of a something (shoes, shirt, gloves, hat, pumpkin head) on the road. She gets progressively scared of what she sees. She has a talk with the pumpkin head and convinces it to become her scarecrow.

"The Little Old Woman Who Lived in a Vinegar Bottle." Margaret Read MacDonald. *Storyteller's Start-Up Book: Finding, Learning, Performing, and Using Folktales Including Twelve Tellable Tales*. August House, 1993. 117-123.

Participation tale of an old whining woman that lives in a vinegar bottle and wishes she lived in a cottage. She is visited by a fairy who grants her wish. The woman is still unhappy, and wishes to live in progressively better places. Her wishes continue to be granted until she wishes to be queen of everything. To this, the fairy puts her back in her bottle moralizing, "After all, contentment comes from the *heart*, not from the *house*."

"Mattresses." Vivian Vande Velde. *Tales from the Brothers Grimm and the Sisters Weird*. Harcourt, 1995. 79-87.

Humorous modern retelling of "The Princess and the Pea" in which a whining and demanding Princess has a horrible night's sleep. Her fussy, impossible-to-please nature makes everyone sigh with relief when she finally goes home in the morning.

"Morgan and the Pot o' Brains" (Welsh). Milbre Birch. *Best-Loved Stories Told at the National Storytelling Festival*. August House, 1991. 153-157.

Morgan is a simpleton who decides to visit the witch on the hill and ask her to sell him a whole pot of brains. He is told to bring her the heart of the thing he loves the best plus answer three riddles.

"Ningun." Margaret Read MacDonald. *The Story-Teller's Start-Up Book*. August House, 1993. 185-194.

Tale of a conceited and beautiful girl who follows a forbidden lover into the forest, only to be eaten by a boa constrictor—one inch at a time.

"Ol' Gally Mander" (American). Nancy Van Laan. *With a Whoop and a Holler*. Atheneum, 1998. 76-81.

Ol' Gally Mander hires a girl as stingy and nasty as herself to clean her house, but tells her not to peek up her chimney. You can guess the rest in this perfectly wonderful tale of exaggerated character and trust.

"Old One Eye" (US). Margaret Read MacDonald. *Twenty Tellable Tales: Audience Participation Folktales for the Beginning Storyteller*. Wilson, 1986. 43-51.

Unique story involving an old woman, a big one-eyed dried fish, three robbers, and a purse of gold hidden in the chimney.

"Old Joe and the Carpenter" (US). Pleasant De-Spain. *Thirty-Three Multicultural Tales to Tell*. August House, 1993. 13-14.

Two feuding neighbors find the true meaning of friendship from a hired hand who builds them a bridge when they wanted a fence.

"Old Woman and Her Pig" (English). Joseph Jacobs. *English Fairy Tales*. Schocken Books, 1967.

Classic cumulative tale of a woman who finds some money and goes to town to buy a pig, only to find the pig won't jump over the stile on her return.

"Parley Garfield and the Frogs." Margaret Read MacDonald. *Twenty Tellable Tales: Audience Participation Folktales for the Beginning Storyteller*. Wilson, 1986. 52-56.

Humorous easy to learn and tell tale of a grandfather who was informed by a family of frogs how deep the crick was each spring.

"Peace and Quiet" (Yiddish). Judy Sierra. *The Flannel Board Storytelling Book*. H. W. Wilson, 1987. 184-189.

Great participation tale in which a farmer cannot sleep at night because his house makes too much noise. He visits the wise woman of the village who instructs him to put various and progressively larger animals in his house. Nothing seems to work until she instructs him to remove the animals. Then, finally, the man gets his peace and quiet.

"Red Lips." Naomi Baltuck. *Crazy Gibberish*. Linnet, 1993. 32-36.

Scary story that ends humorously. "Do you know what I do with these red, red lips and these long, red fingernails?"

"The Snow Queen with the Cold, Cold Heart." Naomi Baltuck. *Crazy Gibberish*. Linnet, 1993. 37-41.

Humorous action and audience participation tale of a Queen, her daughters, and a Prince. Unique feature of this tale is that each character is introduced with actions and sounds.

"Sody Sallyrytus" (US). Margaret Read MacDonald. *Twenty Tellable Tales: Audience Participation Folktales for the Beginning Storyteller*. Wilson, 1986. 79-89.

Classic American tale of a family, consisting of an old man, an old woman, a little boy, a little girl, and a pet squirrel, who each are sent to the grocery store to pick up some "sody" to make the biscuits rise. Each in turn gets eaten by the bear that blocks the bridge. Finally, the little squirrel outsmarts the bear by climbing a tree and jumping to another branch. The bear bursts open and everybody goes home to biscuits.

"Spin! Spin! Reel Off, Skin!" (US). Richard and Judy Dockrey Young. *Scary Story Reader*. August House, 1993. 73-77.

Scary story from the low country of South Carolina. Centers on a man who has discovered that he has married an evil boo-hag and his efforts to rid his life of her.

"The Squeaky Door." Naomi Baltuck. *Crazy Gibberish*. Linnet, 1993. 45-49.

Silly cumulative tale full of sound effects (squeaky door, dog, pig, cat, horse) and repeated phrases (like "Sonny Boy, you're driving me crazy!") that invite participation.

"Strength" (Limba People of West Africa). Margaret Read MacDonald. *Ready-to-Tell Tales: Sure-Fire Stories from America's Favorite Storytellers*. Ed., David Holt and Bill Mooney. August House, 1994. 58-63.

Powerful tale in which the animals decide to hold a contest to determine the strongest of them all. Man brings his gun and shows everyone that he should win, confusing the ability to kill with strength.

"The Tailor" (Yiddish). Naomi Baltuck. *Crazy Gibberish*. Linnet, 1993. 50-51.

Classic tale of a poor tailor who saves his money and finally has enough to buy cloth for a coat. He wears it almost out then cuts it down for a jacket. He wears the jacket almost out then cuts it down for a vest, then a cap, then a button. "At least it *seemed* to be worn out, but when he looked more closely, he could see that there was still enough left of that button to make . . . a story."

"The Teeny Weeny Bop" (US). Naomi Baltuck. *Crazy Gibberish*. Linnet, 1993. 23-31.

Humorous participation tale involving a young girl who finds a silver coin while sweeping her floor. She uses the money to buy a pig that ends up ruining her garden, trades the pig for a cat that made a mess of her living room, trades the cat for a hamster that made a mess of everything, and trades the hamster for an ant that eats her food. She lets the ant loose and finds another coin and whole mess starts over again.

"That Was Good! Or Was It?" John Porchino. *Joining In: An Anthology of Audience Participation Stories and How to Tell Them*. Ed., Teresa Miller. Yellow Moon, 1988. 71-74.

Great redo of the classic participatory that's good/that's bad tale.

"The Three Sillies" (English). Joseph Jacobs. *English Fairy Tales*. Putnam, 1958. 9-14.

Classic tale of a gentleman who decides to try and find three bigger sillies than his future wife and her parents before he will marry her.

"The Tiger, the Brahman, and the Jackal" (India). Heather Forest. *Wonder Tales from Around the World*. August House, 1995. 45-49.

Brahman frees suffering Tiger from his cage only to be told he will be the lion's lunch. Tiger agrees to let the Brahman go if he can find three things who will agree that life is unfair. The Tree, the Ox, and the Road all tell the Brahman that there is no fairness in the world. The Jackal returns with the Brahman and tricks the Tiger back into his cage.

"Tilly" (English). Martha Hamilton and Mitch Weiss. *Stories in My Pocket: Tales Kids Can Tell*. Fulcrum, 1996. 47-49.

Classic jump tale of a girl named Tilly who "begged her parents to let her have her bedroom in the attic because it was the scariest in the house."

Tortoise's Flying Lesson. Margaret Mayo. Harcourt, 1995. 29-35.

After begging Eagle for flying lessons, Tortoise tries it on his own, only to find that while the flying part is easy, it is the landing that is hard.

"Uwungelema" (Bantu). Judy Sierra. *The Flannel Board Storytelling Book*. H. W. Wilson, 1987. 152-153.

A famine has struck and the single remaining source of food is a great magic tree that will only drop its fruit if its name is said out loud. Hare, Eland, and finally Tortoise are sent to the King to bring back the name. Each forgets the name upon return, except slow and sure tortoise who saves the day.

Why Alligator Hates Dog: A Cajun Folktale. J. J. Reneaux. August House LittleFolk, 1995.

When sassy old Dog tricks Alligator, the king of the swamp, it starts a feud that continues to this very day.

"Why Anansi the Spider Has a Small Waist" (West Africa). Martha Hamilton and Mitch Weiss. *Stories in My Pocket: Tales Kids Can Tell*. Fulcrum, 1996. 102-105.

Story which explains how spiders came to have small waists.

"Why Crocodile Does Not Eat Hen" (Bantu people of Africa). Martha Hamilton and Mitch Weiss. *Stories in My Pocket: Tales Kids Can Tell*. Fulcrum, 1996. 56-58.

Folktale in which chicken outsmarts crocodile through courtesy.

Why the Sky Is Far Away: A Folktale from Nigeria. Mary-Jean Gerson. Little, Brown, 1992.

A tale of conservation. The sky was once so close to the Earth that the people cut parts of it to eat. Their waste and greed caused the sky to move far, far away.

Wiley and the Hairy Man (African-American). Jack Stokes. Macrae Smith, 1970.

Hairy Man is going to get Wiley, just like he got Pappy, unless the boy can fool him three times.

The Woman Who Flummoxed the Fairies: An Old Tale from Scotland. Heather Forest. HBJ, 1990.

Asked to make a cake for the fairies, a clever baker woman figures out a way to prevent the fairies from keeping her with them to always bake them her delicious cakes.

CHAPTER EIGHT

Family Story Programs

Family story programs may prove to be the most satisfying in your lineup. Not only do you have the opportunity to meet, in some cases, entire families at one time, but you have the wonderful good fortune of presenting quality literature to all ages at once.

If you are primarily used to doing age specific programs and the idea of such a range of ages as you might find in a family story program makes you nervous, relax. A program of mixed ages is an *easy* one to plan, an *easy* one to practice, and an *easy* one to perform. Still in doubt? Consider the following three simple facts:

1. Wide age ranges mean a wide range of material from which to choose;
2. Since your chance is higher that both parents will attend a family story program, you have double the adult supervision;
3. Family story programs generally have a more relaxed feel about them because they are usually offered in the evenings and on weekends.

Family Story Program Elements

Family story programs may include a wide range of storytelling elements such as poetry, folktales, literary tales, participation stories, creative dramatics, puppetry, and reading aloud. In addition, several transitional elements will be vital to the success of this thirty minute to one hour in length program.

In selecting material for the family program, pay careful attention to appropriateness. While younger stories are usually quite suitable for older children, the reverse is rarely true. To meet this need, consider telling a story geared toward a younger crowd in a different way. For instance, a story you have previously learned and told as a flannel board (such as "The Enormous Turnip" or "Little Red Hen") might easily adapt itself to being a participation tale, presented orally instead of visually. In other words, feel free to include a story for a five-year-old, but tell it in an eight-year-old manner.

Lean on the side of caution when selecting material for family programs. Avoid lengthy stories. Avoid all scary stories as there may be infants or toddlers in the room and you don't want to inspire nightmares. Avoid stories that would be considered inappropriate for the youngest members of your group. Avoid stories requiring a great deal of explanatory remarks, such as personal stories or tales of a highly unusual nature.

If you are planning a themed family program, select themes suitable for the wide range of ages you will encounter. Appropriate family program themes include, but are not limited to, pets, families, travel, bugs, food, space, oceans, nature, seasons, and the home.

While you don't have to necessarily aim the entire program for a specific age level, have several toddler fingerplays and action rhymes available, in the back of your mind, to be used in case they become necessary. Restless toddlers can be quickly soothed with a rendition of "Twinkle, Twinkle" or refocused with "I'm a Little Teapot" or "Teddy Bear, Teddy Bear, Turn Around."

Family Story Books

When choosing books for reading aloud, you might make your selections from the list of recommended picture books provided in chapter nine. If you are working with a theme, there are several sources to aid you in your search. One of the best is *A to Zoo: Subject Access to Children's Picture Books* by Carolyn W. Lima. This source is an outstanding and comprehensive guide that lists children's picture books by title, author, and subject. In some cases, it will be your only access to a list of books by theme as almost all public libraries arrange their children's picture book collection by author, not subject.

Every book you choose to read aloud in your family story program is an advertisement for the book, so be sure to have plenty of extra copies available on your book display for patron checkout. In fact, if your library only owns a single copy of a title, you might want to pass on using the story so prominently in your program. Without meaning to, you might be creating an unpleasant situation when your audience finds that they cannot take a copy home with them.

The primary goal of a library story program is to inspire a life-long love of reading. To facilitate this mission, it is of the utmost importance to create a pleasurable experience. If a child or adult can make some sort of conscious or unconscious connection between pleasure and reading or enjoyment and books, they will be naturally drawn to similarly entertaining encounters on their own.

Not to be crass, but think of your story program as a reading commercial and your books as the hooks upon which you hope to catch some readers, reel them in, and then return them to their daily lives enriched and eager to pursue their new reading interests.

Every parent wants their child to succeed in life, yet not every parent knows how to accomplish this all-important task. You, the librarian, the professional storyteller, the camp counselor, the childcare giver, the teacher, the scout leader, the Sunday school teacher, the parent, are ideally suited to relay the vital message that reading is the way.

Regardless of gender, race, nationality, or socioeconomic background, those children who read the most achieve the most. According to a 1985 report *Becoming a Nation of Readers*, published by the Commission on Reading, under the auspices of the Department of Education, "The single most important activity for building the knowledge required for eventual success in reading is *reading aloud* to children (23)."

In this regard, you have your work cut out for you. Good luck.

Sample Family Story Programs

═══ Bugs ═══

Story Books

Old Black Fly	Jim Aylesworth
In the Tall, Tall Grass	Denise Fleming
Fireflies, Fireflies, Light	
My Way	Jonathan London
The Very Quiet Cricket	Eric Carle

Activities, Songs, and Fingerplays

Mosquito by	
Mary Ann Hoberman	poem
Spider on the Floor	song
I'm Bringing Home a Baby	
Bumblebee	song
Eensie Weensie Spider	activity song
Here Is the Beehive	fingerplay
An Early Worm Got Out of	
Bed by Jack Prelutsky	poem

═══ Food ═══

Story Books

Jake Baked a Cake	B. G. Hennessy
Stop That Pickle!	Peter Armour
The Very Hungry Caterpillar	Eric Carle
Benny Bakes a Cake	Eve Rice
If You Give a Mouse a	
Cookie	Laura Numeroff

Activities, Songs, and Fingerplays

Apples and Bananas	song
The Gingerbread Boy	told story
Sandwiches Are Beautiful	song
Peanut Butter and Jelly	activity
Hot Cross Buns	rhyme
On Top of Spaghetti	song
Take Me Out to the Ball	
Game	song

═══ Family ═══

Story Books

What Baby Wants	Phyllis Root
Gone Fishing	Earlene Long
No, David!	David Shannon
Is Your Mama a Llama?	Deborah Guarrino
Leo the Late Bloomer	Robert Kraus
Little Gorilla	Ruth Bornstein

Activities, Songs, and Fingerplays

Smart by Shel Silverstein	poem
My Aunt Came Back	call/response song
Mother and Father and	
Uncle John	activity

═══ Home ═══

Story Books

The Napping House	Audrey Wood
A House Is a House for Me	Mary Hoberman
Is This the House for a	
Hermit Crab?	Megan McDonald
The Little Old Woman Who	
Lived in a Vinegar Bottle	Margaret Read
	MacDonald

Activities, Songs, and Fingerplays

Home on the Range	song
Roll Over	song
The Three Bears	creative dramatics

Nature

Story Books

Rainbow of My Own	Don Freeman
Listen to the Rain	Bill Martin, Jr.
Why the Sky Is Far Away	Mary-Jean Gerson
Rain Sizes	John Ciardi
Vegetable Garden	Douglas Florian
The Carrot Seed	Ruth Krauss

Activities, Songs, and Fingerplays

The Cloud by Percy Bysshe Shelley	poem
The Rabbit and the Well	told story
Twinkle, Twinkle	song
Mr. Sun	song
Zip-A-Dee-Doo-Dah	song
The Oak and the Rose by Shel Silverstein	poem

Pets

Story Books

Millions of Cats	Wanda Gag
Martha Speaks	Susan Meddaugh
I Swapped My Dog	Harriet Zieffert
Dogzilla	Dav Pilkey
A Whistle for Willy	Ezra Jack Keats
Six-Dinner Sid	Inga Moore
Dog Breath	Dav Pilkey

Activities, Songs, and Fingerplays

King's Prized Possession	told story
How Much Is That Doggie in the Window?	song
B-I-N-G-O	song
Cats Sleep Anywhere by Eleanor Farjeon	poem
The Cat Came Back	song

Oceans

Story Books

The Fish Who Could Wish	John Bush
Baby Beluga	Raffi
An Octopus Followed Me Home	Dan Yaccarino
Swimmy	Leo Lionni
Big Al	Andrew Clements

Activities, Songs, and Fingerplays

Sailor Went to Sea	song
Little Crab and His Magic Eyes	told story
My Bonnie Lies Over the Ocean	song
Popeye the Sailor Man	song

Seasons

Story Books

Planting a Rainbow	Lois Ehlert
Sleepy Bear	Lydia Dabcovich
New Boots for Spring	Harriet Zieffert
The Snowy Day	Ezra Jack Keats

Activities, Songs, and Fingerplays

Alicia and the Leaves by Pyke Johnson, Jr.	poem
The North Wind Doth Blow	creative dramatics
Frosty the Snowman	song
Let It Snow, Let It Snow, Let It Snow	song
That Was Summer by Marci Ridlon	poem

PART THREE

STORYTELLING/
STORYSHARING

CHAPTER NINE

Reading Aloud: The Hand-Held Picture Book

Picture books represent the core of story programs for young children. Since one of the prime goals of the story program is teaching children to love books and reading, picture books should occupy a lion's share of the time allotted to the program.

Choosing the picture books to include in your story program requires thoughtful consideration. You will find the task is simplified if you have read rather widely and have developed a familiarity with many picture books. Ask yourself what is the purpose of your story program. Then consider which picture books will most likely aid you in achieving your goal. Are they appropriate for the intended age level? Do the moods of the selections blend together smoothly? For instance, it would be an unusual story program that would contain both *Play with Me* by Ets and *Fortunately* by Charlip, the former being a delicate nature story and the latter slapstick humor. Does the plot and theme of the books you have chosen begin where the children are and stretch them into new emotions and experiences? Are the illustrations large, uncluttered, and clear enough to be seen easily by every child in the group? Even the finest picture book will fail if the children in the back of the room cannot distinguish the artwork.

You should measure the books you have picked out against one final criterion: are they truly worthy of a place in your story program and will they earn a place in the children's hearts?

You should avoid picture books that are either in a small format or contain cluttered, tiny, or uninteresting illustrations. While these might be the greatest story ever written, the pictures in the books are not accessible in a group setting. You might consider using these titles on a list for recommended reads in a lap time storybook sharing. Likewise, books that contain chapters or are very long, with more than a few paragraphs per page, are not appropriate for a read-aloud program.

Selecting picture books to use in toddler story programs requires taking a look at developmental and experiential levels of the children. Between the ages of eighteen and thirty-six months, children are practicing motor skills using large muscles, are learning the basic language skills, and are discovering themselves as independent individuals. Their experiences and interests are centered around family, animals, and themselves.

Some of the very simplest concept books can be included but may have to be abridged. For instance, Pienkowski's *Shapes* is useful, but only for the basic shapes. Number books such as Peppe's *Circus Numbers* works well with older toddlers, but you may want to count only to five rather than to ten. Several books with very little plot are appropriate for toddlers. Omerod's *Reading*, Oxenbury's *Tom and Pippo* books, and Barton's vehicle series are examples. A few simple picture story books can be included. Among these are

Bornstein's *Little Gorilla*, Martin's *Brown Bear, Brown Bear*, and Hutchins' *Titch*.

For preschoolers, you will fine a rich and abundant supply of picture books from which to choose. Your main problem in selecting books will be narrowing down the field and choosing the most appropriate for your group. This age group can handle more elaborately developed concept books and stories with more detailed and intricate plots. Children enjoy examining illustrations—they pore over the paintings in Brian Wildsmith's *Mother Goose Nursery Rhymes* and count the baby ducks in McCloskey's *Make Way for Ducklings*.

Children's choices for preschool story programs include Butler's *My Brown Bear Barney*, Shannon's *No, David!*, Nodset's *Who Took the Farmer's Hat?*, Keat's Peter books, Zion's Harry tales, Flack's Angus stories, and anything by Mercer Mayer and Dav Pilkey.

You should include enough variety to satisfy the many tales and interests of three- to five-year-olds. You will, however, have to look long and hard to find titles about girls, for in most picture story books even animal main characters are male.

Picture books for primary level children are not quite as plentiful as those for preschoolers, but outstanding selections are available. The Frances books by Hoban, the Madeline books by Bemelmans, and the Frog and Toad books by Lobel are excellent choices, as are titles by Lionni, Keeping,

Ness, and DePaola.

This age group also likes folk tales, such as *Why Mosquitoes Buzz in People's Ears*, *Tikki Tikki Tembo*, *The Funny Little Woman*, *Stone Soup*, *Anansi and the Moss-Covered Rock*, and *Why Alligator Hates Dog*. They enjoy poems, such as *Custard the Dragon*, *The Sneeches and Other Stories*, *Hailstones and Halibut Bones*, and *Chicka Chicka Boom Boom*, and folk songs such as "Old Woman Who Swallowed a Fly," "Mama Mama," "Skip to My Lou," and "I Had a Rooster."

Even though most eight-year-olds can read these picture books independently, they still enjoy them read in the story program and sharing them with others. Preschoolers can also be introduced to good stories which they might not choose to read themselves.

The bibliography included here offers a wide range of suggested picture books. All titles on this list can be used effectively with groups of children in any story program setting. Some outstanding stories have been omitted because they are simply more appropriately read to children on a one-to-one basis rather than in a group.

Begin by using picture books that you especially like and gradually expand your repertoire to include stories appropriate for all ages and all situations. Experiment until you find a selection of stories that you can generally call your own.

Outstanding Books to Use in Story Programs

Aardema, Verna. *Why Mosquitoes Buzz in People's Ears*. Dial, 1975.

The mosquito's boasting creates a chain reaction of events affecting all the animals in the jungle. Read aloud and share the exquisite pictures. Available on filmstrip, film, video, and in poster size.

Also: *Bringing the Rain to Kapiti Plain*. Dial, 1981. Also poster size. *Jackal's Flying Lesson*. Knopf, 1995. *Oh, Kojo! How Could You?* Available on filmstrip.

Adams, Adrienne. *The Shoemaker and the Elves*. Macmillan, o.p.

A pleasantly illustrated version of the folktale in which elves assist a shoemaker by secretly making shoes each night, this book can be used with small groups. The story itself makes a charming puppet play. Available on filmstrip.

Ahlberg, Janet. *Each Peach Pear Plum*. Viking Penguin, 1979.

In this participation story children are asked to "spy" the familiar nursery rhyme and folktale characters hidden within the pictures. The book contains illustrations too small for use in a group setting, but the poster-size edition, filmstrip, and video serve groups well.

Alarcón, Karen Beaumont. *Louella Mae, She's Run Away!* Henry Holt, 1997.

Adorable and well illustrated rhyming story of the missing Louella Mae. Her entire family looks everywhere for her and almost gives up, only to find her in the tub. You don't find out until the last page that Louella Mae is a pig. Read aloud to preschool age crowd.

Aliki. *Hush Little Baby*. Simon & Schuster, 1968.

Warm pictures illustrate the popular folk song in which "Papa's going to buy you a mockingbird." Since the text catalogs a list of items that Papa's going to buy, this story works well on the flannel board as well as a sing-along. Available on film, video, and filmstrip.

Armour, Peter. *Stop That Pickle!* Houghton Mifflin, 1993

A pickle tries to escape being eaten by fleeing through the city pursued by a peanut butter and jelly sandwich, a fat braided pretzel, a lovely green pippin apple, seventeen toasted almonds, a crowd of raisins, a cake doughnut, a cool bottle of grape juice, and an elegant vanilla ice cream cone sprinkled with chocolate. Fanciful illustrations make this a great read-aloud for younger school aged children.

Asch, Frank. *Happy Birthday, Moon*. Simon & Schuster, 1981.

A small bear decides to get a birthday present for the moon in this gentle, warm story. Available on film, video, and filmstrip.

Also: *Bear's Bargain*. Simon & Schuster, 1989. Also available in poster size. *Mooncake*. Simon & Schuster. Available in poster size. *Moongame*. Simon & Schuster, 1984.

Bang, Molly. *Ten, Nine, Eight*. Greenwillow, 1983.

A Caldecott Honor Book, this counting book depicts a loving father putting his small daughter to bed. It is suitable for both toddlers and preschoolers. Available in poster size and on filmstrip.

Barrett, Judy. *Animals Should Definitely <u>Not</u> Wear Clothing*. Atheneum, 1970.

What would animals look like if they wore clothes? Children love these humorous illustrations. Also available in poster size format.

Also: *Animals Should Definitely <u>Not</u> Act Like People*. Atheneum, 1980.

Barton, Byron. *Airport*. Harper, 1982.

Featuring bold, bright illustrations with only a few words per page, *Airport* describes the activities that precede a flight. It is a sure winner with those preschoolers who want informational books.

Also: *Bones, Bones, Dinosaur Bones*. Harper, 1990. *Dinosaurs, Dinosaurs*. Harper, 1989. *I Want to Be an Astronaut*. Harper, 1988. *Machines at Work*. Harper, 1987. *Trains*. Crowell, 1986. *Three Bears*. Harper, 1991.

Bemelmans, Ludwig. *Madeline*. Viking Penguin, 1939.

When Madeline requires an appendectomy and is showered with gifts, the other little girls in her French school long for similar surgery. A well-written verse story, *Madeline* is fun to read aloud. Available on film, filmstrip, video, and in poster size; also dolls in a variety of sizes.

Bishop, Claire. *The Five Chinese Brothers*. Putnam, 1938.

A well-loved tale in which five look-alike brothers, each with a unique characteristic, resist the villagers determined attempts to execute the first brother. It can be told, read aloud, or dramatized. Available on film, video, and filmstrip.

Bornstein, Ruth. *Little Gorilla*. Houghton Mifflin, 1979.

Little Gorilla, who is loved by his family and all the animals in the great green forest, discovers that when he grows up every one still loves him. This book is a must for preschool story hours.

Bright, Robert. *My Red Umbrella*. Morrow, 1985.

Suitable for toddlers as well as preschoolers, this brief story tells of a little girl and all the animals that share her red umbrella during a rain shower. The tiny book can be shared with very small groups. For larger groups, the story works well on the flannel board.

Also: *Georgie*. Doubleday, 1944. Also available on filmstrip, film, and video.

Brown, Marc. *Arthur's Baby*. Little, 1987.

Anticipating a surprise, Arthur is disappointed to receive a baby sister instead of a bicycle. He considers her a real nuisance until the day that she will only stop crying for him. Available on filmstrip. Also an 18 inch Arthur doll.

Also: *Arthur's Nose*. Little, 1976.

Brown, Marcia. *The Three Billy Goats Gruff*. Harcourt, 1957.

Three billy goats Gruff encounter a wicked troll on their way to the hillside to make themselves fat. Brown's version of this Norse folktale is great for reading aloud or learning to tell without the picture book. The story is adaptable to the flannel board, to puppets, and to creative dramatics. Available on filmstrip, film, and video.

Also: *Cinderella*. Macmillan, 1954. Available on filmstrip. *Once a Mouse*. Macmillan, 1961. Available on filmstrip and video. *Stone Soup*. Macmillan, 1947. Available on filmstrip, film, and video.

Brown, Margaret Wise. *Goodnight Moon*. Harper, 1947.

In this classic "good night" story a bunny says good night to familiar objects in his world. Colors in the illustrations change from bright to dusky as night falls. Available on filmstrip and in poster size book.

Also: *Big Red Barn*. Rev. ed. Harper, 1989. Also poster size. *Runaway Bunny*. Harper, 1942.

Bucknall, Caroline. *One Bear All Alone*. Dial, 1986.

The charming counting book is designed with a double-page spread for each number: the numeral and a rhymed couplet appear on one page and a full page picture depicting the verse appears opposite.

Burningham, John. *Mr. Gumpy's Outing*. Holt, 1971.

When Mr. Gumpy goes out in his boat, he warns each of the children and animals who join him not to do certain things. When they all disobey, the boat tips over and everyone gets wet. Mr. Gumpy takes them all home for tea and invites them to come for a ride on another day. Read aloud; for variety interpret on the flannel board. Available on filmstrip.

Also: *Hey! Get Off Our Train*. Crown, 1990. *Mr. Gumpy's Motorcar*. Harper, 1976. Also available on filmstrip.

Burton, Virginia Lee. *Mike Mulligan and His Steam Shovel*. Houghton Mifflin, 1939.

Mike Mulligan and his steam shovel, Mary Ann, win a wager by digging the basement for the town hall in one day. Unfortunately, they allow no means for escaping the excavation, a dilemma solved when a small boy suggests that Mary Ann be converted into a furnace. A favorite read-aloud story available on film, video, and filmstrip.

Also: *Katy and the Big Snow*. Houghton Mifflin, 1973. *The Little House*. Houghton Mifflin, 1978. Available on filmstrip and film.

Butler, Dorothy. *My Brown Bear Barney*. Greenwillow, 1989.

In a series of scenarios familiar to preschoolers, a little girl describes what she will take along and always includes her brown bear Barney. Children love to chime in on the refrain, "and my brown bear Barney," turning it into a delightful participation story. Although the detailed pictures are so tiny that the book can only be used with small groups, the poster size edition renders it suitable for use with more children.

Also: *My Brown Bear Barney in Trouble*. Greenwillow, 1993.

Carle, Eric. *The Very Hungry Caterpillar*. Putnam, 1981.

A multi-faceted concept book in which a caterpillar eats his way through a variety of foods and a week of days to emerge as a beautiful butterfly. Appealing color, intriguing format, and the various concepts invite participation. Available in poster size; also as a stuffed toy.

Also: *Animals, Animals*. Putnam, 1989. *A House for a Hermit Crab*. Picture Book Studio, 1987. *1, 2, 3 to the Zoo*. Putnam, 1989. *Today Is Monday*. Philomel, 1993. *The Very Busy Spider*. Putnam, 1989. *The Very Quiet Cricket*. Putnam, 1990.

Carlson, Nancy. *I Like Me*. Viking Penguin, 1988.

In this ultimate self-concept book a pig admires her strengths and forgives her weaknesses as she declares that she is her own best friend. This cheerful, self-confident pig cannot help but inspire children to feel better about themselves. Available on filmstrip and in poster size.

Chalmers, Mary. *Throw a Kiss, Harry*. New ed. Harper, 1990.

Harry, the mischievous young cat, wanders away when his mother stops to talk to a friend. While playing, he climbs a tree, jumps onto the very high roof of a house, and must be rescued by a fireman. First published in 1956, this new edition is considerably larger and is illustrated in full color. A perfect story for two- and three-year-olds.

Charlip, Remy. *Fortunately*. Macmillan, 1980.

When Ned in New York receives an invitation to a birthday party in Florida, he encounters a series of adventures en route which "fortunately" and "unfortunately" aid and hinder his journey. Since most of the outrageously unexpected events are depicted only in the pictures, reading aloud is imperative. The story can be adapted for telling purposes.

Chase, Edith Newlin. *New Baby Calf.* Scholastic, 1986.

A simple story about Buttercup the cow and her new baby calf, this book features unusual illustrations. The textured clay provides an intriguing three-dimensional effect. Although the pictures are large and easy to see, the poster size edition will enhance story programs for larger groups.

Crews, Donald. *Freight Train.* Greenwillow, 1978.

A Caldecott Honor Book, *Freight Train* features a black steam engine pulling cars of purple, blue, green, yellow, orange, and red. The train zooms through tunnels, over trestles, by cities, in darkness, and in daylight. It is appropriate for both toddlers and preschoolers and is available in poster size and on filmstrip.

Also: *Bigmama's.* Greenwillow, 1991. *Carousel.* Greenwillow, 1982. *Sail Away.* Greenwillow, 1995. *School Bus.* Greenwillow, 1984.

DeAngeli, Marguerite. *Book of Nursery and Mother Goose Rhymes.* Doubleday, o.p.

An extensive collection of nursery rhymes, this classic anthology is illustrated with DeAngeli's delicate sketches. Useful as a source book of rhymes, it contains many full page paintings which can be shared in a story program.

Degen, Bruce. *Jamberry.* Harper, 1983.

This book is a four-year-old's delight because of its wonderful experimentation with words, rhyming words, and made-up rhyming words. "Quickberry, quackberry, pick me a blackberry" is sure to tickle the fancy of most preschoolers. Bright colored pictures and the rhymed text combine for a story hour winner. Available in poster size.

DePaola, Tomi. *Strega Nona.* Simon & Schuster, 1975.

Strega Nona (Grandma Witch) hires Big Anthony to help her with the household chores. While she is away, he uses her magic pasta pot which cooks pasta until it creates a near disaster in the town. Strega Nona saves the day and orders just punishment for Anthony. Available on filmstrip, film, and video; also as a doll.

Also: *Charlie Needs a Cloak.* Simon & Schuster, 1974. Available on filmstrip, film, and video. *Strega Nona Meets Her Match.* Putnam, 1993. *Tomi DePaola's Mother Goose.* Putnam, 1985. *Watch Out for Chicken Feet in Your Soup.* Simon & Schuster, 1974.

DeRegniers, Beatrice Schenk. *It Does Not Say Meow.* Houghton Mifflin, 1979.

A collection of rhymed riddles, each of which describes a familiar animal. The large pictures and participation opportunities of this book make it a successful choice for programs for four- and five-year-old children.

Also: *May I Bring a Friend?* Macmillan, 1964. Also on filmstrip.

Duvoisin, Roger. *Petunia.* Knopf, 1962.

Petunia the goose finds a book and convinces everyone that she is wise. Only after she causes near disaster does she discover that wisdom involves more than carrying around a book. Try creative dramatics with older children. Available on film, video, and filmstrip.

Ehlert, Lois. *Fish Eyes: A Book You Can Count On.* Harcourt, 1990.

Fish in electric colors and imaginative shapes fill the pages of this counting book. An excellent adjunct to programs about the sea, it invites participation.

Also: *Color Farm.* Harper, 1990. *Color Zoo.* Harper, 1989. *Feathers for Lunch.* Harcourt, 1990. Available in poster size. *Growing Vegetable Soup.*

Harcourt, 1987. Available in poster size. *Mole's Hill*. Harcourt, 1994. *Nuts to You*. Harcourt, 1993.

Emberley, Barbara. *Drummer Hoff*. Simon & Schuster, 1974.

The repetitious, cumulative, rhyming text describes the firing of a cannon. Even very young children will join the refrain, "But Drummer Hoff fired it off!" Available on film, video, and filmstrip.

Emberley, Ed. *Go Away, Big Green Monster!* Little, Brown, 1992.

Die-cut pages through which bits of monster are revealed. After you meet the monster you yell "go away" and the monster is taken apart in reverse. Not for toddlers as it may be too scary. Preschoolers, however, will ask for more.

Ericsson, Jennifer A. *No Milk!* Tambourine, 1993.

How the little boy coaxes the milk out of the cow. In this humorous tale, the little city boy must learn gentleness in order to accomplish his task. Big bold illustrations make this a good read-aloud.

Ernst, Lisa Campbell. *Miss Penny and Mr. Grubbs*. Bradbury, 1991.

Mr. Grubbs plans revenge for Miss Penny having a better garden than him: send rabbits over and watch them thrive! Great bold illustrations make this a great read-a-loud for preschool and early school age children.

Also: *Squirrel Park*. Bradbury, 1993.

Ets, Marie Hall. *Play with Me*. Viking Penguin, 1955.

A small girl frightens away the wild meadow animals she wants to play with. When she sits quietly by the stream, all the creatures return. Low-key text and delicate pictures make this an important read-aloud story. Children may want to dramatize it. Available on filmstrip.

Also: *Gilberto and the Wind*. Viking Penguin, 1963. Available on filmstrip. *In the Forest*. Penguin, 1976. Available in poster size and on filmstrip. *Just Me*. Viking Penguin, 1965. Also available on filmstrip.

Field, Eugene. *The Gingham Dog and the Calico Cat*. Putnam, 1990.

Field's classic verse, illustrated by Janet Street, describes the fight-to-the-finish of a pair of stuffed toy animals. With only a few lines of the verse appearing on each double page spread, the book can easily be used with a group of preschoolers.

Also: *Wynkin, Blynkin, and Nod*. Dutton, 1982.

Field, Rachel. *General Store*. Greenwillow, 1988.

Nancy Parker has illustrated in picture book format another classic verse, this one detailing the contents of a general store in pioneer America. This book is useful for its historical value and enjoyable for its entertainment value.

Flack, Marjorie. *Angus and the Ducks*. Doubleday, 1989.

Angus, a curious Scotch terrier, slips outside without his leash and chases two white ducks. When the ducks turn and chase him, he runs inside and hides under the sofa. Read aloud or tell with puppets. Available on filmstrip.

Also: *Angus and the Cat*. Doubleday, 1989. Available on filmstrip. *Ask Mr. Bear*. Macmillan, 1932. Available on filmstrip. *Boats on the River*. Viking, 1946, 1991. *The Story about Ping*. Viking Penguin, 1933. Available on filmstrip, film, and video.

Fox, Mem. *Hattie and the Fox*. Bradbury, 1988.

Hattie the hen warns all the other farm animals that something is in the bushes, but they all ignore the warning until they discover that it is a fox. The refrain is sure to inspire participation. Available in poster size.

Freeman, Don. *A Rainbow of My Own*. Viking Penguin, 1966.

In this imaginative story, a small boy pretends to have a rainbow of his own. Together they play games including hide-and-seek. But when the pretend rainbow disappears, the child is pleased by the rainbow created by the sun shining on his goldfish bowl. Available on filmstrip and video.

Also: *Corduroy*. Viking Penguin, 1968. Also available on filmstrip, film, and video. *Dandelion*. Viking Penguin, 1964. Also on filmstrip.

Fyleman, Rose. *A Fairy Went a-Marketing*. Dutton, 1986.

Full color pictures by Jamichael Henterly illustrate this classic poem about a gentle fairy who buys animals at the market only to set them free.

Gag, Wanda. *Millions of Cats*. Putnam, 1928.

A little old man brings his lonely wife not one cat but "hundreds of cats, thousands of cats, millions and billions and trillions of cats." The cats themselves decide which one will belong to the couple. Read the story aloud and let the children join in on the refrain. Available on film, video, and filmstrip.

Galdone, Paul. *The Three Little Pigs*. Houghton Mifflin, 1979.

The artist presents a humorous interpretation of the traditional tale of the pig who built his house of bricks and outwitted the wolf who had huffed and puffed and blown down the houses of straw and sticks. All of the folktales illustrated by Galdone are worthy of sharing with a group. The stories can be read aloud, told, adapted for the flannel board, or dramatized by children or puppets.

Also: *The Gingerbread Boy*. Houghton Mifflin, 1983. Also on filmstrip. *Henny Penny*. Houghton Mifflin, 1979. *The Little Red Hen*. Houghton Mifflin, 1979. Also on filmstrip, film, and video.

Geisel, Theodor Seuss. *The 500 Hats of Bartholomew Cubbins*. Random, 1990.

Bartholomew Cubbins finds himself in much trouble, for each time he removes his hat before the king, another more elaborate one appears in its place. Written in folktale style, this story offers great opportunities for creative dramatics for preschoolers and school age children.

Also: *And to Think That I Saw It on Mulberry Street*. Random, 1989. *Horton Hatches the Egg*. Random, 1940. Also available on filmstrip and video. *The Sneeches and Other Stories*. Random, 1961. *Yertle the Turtle and Other Stories*. Random, 1954.

Gelman, Rita Golden. *Why Can't I Fly?* Scholastic, 1986.

Minnie is a monkey who wants to fly. Her animal friends try and help her, but alas, Minnie can only run, jump, swing, hang, and climb to the sky. That is, until they hold her aloft on a big blanket. Fantastic story of camaraderie and the importance of not giving up. Available in poster size format.

Gershater, Phillis and David. *Greetings, Sun*. DK Publishing, 1998.

Children greet the sun, the breeze, and all the sights which they encounter throughout the day in this beautifully illustrated poem that must be read aloud to enjoy fully.

Ginsburg, Mirra. *The Chick and the Duckling*. Macmillan, 1972.

A newly hatched duckling explores a number of activities with a chick following after, saying, "Me too." An unsuccessful attempt at swimming cures the chick of blind following. The very brief and simple text is appropriate for reading aloud to the youngest children.

Also: *Mushroom in the Rain*. Macmillan, 1988. Also available on filmstrip. *The Three Kittens*. Crown, 1987.

Grossman, Bill. *My Sister Ate One Hare*. Crown, 1996.

A sister eats a lot of really gross stuff in this superb counting book for preschoolers or school age children. Present as a read-aloud or create a box story.

Harper, Wilhelmina. *The Gunniwolf*. Dutton, 1970.

Little Girl disobeys her mother and wanders into the jungle picking flowers and singing. Accosted by the old Gunniwolf who commands her to "sing that guten, sweeten song again," she eventually sings him to sleep and escapes. This truly outstanding story can be read, told, dramatized with two puppets, or adapted into a puppet play.

Hayes, Sarah. *Eat Up, Gemma*. Lothrop, 1988.

Gemma, a toddler who refuses to eat despite admonishments from all members of her family, attempts to eat the fruit on a lady's hat in church. Later, her big brother tempts her into eating by arranging fruit to resemble the hat.

Hill, Eric. *Where's Spot?* Putnam, 1980.

In this lift-the-flap book mother dog Sally looks for her son Spot in hiding places throughout the house but finds a variety of wild animals before discovering the missing puppy. Spot's story is continued in several titles. Video and stuffed toy available.

Hoban, Russell. *A Birthday for Frances*. Harper, 1968.

Frances the badger experiences growing jealousy over the celebration of her little sister's birthday. Her parents, while concerned and amused, stand by lovingly while she works through her feelings. The universal emotion in this story makes it a great one for creative dramatics. Available on filmstrip.

Also: *A Baby Sister for Frances*. Harper, 1964. *A Bargain for Frances*. Harper, 1970. *Bedtime for Frances*. Harper, 1960. *Best Friends for Frances*. Harper, 1969. *Bread and Jam for Frances*. Harper, 1964. Also available in poster size.

Hoberman, Mary Ann. *A House Is a House for Me*. Viking Penguin, 1978.

Houses of all kinds are mused over in this cleverly rhymed book. Besides the usual houses, such as hives for bees and nests for birds, the author suggests that cartons are houses for crackers and gloves are houses for hands. Available in poster size.

Hoffman, Mary. *Amazing Grace*. Dial, 1991.

Grace, who loves stories and acting, earns the part of Peter Pan in the class play despite being black and a girl. She listens when her Nana says, "If Grace put her mind to it, she can do anything she want." Available on video.

Hogrogian, Nonny. *One Fine Day*. Macmillan, 1971.

An old woman cuts off the tail of a fox who has stolen her milk. She promises to return the tail only when he returns the milk. In cumulative folktale tradition, the fox goes from one situation to another in search of the milk. A great read-aloud. Available on filmstrip.

Hutchins, Pat. *Good Night, Owl!* Macmillan, 1972.

All the little woods creatures disturb Owl's daytime sleep. But when night comes and all is quiet, Owl screeches and wakes everybody up. The simple, repetitive text filled with noisy animal sounds appeals to the youngest. Try using an owl puppet with this story and encourage the children to join in with the animal sounds. Available on filmstrip and in poster size.

Also: *Changes, Changes*. Macmillan, 1987. Available on filmstrip, film, and video. *Don't Forget the Bacon*. Greenwillow, 1976. *The Doorbell Rang*. Greenwillow, 1986. Available in poster size. *My Best Friend*. Greenwillow, 1993. *Rosie's Walk*. Macmillan, 1968. Also available on film, filmstrip, video, and in poster size. *Surprise Party*. Macmillan, 1986. Also available in poster size. *Titch*. Macmillan, 1971. Available on filmstrip. *The Wind Blew*. Macmillan, 1974. Also available in poster size book and on filmstrip.

Jeffers, Susan. *All the Pretty Horses*. Scholastic, o.p.

"Hush-a-bye, don't you cry, go to sleep, little lady." This favorite lullaby is illustrated with a delightful fantasy of ponies, flowers, and a small girl. Read it, sing it, and enjoy the pictures. Available in poster size.

Also: *Three Jovial Huntsmen*. Macmillan, 1987.

Johnson, Crockett. *Harold and the Purple Crayon*. Harper, 1958.

Harold goes for a walk with his purple crayon. He draws his way out of a number of scrapes, draws himself into his own room and his own bed, and draws up the covers. Read it aloud, or draw the story as you tell it. Available on film, video, and filmstrip.

Also: *Harold's Trip to the Sky*. Harper, 1957. *A Picture for Harold's Room*. Harper, 1960. Available on filmstrip, film, and video.

Joosse, Barbara M. *Mama, Do You Love Me?* Chronicle Books, 1991.

Set in the Arctic with puffins, whales, and polar bears, this tale shows a small girl testing her mother's patience as she finds the limits of her independence. Include this one as a read-aloud for preschoolers.

Kalan, Robert. *Jump, Frog, Jump!* Scholastic, 1981.

This cumulative tale about a frog that tries to catch a fly is illustrated in bright, bold colors by Byron Barton. No group of children can resist chorusing the refrain, "Jump, Frog, Jump." Available in poster size.

Also: *Rain*. Greenwillow, 1978. *Blue Sea*. Greenwillow, 1979.

Keats, Ezra Jack. *A Whistle for Willy*. Viking Penguin, 1964.

Peter wishes and wishes that he could whistle and practices constantly without success. When at last he really whistles, his dog Willie races to him. Willie and Peter's parents are properly proud of Peter's accomplishment. Illustrated with bright collage, this story with its universal theme is perfect for reading aloud. Available on film, video, and filmstrip. Also a 11 1/2 inch doll.

Also: *A Letter to Amy*. Harper, 1968. Available on filmstrip, film, and video. *Louie*. Greenwillow, 1983. *Pet Show*. Macmillan, 1972. Available on filmstrip, film, and video. *Peter's Chair*. Harper, 1967. Also poster size, filmstrip, film, and video. *The Snowy Day*. Viking Penguin, 1962. Also available in poster size and on filmstrip, film, and video.

Keller, Holly. *Geraldine's Blanket*. Greenwillow, 1984.

Geraldine, a young pig, refuses to give up her favorite blanket despite repeated pleas by her parents. At last she outwits the adults in her life by making a new dress from the blanket for her new doll.

Also: *Geraldine's Big Snow*. Greenwillow, 1988. *Henry's Happy Birthday*. Greenwillow, 1990. *Horace*. Greenwillow, 1991.

Kennedy, Jimmy. *Teddy Bears' Picnic*. Aladdin, 1989.

Illustrated in color by Renate Kozikowski, this picture song book shows a family of teddy bears preparing for and enjoying a picnic in the woods.

Kent, Jack. *The Caterpillar and the Polliwog*. Simon & Schuster, 1982.

A polliwog becomes so enamored with a caterpillar's metamorphosis into a butterfly, that he fails to notice that he is turning into a frog. Available on film, video, and filmstrip. Also available as dolls.

Also: *Joey*. Simon & Schuster, 1984. *Joey Runs Away*. Simon & Schuster, 1985. Available on filmstrip, film, and video. *Silly Goose*. Simon & Schuster, 1982.

Kraus, Robert. *Leo the Late Bloomer*. Harper, 1987.

Leo the lion can't read, write, or draw very well. His mother says he's just a late bloomer. So his father watches and waits for him to develop. It is a slow process to be sure, but in the end, he does bloom in this charming and beautifully illustrated book for preschoolers. Great read-aloud story.

Also: *Whose Mouse Are You?* Macmillan, 1970.

Krauss, Ruth. *The Carrot Seed*. Harper, 1945.

A small boy plants a carrot seed and steadfastly waters it and pulls up the weeds around it, although everyone tells him that it will not come up. His efforts are rewarded when he harvests a giant carrot. Very good on the flannel board and available in poster size.

Also: *A Hole Is to Dig*. Harper, 1952. Also available on filmstrip. *A Very Special House*. Harper, 1953.

Langstaff, John. *Over in the Meadow*. Harcourt, 1957.

This old folk song about various meadow animal mothers and their children can be read aloud or sung. As a counting activity, you can use the illustrations in the book or pictures on the flannel board. Available in poster size, and on film, video, and filmstrip.

Also: *Frog Went a-Courtin'*. Harcourt, 1955. Also available on filmstrip, film, and video. *A-Hunting We Will Go*. Macmillan, 1974.

Leaf, Munro. *The Story of Ferdinand*. Viking Penguin, 1936.

Ferdinand the bull, unlike his peers, prefers smelling flowers to fighting. He is taken to the bull ring where he sits down and smells the flowers and refuses to fight. He is delighted to return to the cork tree in the meadow. Available on filmstrip, film, and video.

Lewin, Hugh. *Jafta*. Carolrhoda, 1983.

Jafta, a child of South Africa, compares his feelings and actions to animals in this lyrical book. "When I'm happy, said Jafta, I purr like a lion cub, or skip like a spider, or laugh like a hyena." The book's sepia illustrations blend perfectly with the text. Read aloud.

Also: *Jafta's Father*. Carolrhoda, 1983. *Jafta's Mother*. Carolrhoda, 1983.

Lionni, Leo. *Frederick*. Knopf, 1990.

Frederick just sits instead of helping his mouse companions gather food for the winter. During the cold winter when the food supply is gone, Frederick redeems himself by raising everyone's spirit by reciting poetry. Available on filmstrip and video.

Also: *Alexander and the Wind-Up Mouse*. Pantheon, 1970. *The Biggest House in the World*. Pantheon, 1968. *Inch by Inch*. Astor-Honor, 1962. *Swimmy*. Pantheon, 1963. Also filmstrip, film, and video. *Tico and the Golden Wings*. Knopf, 1975.

Lobel, Arnold. *Frog and Toad Are Friends*. Harper, 1970.

Five delightful, humorous stories about two friends, Frog and Toad, are written in easy-to-read vocabulary. Unpredictable events with surprise endings make these short tales fun to read aloud. Available on filmstrip, film, and video.

Also: *Frog and Toad Together*. Harper, 1972. Also on filmstrip, film, and video. *Ming Lo Moves the Mountain*. Greenwillow, 1982. *On Market Street*. Greenwillow, 1981. Also available in poster size and on filmstrip.

McCarthy, Patricia. *Ocean Parade: A Counting Book*. Doubleday, 1990.

Beginning with "1 big fish, 2 little fish" and continuing through "50 pink-and-green-spotted fish, 100 silver fish," *Ocean Parade* presents a stream of shimmering fishes to count. The stunning art for the book consists of batik paintings on silk.

Also: *Animals Galore*. Doubleday, 1989.

McCloskey, Robert. *Make Way for Ducklings*. Viking Penguin, 1941.

When Mrs. Mallard escorts her eight ducklings through busy intersections to the Boston Gardens, she receives assistance from Policeman Michael and his colleagues. Read aloud and share the sepia drawings. Available in poster size, and on film, video, and filmstrip.

Also: *Blueberries for Sal*. Viking Penguin, 1948. Also on filmstrip, film, and video. *One Morning in Maine*. Viking Penguin, 1952. Available on filmstrip.

McDonald, Megan. *Is This the House for a Hermit Crab?* Orchard, 1990.

Hermit Crab steps along the shore, by the sea, in the sand, scritch-scratch, scritch-scratch, looking for a new house. He rejects a rock, a tin can, a piece of driftwood, a plastic pail, a fishing net, and finally, chased by a pricklepine fish, settles into an empty shell that fits just right. The large, attractive pictures can easily be seen by a group in a story program.

McKissack, Patricia. *Flossie and the Fox*. Dial, 1986.

Walking through the woods to deliver a basket of eggs, Flossie encounters the fox her mother warned her about. Flossie out-foxes the fox by pretending that she does not believe that he is a fox. Continuing to stall until her destination is in sight, Flossie delights in telling him that she knew his identity all along. Available on film, video, and filmstrip.

Also: *Mirandy and Brother Wind*. Knopf, 1988.

McMillan, Bruce. *Growing Colors*. Lothrop, 1988.

This exceptional color book features fruits and vegetables with corresponding color names. On each left hand page are a small photograph of plant bearing fruit or vegetables and the appropriate color word; on the opposite page is a large close-up photo of the fruit or vegetable.

McPhail, David. *Emma's Pet*. Dutton, 1985.

Emma, a small bear, wants a big, soft, cuddly pet. After trying out a bug, a fish, a turtle, a cat, a dog, a bird, and a snake, she discovers the perfect pet: her father. Available on filmstrip.

Also: *Pig Pig Grows Up*. Dutton, 1985. Also available on filmstrip.

Mahy, Margaret. *17 Kings and 42 Elephants*. Dial, 1987.

Written in whimsical, nonsensical verse, the text of this book commands attention with its pulsating jungle rhythms. Patricia McCarthy's dazzling batik pictures blend perfectly with the text.

Marshall, James. *George and Martha*. Houghton Mifflin, 1972.

George and Martha, a pair of personable hippopotamuses, are best friends and the subject of five brief stories. The subtle humor will appeal to older children. Available on filmstrip.

Also: *Hansel and Gretel*. Doubleday, 1990. *Goldilocks and the Three Bears*. Dial, 1987. Available on film and video. *Red Riding Hood*. Dial, 1987. Also on film and video.

Martin, Bill. *Chicka Chicka Boom Boom*. Simon & Schuster, 1989.

In this zany alphabet book anthropomorphized letters climb a tree, fall down, and take their battered selves home. The rollicking verse text is punctuated with "Chicka chicka boom boom, will there be enough room." Participation is guaranteed.

Also: *Brown Bear, Brown Bear, What Do You See?* Holt, 1983. Available in poster size. *Here Are My Hands.* Holt, 1987. *Knots on a Counting Rope.* Holt, 1987. *The Maestro Plays.* Holt, 1994, 1970. *Polar Bear, Polar Bear, What Do You Hear?* Holt, 1991. Available in poster size.

Mayer, Mercer. *What Do You Do with a Kangaroo?* Scholastic, 1987.

A small girl is faced with the dilemma of finding a kangaroo in her bed, an opossum with her toothbrush, a raccoon with her cereal, etc. When she cannot throw them out, she lets them all stay. Delightful pictures and text appeal to primary level children. Available in poster size.

Also: *There's an Alligator under My Bed.* Dial, 1987. *There's a Nightmare in My Closet.* Dial, 1990. *There's Something in My Attic.* Dial, 1988. *One Frog Too Many.* Dutton, 1985.

Meddaugh, Susan. *Martha Speaks.* Houghton Mifflin, 1992.

Big problems arise when the family dog, Martha, eats some alphabet soup and learns to speak. Great for preschoolers. Also makes a wonderful puppet story.

Miller, Jane. *Farm Noises.* Simon & Schuster, 1989.

Illustrated with beautiful color photographs, *Farm Noises* includes the standard farm animals (one per page) plus mice, owls, frogs, streams, combine harvesters, and tractors. The text merely states the object or animal and the sound it makes. Useful with toddlers.

Also: *Farm Counting Book.* Prentice-Hall, 1983. *Farm Alphabet Book.* Prentice-Hall, 1984.

Miller, Margaret. *Whose Hat?* Greenwillow, 1988.

Another picture book filled with clear color photographs, this one includes hats used by a variety of workers and community helpers. An interesting participation book for preschoolers.

Mosel, Arlene. *Tikki Tikki Tembo.* Holt, 1968.

The first and honored son Tikki Tikki Tembo receives a great long name which almost costs him his life. This folktale explains why Chinese names are now short. After reading this story aloud, try dramatizing parts of it. Available in poster size and on film, video, and filmstrip.

Also: *The Funny Little Woman.* Dutton, 1972. Also available on filmstrip.

Mwenye Hadithi. *Hot Hippo.* Little, 1986.

Large pictures in brilliant colors illustrate the story of Hippo, who is so hot living on the land that he bargains with Ningai, the god of everything and everywhere, to live in cool water by day and on land by night. A good read-aloud story, it is available on film, video, and filmstrip.

Also: *Lazy Lion.* Little, 1990. *Tricky Tortoise.* Little, 1988.

Nash, Ogden. *Custard the Dragon.* Little, 1973.

Custard, a "realio, trulio cowardly pet dragon," becomes fierce and brave when a terrible pirate threatens. Children enjoy dramatizing this verse story. Available on film, video, and filmstrip.

Ness, Evaline. *Sam, Bangs, and Moonshine.* Holt, 1966.

Sam (Samantha) lives in a world of make-believe until her moonshine almost causes disaster for her friend Thomas and her cat Bangs. This delicate mood story has a perfect blend of text and pictures. Available on filmstrip, film, and video.

Nodset, Joan. *Who Took the Farmer's Hat?* Harper, 1963.

When the farmer loses his beloved old brown hat, he asks various animals if they have seen it. All have, but all perceive it as something else. After discovering that Bird is using it for an "old brown nest," the farmer gets a new hat. Available in poster size.

Numeroff, Laura. *If You Give a Mouse a Cookie*. Harper, 1985.

In this predictable, circular tale, a little boy speculates that "if you give a mouse a cookie, he's going to ask for a glass of milk" and "when you give him the milk, he'll probably ask you for a straw." And so the story goes, as one preposterous event leads to another and finally back to a second cookie. A sure winner with five- and six-year-olds, it is available in poster size. Also a 7 inch doll.

Also: *If You Give a Moose a Muffin*. Harper, 1991.

O'Neill, Mary. *Hailstones and Halibut Bones*. 2nd ed. Doubleday, 1989.

In this collection each poem explores a color in terms of emotion and the five senses. The crisp imagery and thought-provoking metaphors strike a responsive chord in primary level children. The 1989 edition contains new illustrations by John Wallner.

Omerod, Jan. *Dad's Back*. Lothrop, 1985.

Designed for the youngest toddler, this book uses few words on few pages to show a small child's delight that Dad has returned home.

Also: *Reading*. Lothrop, 1985.

Oxenbury, Helen. *Tom and Pippo Make a Friend*. Macmillan, 1989.

Tom and his stuffed monkey, Pippo, have a confrontation with a little girl in the park but resolve it and share their toys. Another book designed for toddlers.

Also: *Tom and Pippo and the Dog*. Macmillan, 1989. *Tom and Pippo Go for a Walk*. Macmillan, 1988.

Payne, Emmy. *Katy No-Pocket*. Houghton, 1973.

Katy, a mother kangaroo with no pocket, worries about how to carry her baby. She solves her dilemma by wearing a carpenter's apron which has a pocket for her child and others to share with various animal babies.

Peppe, Rodney. *Circus Numbers*. Delacorte, 1986.

This dual purpose book is valuable both for its circus theme and for showing number concepts. Each number is illustrated by circus performers, e.g., one ringmaster, two horses.

Petersham, Maud and Miska. *The Box with Red Wheels*. Macmillan, 1949.

All the farm animals are curious about the contents of the box with red wheels which sits in the yard. They are delighted that it contains a baby who in turn is delighted with them. Read it aloud or try it on the flannel board. Available on filmstrip.

Also: *Circus Baby*. Macmillan, 1968. Also available on filmstrip, film, and video.

Pienkowski, Jan. *Shapes*. Simon & Schuster, 1989.

One of the simplest books dealing with the concept of shapes, this volume includes all the common shapes and associates them with familiar objects, e.g., the circle is the wheel of a tractor. The brightly colored pictures are appealing.

Also: *Colors*. Simon & Schuster, 1989.

Pilkey, Dav. *The Paperboy*. Orchard, 1996.

A day in the life of a paperboy. Exquisite illustrations.

Also: *Dog Breath*. Blue Sky Press, 1994. *Dogzilla*. Harcourt, 1993.

Plourde, Lynn. *Pigs in the Mud in the Middle of the Rud*. Blue Sky Press, 1997.

Grandmother and family struggles to get a mess of farm animals out the road so they can pass in their Model T Ford.

Potter, Beatrix. *The Tale of Peter Rabbit*. Warne, 1902.

Peter Rabbit disobeys his mother by sneaking into Mr. MacGregor's garden and stealing his vegetables. Peter escapes but loses his jacket and shoes. The exquisite paintings are so tiny that you can use this book only with small groups. Available on filmstrip and in poster size; also dolls in various sizes.

Also: *The Tale of Benjamin Bunny*. Warne, 1904. Also on filmstrip. *The Tale of Jemima Puddleduck*. Warne, 1908. *The Tale of Mrs. Tiggy Winkle*. Warne, 1905.

Pomerantz, Charlotte. *One Duck, Another Duck*. Greenwillow, 1984.

Danny, a young owl, and his grandmother go to the pond where he counts the ducks. When his grandmother gets tired and tells him not to count the swans, he silently decides to count the stars. A delightful counting book.

Raffi. *Shake My Sillies Out*. Crown, 1987.

In picture book format, this boisterous activity song is illustrated in equally boisterous color drawings. This book will provide a participation opportunity in programs for primary children.

Also: *Down by the Bay*. Crown, 1987. *Five Little Ducks*. Crown, 1988. *One Light, One Sun*. Crown, 1988. *Tingalayo*. Crown, 1989.

Ray, Mary Lyn. *Mud*. Harcourt Brace, 1996.

Lavishly illustrated poem about winter melting into spring, producing magnificent mud. Oversized format makes this an ideal read-aloud for preschoolers and school aged children.

Reiss, John T. *Colors*. Bradbury, 1969.

Brilliant, vivid colors depict a balance of familiar and unfamiliar objects. Four full pages are devoted to each color.

Also: *Numbers*. Bradbury, 1971. *Shapes*. Bradbury, 1974.

Rey, Hans A. *Curious George*. Houghton Mifflin, 1973.

George, a lovable monkey, allows his curiosity to get him into incredible predicaments and invariably is rescued by his friend, the man with the yellow hat. Children adore George and repeatedly want to hear of his escapades. Available on filmstrip, film, video, and in poster size; also dolls in a variety of sizes.

Also: *Curious George Gets a Medal*. Houghton Mifflin, 1957. Available on filmstrip. *Curious George Rides a Bike*. Houghton Mifflin, 1952.

Rice, Eve. *Benny Bakes a Cake*. Morrow, 1984.

Benny and his mother bake his birthday cake, then go for a walk. Returning to find that his dog has eaten the cake, Benny cannot be comforted until his father comes home and there is a party after all.

Also: *Goodnight, Goodnight*. Greenwillow, 1980. *Sam Who Never Forgets*. Greenwillow, 1977.

Root, Phyllis. *What Baby Wants*. Candlewick Press, 1998.

Various family members try to stop the baby from crying, but only his brother can figure out what the infant wants: a cuddle, a kiss, and a lullaby.

Rosen, Michael. *We're Going on a Bear Hunt*. Macmillan, 1989.

Both preschool and school age children will love this version of the traditional activity story. Illustrated by Glen Rounds, the rollicking tale contains enough action to please the squirmiest child. Appropriate for both preschoolers and early school age children.

Schlein, Miriam. *Big Talk*. Rev. ed. Bradbury, 1990.

First published in 1955, *Big Talk* has been reissued with appropriate color illustrations. It recounts the playful boasting of Little Kangaroo who is encouraged and supported by his mother. Typical questions and answers include the following. "How high can you jump?" "I can jump as high as the sun." "How fast can you run?" "I can run as fast as the wind." A preschoolers delight.

Scieszka, Jon. *The Stinky Cheese Man & Other Fairly Stupid Tales*. Viking, 1992.

Ingeniously illustrated collection of silly tales, including "Chicken Licken," "The Princess and the Bowling Ball," "The Really Ugly Duckling," "The Other Frog Prince," "Little Red Running Shorts," "Jack's Bean Problem," "Cinderumpelstiltskin," "The Tortoise and the Hair," "The Stinky Cheese Man," and "The Boy Who Cried 'Cow Patty'."

Also: *The True Story of the Three Little Pigs*. Viking, 1989. *The Frog Prince, Continued*. Viking, 1991. *The Book That Jack Wrote*. Viking, 1994.

Scott, Ann Herbert. *Sam*. McGraw-Hill, 1967.

As the youngest member of the family, Sam gets shuttled from one person to another until his outburst of tears causes everyone to recognize his position. The sensitive illustrations help depict Sam's feelings.

Also: *On Mother's Lap*. McGraw-Hill, 1972.

Sendak, Maurice. *Where the Wild Things Are*. Harper, 1963.

When Max, dressed in his wolf suit, is sent to bed without supper for being a "wild thing," he sails to where the wild things are and becomes king of all wild things. Feeling lonely, he returns to his room where his supper is waiting for him. Children enjoy dramatizing this story. Available on film, video, and filmstrip; also as a set of dolls.

Also: *Alligators All Around*. Harper, 1962. Available on filmstrip, film, and video. *Chicken Soup with Rice*. Harper, 1962. Also available on filmstrip, film, video, and poster size. *In the Night Kitchen*. Harper, 1970. Also available on filmstrip, film, and video. *One Was Johnny*. Harper, 1962.

Available on filmstrip, film, and video. *Pierre*. Harper, 1962. Also available on filmstrip, film, and video.

Serfozo, Mary. *Rain Talk*. Macmillan, 1990.

A little girl describes the various sounds of falling rain in a brief text which is illustrated with lively watercolor paintings. This lovely book is a delightful addition to programs relating to weather.

Also: *Who Said Red?* Macmillan, 1988. Also available in poster size.

Shannon, David. *No, David!* Blue Sky Press, 1998.

David gets into a lot of trouble in this fantastic little book. Hug-filled ending is guaranteed to produce a roomful of "ahhs." Great read-a-loud for preschool, toddler, and early school ages.

Shute, Linda. *Clever Tom and the Leprechaun*. Lothrop, 1988.

Clever Tom catches a leprechaun and forces the little fellow to lead him to buried treasure. The leprechaun, however, outwits Tom, who, years later, continues to tell how he nearly found gold.

Shaw, Charles. *It Looked Like Spilt Milk*. Harper, 1947.

White silhouettes on a blue background depict changing cloud formations. Children love to participate by naming the shapes as you read the text: "Sometimes it looked like spilt milk, but it wasn't spilt milk." The story succeeds on the flannel board. Available in poster size.

Slobodkina, Esphyr. *Caps for Sale*. W. R. Scott, 1947.

A peddler, who carries his wares (caps) stacked upon his head, goes to sleep leaning against a tree. During his nap, monkeys take all his caps and return them when he least expects it. This story is ideal for creative dramatics or done as a told story for preschoolers. Available on film, video, filmstrip, and in poster size.

Spier, Peter. *The Fox Went Out on a Chilly Night*. Doubleday, 1961.

This old folk song tells of the fox who went to town, stole a goose and a duck, and took them home to his wife and ten children. The catchy tune is fun to sing, and Spier's illustrations are fun to look at. Available on film, video, and filmstrip.

Also: *London Bridge Is Falling Down*. Doubleday, 1967. Available on filmstrip.

Stevenson, Robert Louis. *Block City*. Dutton, 1988.

This well-known poem about a boy who, while playing with blocks, creates a world of his own imagination is delightfully illustrated by Ashley Wolff. The bold, colorful pictures can easily be seen by the story hour crowd.

Also: *My Shadow*. Putnam, 1990.

Tafuri, Nancy. *Spots, Feathers, and Curly Tails*. Greenwillow, 1988.

Large, bold pictures of farm animals fill this guessing-game book. Each question is accompanied by an incomplete picture of an animal followed on the next page by the answer with the complete animal. Preschoolers enjoy this one.

Also: *The Ball Bounced*. Greenwillow, 1989. *Early Morning in the Barn*. Greenwillow, 1983. *Have You Seen My Duckling?* Greenwillow, 1984.

Taylor, Judy. *My Cat*. Macmillan, 1988.

Large, uncluttered pictures and a few words of text per page tell a simple story about a cat from kittenhood to motherhood. Most suitable for toddlers.

Also: *My Dog*. Macmillan.

Tudor, Tasha. *Mother Goose*. Random, 1989.

Delicate pastel drawings illustrate this small volume of nursery rhymes. Costumes in the book are authentic for the historical period they represent. Could be used effectively with groups small enough to see the intricate detail in the pictures.

Turkle, Brinton. *Thy Friend, Obadiah*. Penguin, 1982.

Obadiah Starbuck, a small Quaker boy of Nantucket, is distressed because a sea gull insists on following him everywhere. The bird disappears for a few days and reappears with a fish hook in his beak. Obadiah, who has missed the gull, removes the hook and is glad to have his friend back again. Available on filmstrip.

Also: *Rachel and Obadiah*. Dutton, 1978.

Tworkov, Jack. *The Camel Took a Walk*. Dutton, 1951.

When a beautiful camel goes for a walk in the jungle, a tiger decides to pounce on her, the monkey plans to drop a coconut on the tiger, the squirrel wants to bite the monkey's tail, and the bird thinks he will pounce on the squirrel. The camel surprises them all by turning around and going back. Available on film, video, and filmstrip.

Udry, Janice May. *A Tree Is Nice*. Harper, 1956.

In a low-key style, this book enumerates all the good things about trees—"They fill up the sky . . . Cats get away from dogs by going up the tree." Children identify with the simplistic statements and stylized illustrations. Available on filmstrip.

Also: *Let's Be Enemies*. Harper, 1961. *The Moon Jumpers*. Harper, 1959. *What Mary Jo Shared*. Albert Whitman, 1966.

Viorst, Judith. *Alexander and the Terrible, Horrible, No Good, Very Bad Day*. Macmillan, 1972.

Alexander wakes up with gum in his hair, the beginning of his terrible, horrible, no good, very bad day. All day long everything goes wrong. When he threatens to go to Australia, his mom tells him that there are days like that, even in Australia. Try creative dramatics with this one. Available on film and video.

Waber, Bernard. *Ira Sleeps Over*. Houghton Mifflin, 1972.

Invited to spend the night with a friend, Ira must decide whether to take along his teddy bear. He is torn between fear of appearing babyish and fear of sleeping without his bear. He is relieved to find that his friend also sleeps with a bear. Available on film, video, and filmstrip.

Also: *I Was All Thumbs*. Houghton Mifflin, 1975. *Lyle, Lyle Crocodile*. Houghton Mifflin, 1965. Also available on filmstrip.

Ward, Lynd. *The Biggest Bear*. Houghton Mifflin, 1952.

Johnny, who goes hunting for a bearskin for his barn, finds a bear cub. The pet cub becomes the biggest bear and the biggest pest in the valley. Just before Johnny has to shoot him, he is taken to the zoo in the city. Available on filmstrip.

Wheeler, Cindy. *Marmalade's Nap*. Knopf, 1983.

Marmalade is looking for a quiet place to sleep, but all over the farm the cat finds only noisy, playful baby animals. The perfect spot is in the house where the baby is taking a nap. Written for toddlers, the book features only a few words of text per page.

Watanabe, Shigeo. *Daddy Play with Me*. Putnam, 1985.

A small bear cajoles his father to play train and horsy, to give piggyback rides, and to read books. With only a few words per page, this engaging story of a father-child relationship is perfect for toddlers.

Also: *How Do I Put It On?* Putnam, 1984. *What a Good Lunch*. Putnam, 1981.

Wildsmith, Brian. *The Lazy Bear*. Oxford University Press, 1987.

A kind, thoughtful bear finds a wagon and loves riding in it. He gives down-hill rides to his friends but frightens them into pushing him up the hill. They trick him out of his selfishness and help him regain his kind personality.

Also: *Mother Goose Nursery Rhymes*. Oxford University Press, 1987. *The Owl and the Woodpecker*. Oxford University Press, 1987.

Williams, Jay. *Everyone Knows What a Dragon Looks Like*. Macmillan, 1976.

When the Wild Horsemen of the North bring war into China, the people of Wu pray to the Great Cloud Dragon for help. But no one except Han, the gate-sweeper lad, recognizes the dragon when he sees him.

Wood, Audrey. *The Napping House*. Harcourt, 1984.

In a humorous, cumulative text this story recounts what happens when snoring Granny is joined by a dreaming child, a dozing dog, a snoozing cat, and a slumbering mouse who is awakened by a biting flea. Available on film, video, filmstrip, and in poster size.

Also: *King Bidgood's in the Bathtub*. Harcourt, 1985. Also available on filmstrip and in poster size.

Yashima, Taro. *Umbrella*. Viking Penguin, 1958.

On Momo's third birthday she receives boots and an umbrella which she contrives to use in sun and wind. When at last it rains and she carries her umbrella, she crosses the street without holding anyone's hand. Available on filmstrip.

Zemach, Harve and Margot. *Mommy, Buy Me a China Doll*. Farrar, 1975.

A small girl solves all kinds of problems while coaxing her mother to buy her a china doll. A beautifully illustrated version of an Ozark folk song, this book can be read or sung. Appropriate for preschool age children. Also available in filmstrip format.

Also: *The Judge*. Farrar, 1969. Available on filmstrip.

Yolen, Jane. *Owl Moon*. Philomel, 1987.

A little girl treks through the snow-filled woods on a moonlit night in hopes of seeing an owl. Soft, sensitive paintings and text set a mood of quiet calm. Appropriate for the preschooler and early school age crowd. Available on film, video, and filmstrip.

Ziefert, Harriet. *I Swapped My Dog*. Houghton Mifflin, 1998.

Incredibly vivid illustrations make this humorous story of a farmer who makes a series of trades, ending up with the dog he had at the beginning, an ideal read-aloud for large and small groups of preschoolers or younger school age children.

Zion, Eugene. *Harry the Dirty Dog*. Harper, 1956.

Harry, a black dog with white spots, loves everything except taking baths. He runs away and gets so dirty that his family does not recognize him, forcing him to beg for a bath to reestablish his identity. Available on film and filmstrip.

Also: *Harry by the Sea*. Harper, 1965. Also available on filmstrip. *No Roses for Harry*. Harper, 1958. Also on filmstrip.

Zolotow, Charlotte. *Do You Know What I'll Do?* Harper, 1958.

A little girl recounts to her younger brother all the things she will do for him, including building him a snowman, bringing him a shell to hold the sound of the sea, and buying him a surprise in the city. This warm, loving story is nice to read aloud.

Also: *Hold My Hand*. Harper, 1972. *Mr. Rabbit and the Lovely Present*. Harper, 1962. Available on filmstrip. *Say It*. Greenwillow, 1980. *The Sleepy Book*. Harper, 1988. *William's Doll*. Harper, 1972.

CHAPTER TEN

Flannel Board Stories

The flannel board, if used prudently, can add variety and fun to the story program. In using the flannel board, the selection of material to be presented is of prime importance. You should consider carefully what kinds of story activities can be done more effectively on the flannel board than in any other format. For instance, the flannel board is not a substitute for picture books. Few of us have the artistic ability to create pictures for the flannel board which in any way could compare favorably with the beautiful art in many picture books. These stories should only be used with their original art.

On the other hand, some stories are well-suited for the flannel board. A story told with the flannel board should have few characters, definite action, and a story line simple enough that it can be interpreted without a great deal of background or detail. You should be able to read the story and easily select those characters and props which are essential to the story.

For the toddler, the flannel board is practically magic, for by a mere touch of the hand, the pieces stay put on the board. Since toddlers must have very short and very simple stories, the flannel board serves as an effective tool. Triangles, circles, squares, and rectangles cut in varying sizes from brightly colored poster board or felt can be used to reinforce concepts of shapes, sizes, and colors.

Some fingerplays can first be presented on the flannel board, then repeated as finger games. When singing simple songs, such as "Old MacDonald Had a Farm," you can place the flannel board pieces on the board sequentially thus giving the youngster visual clues for the next verse of the song. Nursery rhymes and very simple stories can also work well for toddlers.

Preschoolers love to use the flannel board, so whenever possible, you should consider incorporating stories in which they can participate. If you are telling *My Red Umbrella*, let the children take turns placing and removing the animals. The song "Jennie Jenkins" can be used to practice color recognition and simultaneously provide for individual participation. While most poems should not be illustrated, for the visual images form imaginatively in each young mind, some poems are very adaptable for use on the flannel board.

Although primary level children have outgrown the feeling that flannel boards are magic, they enjoy the fun and participation experiences which can be presented on the flannel board. They can practically learn a cumulative verse or story such as "The House That Jack Built" or "The Old Woman and Her Pig" in one story program session by using the flannel board pieces as clues for sequence. Sometimes a group of children will possess quite underdeveloped listening skills. These children will benefit from the visual images which help to hold their attention as they learn to listen.

Building a Simple Flannel Board

If you do not have access to a flannel board, you can construct one easily from heavy corrugated cardboard, fiberboard, or even wood. Stretch a plain piece of flannel, felt, or a receiving blanket over a board at least 24 by 30 inches. Fasten the cloth to the back of the board with tape, staples, glue, or tacks.

Be sure to keep the cloth extremely clean, for the flannel board pieces will not adhere securely to a dirty board. Wash the flannel or brush the felt frequently to ensure that the cloth is filled with static electricity.

Included in this chapter are sample verses, songs, and stories suitable for toddlers, preschoolers, and primary level children. Traceable patterns and instructions for making and using the flannel board pieces accompany each sample. Be sure to glue flannel, felt, or velcro on the back of each piece.

Toddler Flannel Board Stories

The Train

Chug, chug, choo, choo, choo down the track.
First comes the engine with the coal car in back;
Boxcar, flat car, boxcar again;
Last the caboose at the end of the train.

—C. S. Peterson

Directions

Trace the cars on poster board, heavy white paper, or Pelon, making two boxcars. Color the trains as desired and outline in black. (Make the boxcars two different colors.) Place the engine on the board, and follow with the other cars as the poem dictates.

You will have to say the poem slowly the first time so you can put the train on the board. You may want to repeat the poem, increasing the speed and creating the rhythm of a moving train.

You may also choose to forgo using a flannel board altogether if your toddlers are very active reachers and walkers and instead hold up the pieces as you say the poem. In this case, you would want to use a heavy cardboard for the train pieces.

Parts of the Body

This flannel board activity is ideal for a story program featuring self-concept for two- and three-year-olds. After sharing "I'm Glad I'm Me" by Stone, for instance, allow the children to place the various features on the flannel board model.

Directions

Trace the boy's legs onto a large sheet of white poster board, then center the top of his body over the legs, joining at his waist. Trace the top of his body onto the poster board. Trace the remaining pieces onto poster board and cut out.

Before you add color, glue small squares of velcro on the hair, eyes, ears, nose, mouth, hands, and feet of the boy. Color the boy with crayons or felt tip pens, covering the velcro. Color the extra pieces, hair, eyes, ears, etc., to match those of the boy. Glue small squares of velcro on the back of each extra piece to allow you to stick them where they belong on the boy.

Note: Draw the mouth with thick red lines and cut it out, leaving some white around it to make it large enough to handle.

"The Train" Flannel Board Pieces

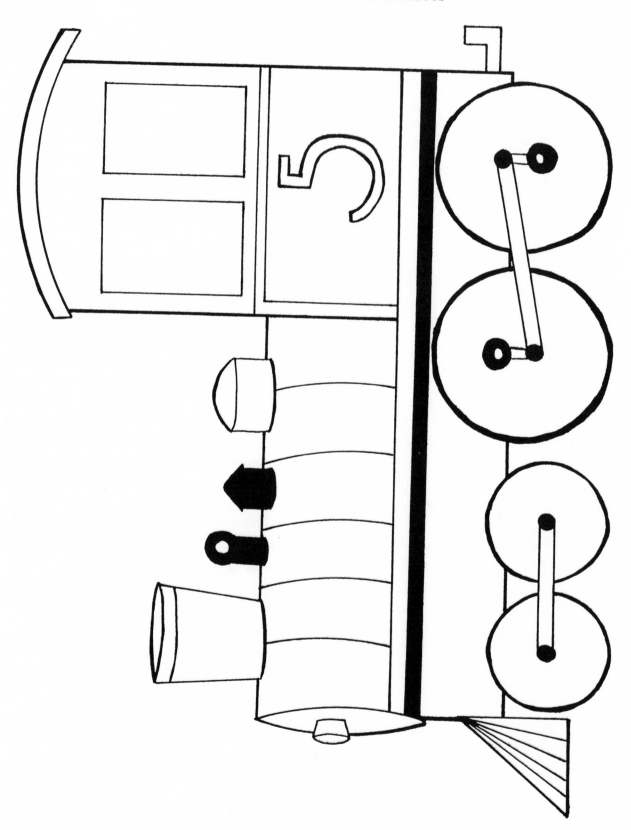

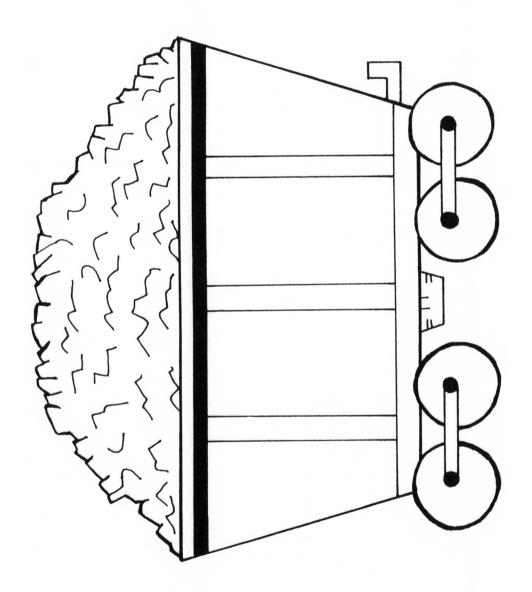

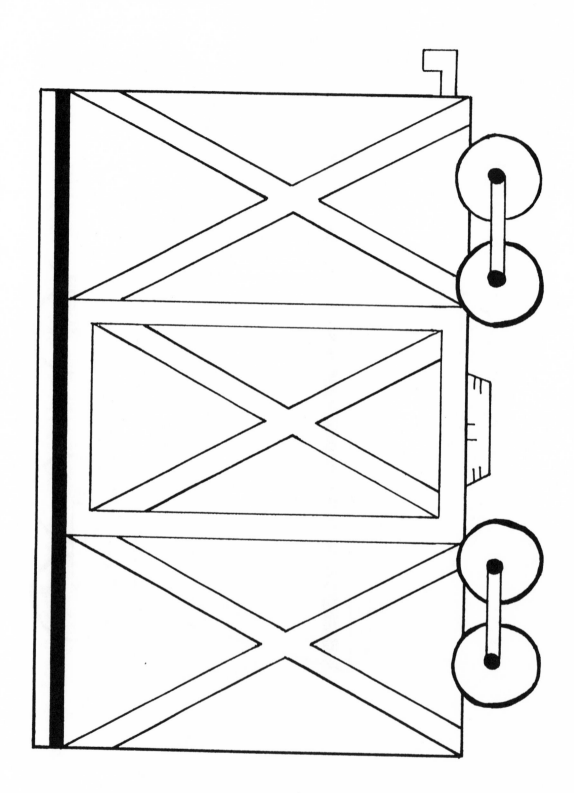

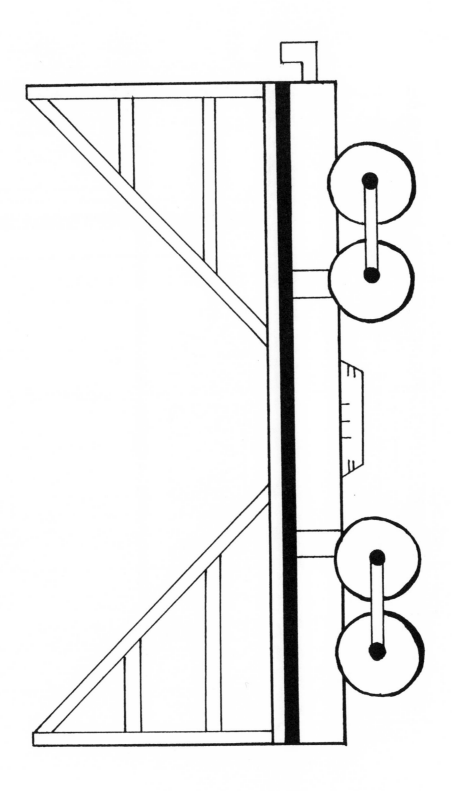

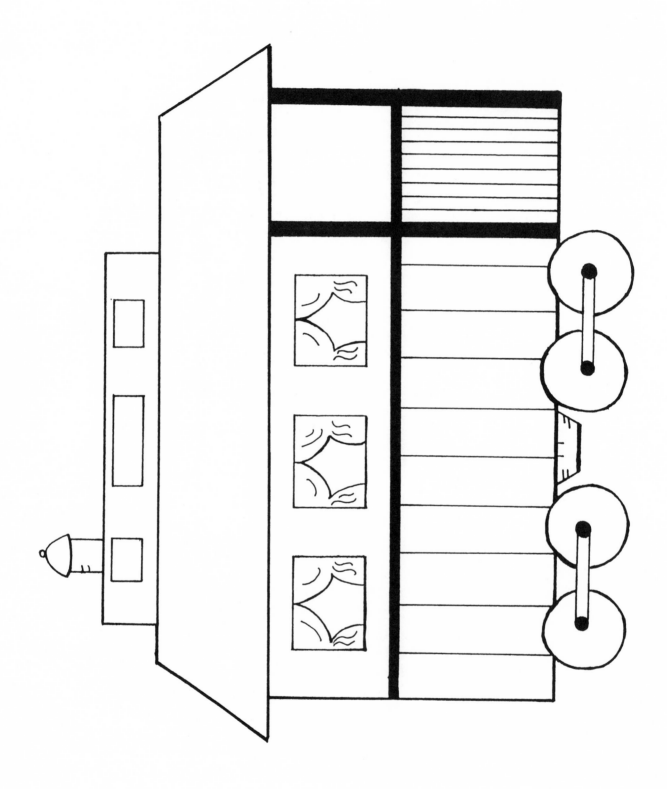

"Parts of the Body" Flannel Board Pieces

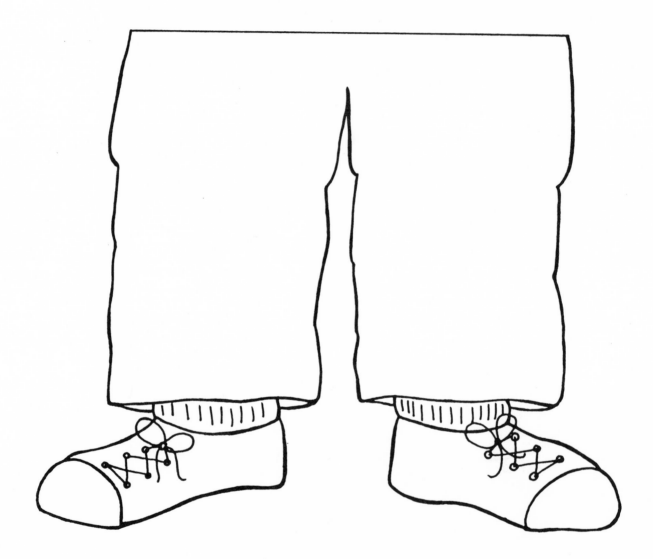

The Three Little Kittens

Three little kittens lost their mittens,
And they began to cry,
"Oh, mother dear, we very much fear
Our mittens we have lost."
"What! Lost your mittens! You naughty kittens!
Then you shall have no pie."
"Mee-ow, mee-ow, mee-ow."
"No, you shall have no pie."

The three little kittens found their mittens,
And they began to cry,
"Oh, mother dear, see here, see here!
Our mittens we have found."
"Put on your mittens, You silly kittens,
And you shall have some pie."
"Purr, purr, purr.
Oh, let us have the pie!"

The three little kittens put on their mittens,
And soon ate up the pie.
"Oh, mother dear, we greatly fear,
Our mittens we have soiled!"
"Soiled your mittens! You naughty kittens!"
Then they began to sigh,
"Mee-ow, mee-ow, mee-ow."
And they began to sigh.

The three little kittens washed their mittens,
And hung them up to dry.
"Oh, mother dear, do you not hear,
Our mittens we have washed?"
"What! Washed your mittens! You darling kittens,
But I smell a rat close by.
Hush! Hush! Mee-ow, mee-ow.
"We smell a rat close by."

—Unknown

Directions

Trace the characters onto poster board or heavy paper making three sets of mittens. Color the kittens as desired and outline them in black, using crayons or felt tip pens. To have the kittens actually wear their mittens, put a small square of velcro between the kittens' paws and color the velcro to match their fur. Put another small square of velcro on the back of each pair of mittens.

Place the mother and three kittens on the board before you start; then say the first stanza. Place the mittens on the kittens at "Oh, mother dear, see here, see here" in the second stanza. Place the pie on the board at "And you shall have some pie" in the second stanza. Remove the pie at "And soon ate up the pie" in the third stanza. Finally, take off the mittens at the beginning of the fourth stanza, and put up the mittens on the clothes line to end the story.

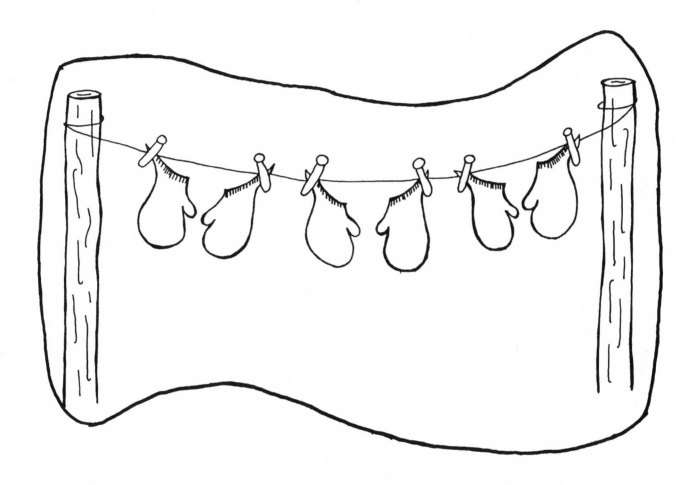

Mittens on the Line

Preschool Flannel Board Stories

A Secret

I have a secret, I and a tree.
And a mother robin, just we three.
I climbed the tree to a very high limb;
I saw the nest and I peeped in.

The robin stood up to stretch her legs,
And there in the nest were three small . . .
Oh dear, I must not slip and tell
The secret we three know so well.

Though I promise not to say a word,
And the tree won't talk, nor will the bird,
When the babies hatch and fly about,
Then our whole secret will be out.

— C. S. Peterson

Directions

Trace the characters onto white poster board. Color as desired and outline in black. Put a small piece of velcro in the center of the tree, and color it to match. Put a small piece of velcro on the back of both nests, and another piece on the front of the nest with eggs, placing the velcro just below the eggs. Again, color to match. Finally, put velcro on the back of the mother robin at the top of her tail.

To start, place the tree in the center of the board and secure in place with pins or tacks. Put the nest with eggs on the tree, and the mother robin on the nest so she hides the eggs. Place the girl beside the tree.

In the second stanza remove the robin from the nest and put her on the ground. In the final line, remove the nest with eggs and replace it with the nest with baby birds to finish the poem.

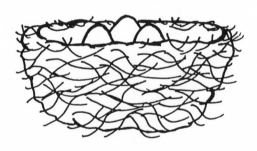

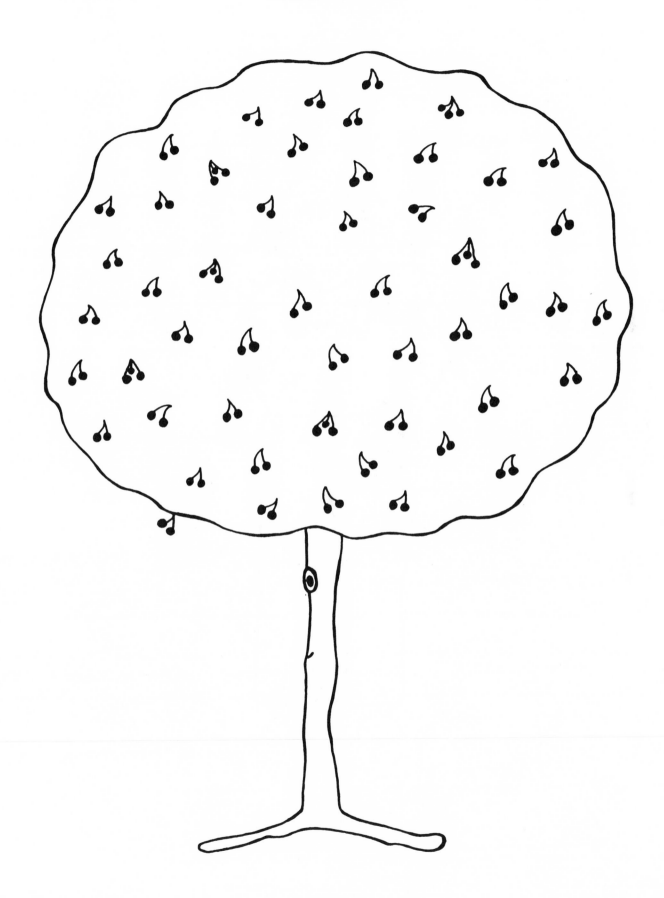

Jennie Jenkins

Oh, will you wear red, oh my dear, oh my dear,
Oh will you wear red, Jennie Jenkins?
No, I won't wear red, It's the color of my head.

Chorus: Gonna buy me a fill-dy, foll-dy,
Seek-a-double, use-a cause-a
Roll, the find me! Roll, Jennie Jenkins, roll!

Oh, will you wear blue, etc.
No, I won't wear blue,
It's the color of my shoe, etc.

Oh, will you wear green, etc.
No, I won't wear green,
It's the color of a bean, etc.

Oh, will you wear purple, etc.
No, I won't wear purple,
It's the color of my turtle, etc.

Oh, will you wear white, etc.
No, I won't wear white,
For the color's not right, etc.

Then, what will you wear, etc.
Don't know what I'll wear,
But I won't go bare, etc.

Directions

Trace Jennie onto white poster board or heavy paper. Outline with black and color as desired, using a light color for her underclothes. Trace the dress five times onto a heavy grade of Pelon (interfacing material used in sewing). Color each dress as described in the song and outline in black, using felt tip pens or crayons. If crayons are used, cover the dresses with an old cloth and press lightly with a cool iron. This will melt the wax and keep colors from smearing.

Secure Jennie to the flannel board with tacks or pins. Place the red dress on her at the beginning. Remove the red dress during the chorus, and then place the blue dress on her for the next stanza. Continue as the song describes. If the dresses slip, glue a small square of white flannel or velcro on her chest, and color it the same as her underclothes. When you place the dresses on Jennie, press each dress firmly against the velcro and it will stick.

The Little Red Hen

Once upon a time a Little Red Hen lived in a very small house in a clearing near a village. She shared her cozy little home with her three friends: a tabby cat, a curly dog, and a big pink pig.

Now although Little Red Hen was hardworking and generous, her friends were rather lazy and selfish. So most of the work fell to Little Red Hen. She cleaned the house, she cooked the meals, she made the beds, she raked the yard, she washed the windows, she mopped the floors, she dusted the furniture, and she worked in the garden all by herself while the tabby cat, the curly dog, and the big pink pig leisurely sunned themselves all day long.

And so it happened that one day Little Red Hen was busily working in the yard when she found a grain of wheat.

"Oh my oh!" she exclaimed. "A grain of wheat! How fortunate am I to find a grain of wheat!" And turning to her lazy friends, she said, "Who will help me plant this wheat?"

"Not I," said the tabby cat, licking her paws.

"Not I," said the curly dog, scratching his nose.

"Not I," said the big pink pig, sitting down in a mud puddle.

"Very well then, I shall do it myself," said Little Red Hen. And so she did.

Days and weeks passed and the wheat grew and at last ripened, tall and golden.

Little Red Hen looked at her three friends and said, "Who will help me cut this wheat?"

"Not I," said the tabby cat, pouncing on a bug.

"Not I," said the curly dog, holding a bone under one paw.

"Not I," said the big pink pig, turning over on his other side.

"Very well then, I shall do it myself," said Little Red Hen. And so she did.

So Little Red Hen cut the wheat and carefully bundled it up to take to the mill to be ground into flour.

Then she sought out her three lazy companions and asked them, "Who will help me take this wheat to the mill to be ground into flour?"

"Not I," said the tabby cat, batting a blade of grass with her paw.

"Not I," said the curly dog, tossing his bone in the air.

"Not I," said the big pink pig, rolling over on his back.

"Very well then, I shall do it myself," said Little Red Hen. And so she did.

The hard-working Little Red Hen shouldered the bundle of wheat and trudged with it to the mill. After the miller had ground the grain into flour for her, she lugged the sack of flour home again.

Little Red Hen looked from one of her friends to another. Then she said, "Who will help me make this flour into bread?"

"Not I," said the tabby cat, washing her fluffy tail.

"Not I," said the curly dog, chewing his bone.

"Not I," said the big pink pig, oozing deeper into the mud.

"Very well then, I shall do it myself," said Little Red Hen. And so she did.

The tabby cat, the curly dog, and the big pink pig all moved to a sunny spot for their naps. Little Red Hen bustled about sweeping and dusting their little house.

Meanwhile, the lovely smell of baking bread filled the air. One by one the tabby cat, the curly dog, and the big pink pig sniffed the delicious smell and came eagerly to the kitchen where they stood around sniffing and licking their lips.

At last the bread was baked. Carefully Little Red Hen removed from the oven a delicious-smelling, golden brown loaf of bread. "And now," she said rather meaningfully, "who will help me eat this bread?"

"I will!" said the tabby cat, jumping on her chair.

"I will!" said the curly dog, wagging his tail.

"I will!" said the big pink pig, coming to the table.

"Oh, no, you won't!" said Little Red Hen. "By myself I planted the wheat, by myself I cut the wheat, by myself I took the wheat to the mill to be ground into flour, and by myself I made the flour into bread. And by myself I'm going to eat it too." And so she did. And you can just bet dollars to donuts that the next time Little Red Hen has some housework to be done, she has three very eager helpers.

—Retold by C. S. Peterson and S. Koorey

Directions

Trace the characters onto white poster board or heavy paper. Color as desired and outline in black with crayons or felt tip pens.

Place the hen on the board as you begin the story. Add the cat, dog, and pig as you come to them.

Place the wheat on the board at "and at last ripened, tall and golden." Remove the wheat at "Little Red Hen cut the wheat and carefully bundled it up."

Place the flour on the board at "after the miller had ground the grain into flour for her." Remove the flour after she asks who will help her make the bread and says "Very well then, I'll do it myself."

Place the bread on the board at "The Little Red Hen removed from the oven . . . loaf of bread." Remove the bread at "I'll eat it myself. And she did."

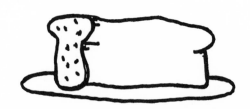

I Had a Rooster

I had a rooster and the rooster pleased me.
I fed my rooster 'neath the green apple tree.
And my old rooster went, "Cock-a-doodle-do,
De-doodle, De-doodle, De-doodle, De-do."

I had a cat and the cat pleased me.
I fed my cat 'neath the green apple tree.
And my old cat went, "Me-ow, Me-ow."
And my old rooster went, "Cock-a-doodle-do,
De-doodle, De-doodle, De-doodle, De-do."

I had a dog and the dog pleased me.
I fed my dog 'neath the green apple tree.
And my old dog went, "Ruff, Ruff, Ruff."
And my old rooster went, "Cock-a-doodle-do,
De-doodle, De-doodle, De-doodle, De-do."

I had a pig and the pig pleased me.
I fed my pig 'neath the green apple tree.
And my old pig went, "Oink, Oink, Oink."
And my old rooster went, "Cock-a-doodle-do,
De-doodle, De-doodle, De-doodle, De-do."

I had a cow and the cow pleased me.
I fed my cow 'neath the green apple tree.
And my old cow went, "Moo, Moo, Moo."
And my old rooster went, "Cock-a-doodle-do,
De-doodle, De-doodle, De-doodle, De-do."

I had a horse and the horse pleased me.
I fed my horse 'neath the green apple tree.
And my old horse went, "Neigh, Neigh, Neigh."
And my old rooster went, "Cock-a-doodle-do,
De-doodle, De-doodle, De-doodle, De-do."

I had a LION, and the LION pleased me.
I fed my LION 'neath the green apple tree.
And my old LION went,
"GGGRRRRRRRRAAAAAARRRRRR!"
And my old cat went, "Me-ow, Me-ow."
And my old dog went, "Ruff, Ruff, Ruff."
And my old pig went, "Oink, Oink, Oink."
And my old cow went, "Moo, Moo, Moo."
And my old horse went, "Neigh, Neigh, Neigh."
And my old rooster went, "Cock-a-doodle-do,
De-doodle, De-doodle, De-doodle, De-do."

Notes on Telling the Tale

This is a great piece-together story. If you don't want to make a special flannel board set for this song, you can always pull animals from other flannel board sets you own. In fact, you don't even have to use these animals at all. Instead, you can easily change the song to suit your collection of animal flannel board pieces.

The lion, however, is the most important part, and I would recommend not adapting the ending. I have found that it works quite well for the teller to act scared of the lion when you pull it out for placement on the flannel board and really play up the growl.

Also be sure to end this song with a bang and a bow, drawing out the last line to let them know it's really over. Otherwise, your audience might be expecting more.

—S. Koorey

Primary Level Flannel Board Stories

Chicken Little

One day Chicken Little was in the barnyard scratching for bugs. All at once an acorn dropped from a tree and landed ker-plunk right on top of Chicken Little's head.

"Oh, dear," she cried, "the sky is falling! The sky is falling! I must go and tell the king!"

So Chicken Little went running across the barnyard until she came to Henny Penny.

"Good Morning, Chicken Little and where are you going?" asked Henny Penny.

"The sky is falling, the sky is falling, and I must go and tell the king," answered Chicken Little.

"May I come, too?" asked Henny Penny.

"Certainly," said Chicken Little. And Chicken Little and Henny Penny hurried on across the barnyard. Soon they met Cocky Locky.

"Good morning Chicken Little and Henny Penny. Where are you going?" asked Cocky Locky.

"The sky is falling, the sky is falling, and we are going to tell the king," said Chicken Little and Henny Penny.

"May I come along?" asked Cocky Locky.

"Certainly," said Chicken Little.

So Chicken Little, Henny Penny, and Cocky Locky went along and went along until they came to the pond. There they met Ducky Lucky.

"Good morning Chicken Little, Henny Penny, and Cocky Locky. Where are you going?" asked Ducky Lucky.

"The sky is falling, the sky is falling, and we are going to tell the king," replied Chicken Little, Henny Penny, and Cocky Locky.

"Oh, May I come with you?" asked Ducky Lucky.

"Certainly," answered Chicken Little. So Chicken Little, Henny Penny, Cocky Locky, and Ducky Lucky went along and went along until they came to the far edge of the barnyard where they met Turkey Lurkey.

"Good morning all. Where are you going?" asked Turkey Lurkey.

"The sky is falling, the sky is falling, and we are going to tell the king," said Chicken Little, Henny Penny, Cocky Locky, and Ducky Lucky.

"May I go with you?" asked Turkey Lurkey.

"Certainly," answered Chicken Little. So Chicken Little, Henny Penny, Cocky Locky, Ducky Lucky, and Turkey Lurkey went along and went along until they met Goosey Loosey.

"Good morning friends. Where are you going?" asked Goosey Loosey.

"The sky is falling, the sky is falling, and we are going to tell the king," said Chicken Little, Henny Penny, Cocky Locky, Ducky Lucky, and Turkey Lurkey.

"May I come with you?" asked Goosey Loosey.

"Certainly," replied Chicken Little. So Chicken Little, Henny Penny, Cocky Locky, Ducky Lucky, Turkey Lurkey, and Goosey Loosey went along and went along until they entered the woods. There they met Foxy Loxy.

"Oh, hello there Chicken Little, Henny Penny, Cocky Locky, Ducky Lucky, Turkey Lurkey and Goosey Loosey. Where are you going?" asked Foxy Loxy.

"The sky is falling, the sky is falling, and we are going to tell the king," said Chicken Little.

"Would you like to come with us?"

"Oh, yes, indeed!" replied Foxy Loxy. "But you are going in the absolutely wrong direction. Follow me and I shall show you the proper way."

So Chicken Little, Henny Penny, Cocky Locky, Ducky Lucky, Turkey Lurkey, an Goosey Loosey all followed Foxy Loxy to find the king and tell him that the sky was falling.

They went along and they went along and they went along until they came to Foxy Loxy's deep dark cave.

"Follow me and we will take a short cut to the king's palace," said Foxy Loxy as he entered the cave.

So Chicken Little, Henny Penny, Cocky Locky, Ducky Lucky, Turkey Lurkey, and Goosey Loosey all followed Foxy Loxy into the cave. And they never were seen again. But Foxy Loxy and his wife and little foxes remembered their fine dinner for a long time.

No one ever told the king that the sky was falling. But that was just as well, for the sky never did fall anyway.

—Retold by C. S. Peterson and S. Koorey

Directions

Trace the characters onto white paper, poster board, or a heavy grade of Pelon (interfacing material used in sewing). Outline with black and color as desired with crayons or felt tip pens.

If using crayons on Pelon, cover the Pelon with an old cloth and press lightly with a cool iron. This will melt the wax and keep colors from smearing. Place the characters on the board as you come to them in the story. Since this is a cumulative story, leave each piece on the board throughout. Be sure to start at the top of the board and allow enough room for all of the characters.

Notes on Telling the Tale

When I first started to work with this story, I wondered whether it had lost its appeal based on its rather violent ending. I remembered liking the story as a child so I proceeded to "adapt" it for a modern audience's sensibilities, without reworking the final outcome.

For starters, I found that using distinctly different character voices for each animal was a sure way to avoid any tone of doom and death that may accompany the reading. In this way, it became a bit of a cartoon, exaggerated and humorous.

Yet, after the fun of the repeating storyline, the ending and its implications still posed a problem. Quite by accident, I one day accompanied my introduction to the character of Foxy Loxy with a musical motif "Dum-de-dum-dum, Dum-de-dum-dum-dum!" as if admitting that the worst was on its way. In this manner, my audience was not that taken aback when these ditzy friends become supper for the fox.

Additionally, I found that introducing the story with a bit of animal background worked well. For instance, asking my audience for the names of some animals that may live on a farm, then jumping in with the fox. I admonish them to "never ever trust a fox" and then begin my telling.

This story also works well as a participation tale, with the audience working together on the "the sky is falling" parts.

—S. Koorey

The House That Jack Built

This is the house that Jack built.

This is the malt
That lay in the house that Jack built.

This is the rat,
That ate the malt
That lay in the house that Jack built.

This is the cat,
That killed the rat,
That ate the malt
That lay in the house that Jack built.

This is the dog,
That worried the cat,
That killed the rat,
That ate the malt
That lay in the house that Jack built.

This is the cow with the crumpled horn,
That tossed the dog,
That worried the cat,
That killed the rat,
That ate the malt
That lay in the house that Jack built.

This is the maiden all forlorn,
That milked the cow with the crumpled horn,
That tossed the dog,
That worried the cat,
That killed the rat,
That ate the malt
That lay in the house that Jack built.

This is the man all tattered and torn,
That kissed the maiden all forlorn,
That milked the cow with the crumpled horn,

That tossed the dog,
That worried the cat,
That killed the rat,
That ate the malt
That lay in the house that Jack built.

This is the priest all shaven and shorn,
That married the man all tattered and torn,
That kissed the maiden all forlorn,
That milked the cow with the crumpled horn,
That tossed the dog,
That worried the cat,
That killed the rat,
That ate the malt
That lay in the house that Jack built.

This is the cock that crowed in the morn,
That waked the priest all shaven and shorn,
That married the man all tattered and torn,
That kissed the maiden all forlorn,
That milked the cow with the crumpled horn,
That tossed the dog,
That worried the cat,
That killed the rat,
That ate the malt
That lay in the house that Jack built.

This is the farmer that grew the corn,
That fed the cock that crowed in the morn,
That waked the priest all shaven and shorn,
That married the man all tattered and torn,
That kissed the maiden all forlorn,
That milked the cow with the crumpled horn,
That tossed the dog,
That worried the cat,
That killed the rat,
That ate the malt
That lay in the house that Jack built.

Directions

Trace the characters onto heavy white paper or poster board. Color as desired and outline in black with crayons or felt tip pens.

Cut out, leaving some white showing around smaller details, such as the rat's tail, for reinforce-ment. Place the characters on the board as you come to them in the story.

Since this is a cumulative story, leave each piece on the board throughout. Be sure to start at the top of the board, and allow enough room for all the characters.

Michael Finnegan

There was a man named Michael Finnegan;
He grew long whiskers on his chin-igan.
A wind came up and blew them in again.
Poor old Michael Finnegan. Begin again.

Directions

Trace head of Michael Finnegan, including the dotted line beneath his beard on his chin, and the separate beard piece onto heavy paper or poster board.

To draw the beard, make a rough outline of the shape and fill this in by drawing overlapping curved lines, using a brown or black felt tip pen or crayon. Use the same color to draw the lines of Finnegan's hair and mustache. Cut along the dotted line and insert the separate beard piece.

Place head on your flannel board, and tack at the top with pins or thumbtacks to keep it from falling when you move the beard.

At the beginning of the song, have the beard pulled down; during the line, "A wind came up and blew them in again," slide the beard up to expose Finnegan's chin.

Repeat this process for each chorus you sing. If the separate beard piece tends to slip, put a small strip of felt at the top.

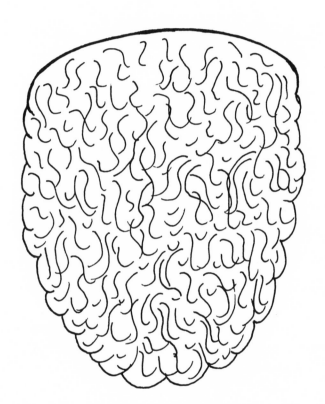

CHAPTER ELEVEN

Puppets in Story Programs

Puppets lend a kind of magic to the story program, for children of all ages are fascinated by the doll-like figures. Using the simplest puppets, you can brighten your story program and simultaneously introduce children to the rudiments of theater; assist children in interpreting stories, poems, or songs; stimulate children's imaginations, and allow them to participate in the story vicariously by identifying with the little representational characters.

Simple puppets are best to use in story programs for two- to eight-year-olds. First of all, they allow the children more room to exercise their imaginations as they mentally assign characteristics to a rather stylized puppet. For example, if you tell the group that your wooden spoon puppet is Little Red Riding Hood, they will reconstruct her physical appearance and personality to fit their interpretations of the character. Second, especially with the toddlers, it is imperative that you permit the youngsters to touch the puppets, e.g., pet the cat. You will feel much more relaxed and less protective of your puppet if it is a simple one, inexpensive and easy to replace. Third, with young children, fancy and elaborate puppets may tend to overpower the piece of literature they are interpreting, thus becoming the focal point in the story program rather than a vehicle for carrying a message. Simple puppets are less apt to intrude in this way. You may have to remind yourself peri-

odically that puppetry in your story program is a means of interpreting literature for young children rather than an end unto itself.

In the story program for toddlers, soft sock puppets, paper bag puppets, and stick puppets are all effective. With this age group it is best to use only one or two puppets to interpret a very short verse, rhyme, or story. Since toddlers do not distinguish between the real and unreal, you should allow the children to touch the puppets to determine for themselves that the puppets are only toys.

Preschoolers are fascinated with puppets and almost any kind of puppet is appropriate for them. They can enjoy verses, songs, or stories interpreted with one or more puppets. They can also relate to very short and simple puppet plays produced on stage. If possible, the play should have no more than two or three characters, should have only a fine plot line, and should be based on a familiar story. *The Gunniwolf*, "The Tortoise and the Hare," and "The Lion and the Mouse" are good examples.

At the primary level, children generally can follow a puppet play performed on stage. They enjoy plays based on fairy tales and folktales, such as "The Frog Prince," "The Three Bears," "The Shoemaker and the Elves," "Rumpelstiltskin," "Tikki-Tikki-Tembo," and "The Three Billy Goats Gruff." Youngsters in grades one through three still enjoy seeing a story interpreted with only one or two puppets. *The Blueberry Pie Elf*, *Angus and the Ducks*, and *The Gunniwolf* can all be told with a puppet or two. Songs and verses illustrated with puppets can also be used effectively in the primary story program.

One or two puppets can be used in several ways to tell a story or poem. Since you are not using a stage, hold the puppet in your lap with your other hand across the bottom as a base. You could also hold a small box on your lap and have the puppet emerge from behind the box.

In some instances, you may want the puppet to interpret the action of the story through simple gestures. In others, you may simply talk to the puppet or have the puppet talk to the children. If you are doing *Angus and the Ducks*, the characters, a dog and the ducks, could perform the story. In *The Gunniwolf*, you, acting as the little girl, and a wolf puppet could provide the action. The poem, "The Little Elfman," could be done with you simply talking to the puppet.

Using puppets on a stage to perform a puppet play is considerably more complicated. A play will usually call for more characters whose actions must carry the story with little outside narration. Therefore, more thorough planning and preparation is necessary.

Sample stage directions, or blocking, are included as completely as possible for three puppet plays to illustrate the type of planning involved. The action is kept simple, with many props imagined. You can add real props and have the puppets use them accordingly for a more complex production.

As you go through the dialogue, think of other actions you might use if you were actually in the play and have the puppets do the same. For instance, in "The Frog Prince," as the princess is crying at the well, she would bow her head and cover her face with her hands. Then when the frog enters, she would look up suddenly and say, "Oh, it's you, old water-splasher." In a puppet play you want to try to have your puppets responding and moving as naturally as possible. This not only will keep the play lively but also make it believable. But remember, since the audience cannot usually see a mouth moving, it is best to let the talking puppet do the actions while the others remain almost stationary. Once you find an action that suits the dialogue, use it for each performance.

As you go through the play for the first time, it may be helpful to draw a diagram of the stage to best visualize the stage directions. For instance, in "The Frog Prince," scene II would be visualized as shown below.

Once you form a mental picture of the action, it will be much easier to do the performance. Notice also that the stage directions are planned for easiest movements by not only the puppets but also the puppeteers behind stage.

In the foregoing example, the king and princess are played by the same puppeteer. When the king exits Stage L, the princess will have to move Stage L also so the puppeteer can reach across the stage to make the exit. Depending on the width of the

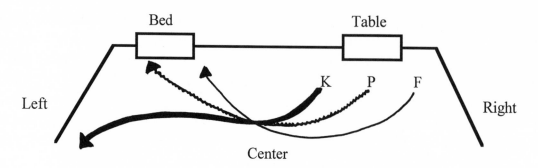

stage, the puppeteers may have to shift positions from one side to the other behind the stage.

Most props for a puppet play will be imagined by the audience, except those which are necessary for the action or to set the stage.

Patterns for cardboard props are given for both "The Frog Prince" and "The Shoemaker and the Elves." Trace the patterns for each prop and transfer them to white poster board. Color them with crayons, felt tip pens, or paint, and outline in black. Cut the props out, leaving some white cardboard around the smaller details, such as the food on the table in "The Frog Prince." Tape two ice cream sticks or dowels to the back of the props at either end. Locate the props on the stage, and tape the sticks to the back of the stage so the audience can see only the props.

One of the most common puppets used in story programs is the simple hand puppet. The basic pattern for hand puppets can be adapted for any human or animal character by creating appropriate features and costumes. Included here are instructions for making and manipulating eleven different types of puppets. They include: simple hand puppets, sock puppets, paper towel puppets, paper bag puppets, styrofoam ball puppets, paper plate puppets, stick puppets, spoon puppets, glove puppets, washcloth puppets, and coat hanger puppets.

We will begin with the simple hand puppet.

Body Pattern for Hand Puppet

- Trace top and bottom pieces of pattern onto tracing paper. Include marking ●'s. Cut out.
- Overlap top and bottom pieces, matching solid lines; tape together forming whole puppet body pattern.
- Fold your fabric so that you place what will be the outside of the puppet together.

- Pin the pattern in place onto what will be the inside of the puppet, and cut along outer, solid line.
- Mark sewing line at ●'s; remove pattern, and pin front and back pieces together.
- Sew around sides and top allowing 5/8 inch seam allowance. (Use very fine stitch around curves to make a smooth, straight seam.)
- Follow marking ●'s to maintain 5/8 inch seam around neckline, remembering to leave the bottom edge unsewn.
- Trim all of the curved seams close to the stitching line. Turn the puppet right side out, press the seams flat. Hem or zigzag bottom (optional).

Hand Puppet with Shirt and Pants

To make the appearance of a puppet wearing a shirt and a pair of pants, trace the top and bottom pattern pieces separately as shown onto tracing paper. (Do not overlap to form whole body at this time.) Add a 5/8 inch extension for seam allowance to the bottom pattern piece.

Choose contrasting fabrics; dark color for the bottom, light for the top. Pin the patterns to the chosen fabric and cut two of each. Using light colored thread, stitch a line down the center of the bottom piece to give the impression of trousers. If you wish, this can also be drawn with a felt tip pen.

Place what will be the outside of the top and bottom parts together and stitch across the edge forming the complete front and back pieces for the puppet's body. Press the seam open. Place what will be the outside of the the front and back pieces together and stitch around the sides and top.

Now complete the puppet as described for the basic hand puppet body. Add a strip of felt for a belt, either gluing or sewing in place.

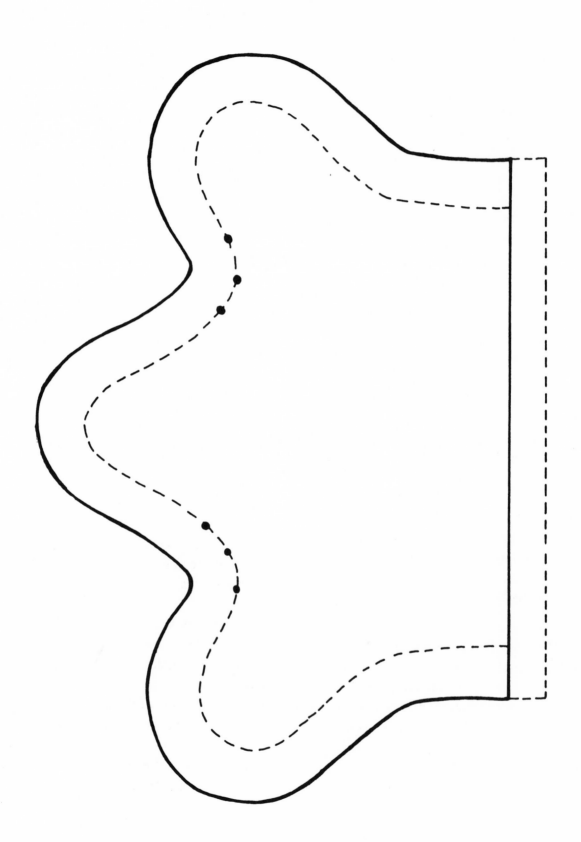

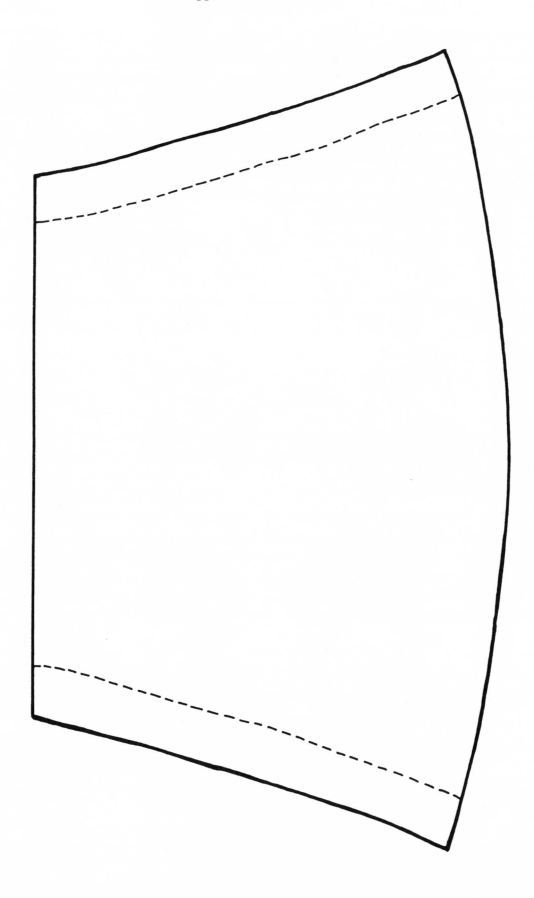

Operating a Hand Puppet

To operate your puppet, place the body on your hand. Using either an open palm or curved finger method, push the styrofoam head onto your index finger. This placement should allow you greatest mobility. In the open palm method, put your thumb in one arm, your index finger in the neck, and the remaining three fingers in the other arm. Moving your puppet's arms in various actions should be easy and comfortable.

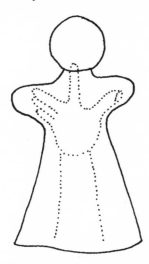

The second, curved finger, method calls for holding your ring and little fingers against your palm. This may be necessary, depending on the size of your hand or your own preference. Practice moving your fingers in different positions to create various "human" actions.

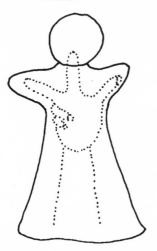

For instance, curve your fingers toward the palm and the puppet delivers oratory. This stance can also indicate taking a pledge or expressing honesty.

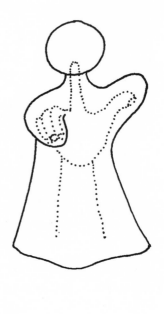

If you bring your thumb and fingers together in front, your puppet can clap, give the appearance of singing, or pick up props.

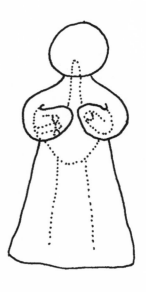

If you bend your index finger at its lower joint, the puppet nods or looks down at the ground.

When you bend your hand at the wrist, your puppet bows. By sweeping your fingers toward your palm while bowing, the gesture becomes even more dramatic.

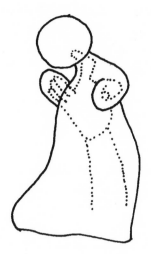

Toddler Puppets

I Love Little Kitty

I love little kitty,
Her coat is so warm;
And if I don't hurt her,
She'll do me no harm.

So I'll not pull her tail,
Nor drive her away,
But kitty and I
Very gently will play.

—Jane Taylor

Directions for Kitty Puppet

For the kitten puppet, use a fuzzy white sock. Place the sock on your hand with your fingers in the toe of the sock. Insert some stuffing (a ball of nylon stocking will do) over the top of your fingers. This will add a bit of bulk to the head above your knuckles in the head of the sock. Add features such as eyes, ears, nose, and whiskers by gluing or sewing as needed.

TIP: To properly place the kitty's features, curve your hand as if you are operating the puppet. Then locate the features and mark their placement on the head. Then remove the sock and glue or sew the features onto the sock.

To operate the puppet, curve your hand with your fingers pointing down so your audience can see the kitty's face. To form the mouth, tuck a portion of the sock between your fingers and thumb. Move your fingers up and down to make the puppet talk. Practice.

KITTY'S EARS: Cut two ears from felt and stitch to the top of the kitty's head. To stiffen ears and make them stand up, mix half white glue and water. Paint the solution on the ears and allow them to dry for several hours.

KITTY'S EYEBROWS: Cut two from felt and glue above eyes. For nose, cut from black or pink felt. Glue in place. For whiskers, use pipe cleaners and sew in place. Finish off with a ribbon or felt bow and sew or glue in place.

KITTY'S EYES: Use black and white felt and cut two sets of each. For eyelashes, clip the felt extensions. Glue white on outer eye, then center black pupil over white. Glue in place on puppet, centering eyes in the middle of the face.

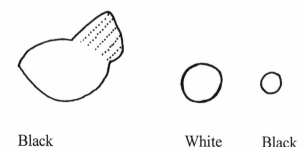

Black   White   Black

Mary Had a Little Lamb

Mary had a little lamb,
It's fleece was white as snow;
And everywhere that Mary went
The lamb was sure to go.

It followed her to school one day;
That was against the rule;
It made the children laugh and play
To see a lamb at school.

—Sara Joseph Hale

Directions for Mary Spoon Puppet

Use a square piece of fabric, about 10 inches by 10 inches. Attach it to the bowl of a wooden spoon with a rubber band. Fold cloth down over handle to make costume.

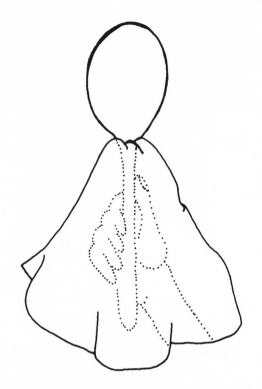

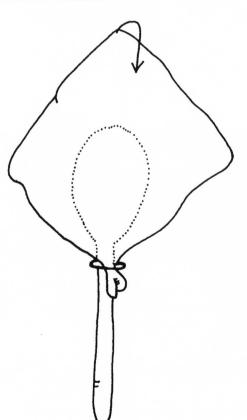

FACE: Draw features on back of spoon with felt tip pen. Put the eyes at center of spoon. Use black for eyes, brows, nose; red for mouth, cheeks.

HAIR: Use thick yarn. Bring top strands down over forehead, gluing to the spoon. For curls, wrap the yarn around a pencil to the length of one curl, about 2 inches. Use a needle and thread and run the needle through each strand on two or three sides of the pencil. Knot to fasten tightly. Remove the curl and glue at the side of the head. Repeat until you have enough curls to make a full head of hair.

TO OPERATE: Grasp handle and move puppet as desired.

Directions for Lamb Stick Puppet

Trace the lamb below, transferring it to poster board. Outline the lamb with black felt tip pen. Glue balls of cotton to the body for a 3D look and soft texture. Tape ice cream sticks to the back of the lamb puppet.

TO OPERATE: Grasp the stick and move the puppet back and forth. Be sure to keep hand below the stage level if using the puppet in a theater.

For a better effect, make a two-sided lamb that can walk back and forth. To make two-sided, trace and transfer the lamb as described above. Repeat process, but turn tracing over before transferring to poster board to have lamb going in the opposite direction. Finish lamb as described above. Tape ice cream sticks to the back of the lamb and glue the two lambs together, back to back.

My Puppy

My fat fuzzy puppy
Comes running to greet me.
He barks and he jumps
And wig-waggles his tail.

My fat fuzzy puppy
Is so glad to see me.
He jiggles all over
And wig-waggles his tail.

My fat fuzzy puppy—
He really DOES love me—
I can tell by the way
He wig-waggles his tail.

—C. S. Peterson

There Was a Little Puppy

There was a little puppy
And he said, "bow wow."
He had a little spot
Upon his little brow.
And every time he looked at me,
His tail would start to wag.
As if he wanted me to play a game of tag.

I love my little puppy.
He is so very dear.
He never asks for anything
And never sheds a tear.
He is so nice and gentle,
That I never could forget,
That lovely little puppy is my special pet.

—Anonymous

Directions for Puppy Sock Puppet

For both the fat fuzzy puppy and little puppy puppet, use a thick fuzzy sock, white or brown. Slit the toe of the sock about halfway to the heel.

MOUTH: Cut four pieces of poster board, about 1/4 inch shorter than the slit in the sock.

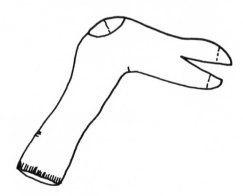

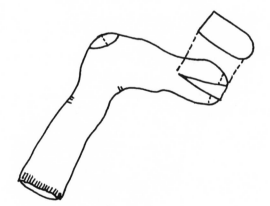

Tape the pieces together on one side, forming a hinge.

Repeat with the remaining two poster board pieces. Insert one mouth piece into slit in the sock.

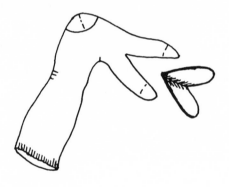

Pull edges of sock over the mouth and tape securely.

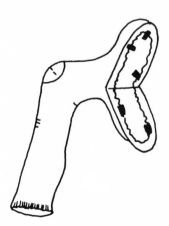

Glue other mouth piece over the first one to hide the tape.

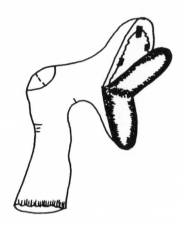

Stuff the top of the puppy's mouth with nylon stockings to form rounded head.

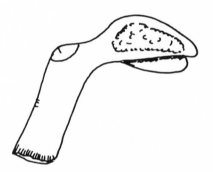

Add features by gluing or sewing as needed.

EARS: Cut two ears, reversing the pattern for a matching pair. You may use fake fur for a fuzzy texture. Sew in place at the top of the head.

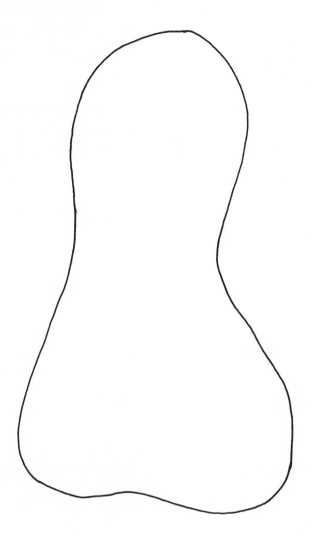

EYES: Use felt, cut two sets of each. Glue white on outer eye, then center the pupil over white. Glue in place. To determine proper placement, put puppet on hand and center eyes about 2/3 of the way up from the end of the puppet. Mark with pen, remove puppet and glue eyes in place.

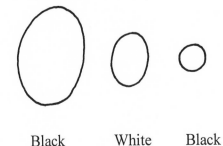

Black   White   Black

TONGUE: Cut from felt, either red or pink. Glue on lower mouth piece, placing back of tongue at hinge in the puppy's mouth.

To finish, cut some eyebrows in quarter moon shapes out of felt and glue over eyes. Make the puppy's nose from a small ball of yarn. Tack with needle and thread in several places to keep shape. Sew nose at end of puppet.

TO OPERATE: Slide your hand inside the puppy puppet with your fingers on the top of the mouth and your thumb on the bottom. Move your fingers up and down to make the puppy talk.

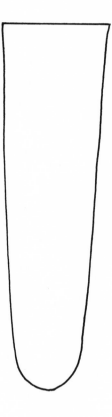

Preschool Puppets

Little Miss Muffet (traditional)

Little Miss Muffet
Sat on a tuffet,
Eating her curds and whey;
Along came a spider,
And sat down beside her,
And frightened Miss Muffet away.

Little Miss Muffet (variation three)

Little Miss Muffet,
She likes Jimmy Buffet,
And Elvis and Dylan and Sting,
Along came a spider,
Who sat down beside her,
And together they boogied 'til Spring.

Little Miss Muffet (variation one)

Little Miss Muffet
Sat on a tuffet,
Eating her curds and whey;
Along came a spider,
And sat down beside her,
And she frightened that spider away.

Little Miss Muffet (variation four)

Little Miss Muffet,
Sat on a tuffet,
Wondering what to eat next;
Along came her brother
Who teased her and taunted,
And left that poor girl quite perplexed.

Little Miss Muffet (variation two)

Little Miss Muffet,
Sat on a tuffet,
Eating her peas porridge hot,
Along came a spider,
Who slid down beside her,
And she offered him some on the spot.

Little Miss Muffet (variation five)

Little Miss Muffet,
Sat on her tuffet,
Eating a Big Mac and fries;
She ate it so quickly,
And then felt so sickly,
She realized that wasn't so wise.

Directions for Miss Muffet Puppet

HEAD: Cut two inches from paper towel roll. Cover with strip of paper, keeping seam in the back.

BODY: Cut a 14 by 14 inch square of fabric. Fold in half and cut three holes about 1 inch apart from each other.

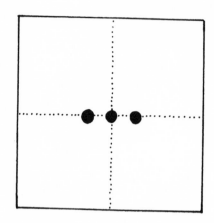

HAIR: Use yellow, red, or black yarn. Make a thick wrap of yarn, about 5 inches long.

TO OPERATE: Place fingers through the three holes. Use middle finger to hold head. Use other fingers for arms of the puppet.

Drape hair across the top of the tube, gluing at the sides (bows will cover any glue marks). Make bows, using felt or ribbon, and glue at sides of head. Draw features with felt tip pens, placing eyes in the the middle of her face. Use black for eyes, eyebrows, and nose, and red for her mouth.

Directions for Spider Glove Puppet

For the spider, use a black evening glove.

EYES: Use felt or buttons. For felt, cut two white circles and two smaller black circles. Glue black pupil on the white, and glue the eyes on the face. For white buttons, cut two black felt circles and glue on buttons as pupil. Sew on the glove.

MOUTH: Embroider a smile with red thread or use red felt, gluing in place.

TO OPERATE: Put the spider glove on your hand and move your fingers to make the spider creep and crawl.

Old MacDonald Had a Farm

Old MacDonald had a farm, E-I-E-I-O.
And on this farm he had a cow, E-I-E-I-O.
With a moo, moo here; And a moo, moo there;
Here a moo, there a moo, everywhere a moo, moo.
Old MacDonald had a farm, E-I-E-I-O.

Old MacDonald had a farm, E-I-E-I-O.
And on this farm he had a duck, E-I-E-I-O.
With a quack, quack here; etc.

Old MacDonald had a farm, E-I-E-I-O.
And on this farm he had a pig, E-I-E-I-O.
With an oink, oink here; etc.

Old MacDonald had a farm, E-I-E-I-O.
And on this farm he had a chicken, E-I-E-I-O.
With a chick, chick here; etc.

Old MacDonald had a farm, E-I-E-I-O.
And on this farm he had a turkey, E-I-E-I-O.
With a gobble, gobble here; etc.

Old MacDonald had a farm, E-I-E-I-O.
And on this farm he had a goat, E-I-E-I-O.
With a maa, maa here; etc.

Old MacDonald had a farm, E-I-E-I-O.
And on this farm he had a horse, E-I-E-I-O.
With a neigh, neigh here; etc.

Old MacDonald had a farm, E-I-E-I-O.
And on this farm he had a dog, E-I-E-I-O.
With a ruff, ruff here; etc.

Old MacDonald had a farm, E-I-E-I-O.
And on this farm he had a cat, E-I-E-I-O.
With a meow, meow here; etc.

Old MacDonald had a farm, E-I-E-I-O.
And on this farm he had a rooster, E-I-E-I-O.
With a cock-a-doodle here; etc.

Old MacDonald had a farm, E-I-E-I-O.
And on this farm he had a lamb, E-I-E-I-O.
With a baa, baa here; etc.

Old MacDonald had a farm, E-I-E-I-O.

Or add the following animals for variety and fun:

peacock
lion
manatee
monkey
turtle
zebra
fly
goldfish
buffalo
eagle
llama
gorilla
tadpole
goose
horse-shoe crab
albino armadillo
ferret
waskaly wabbit
roadrunner
puma
panda
red-bellied sapsucker

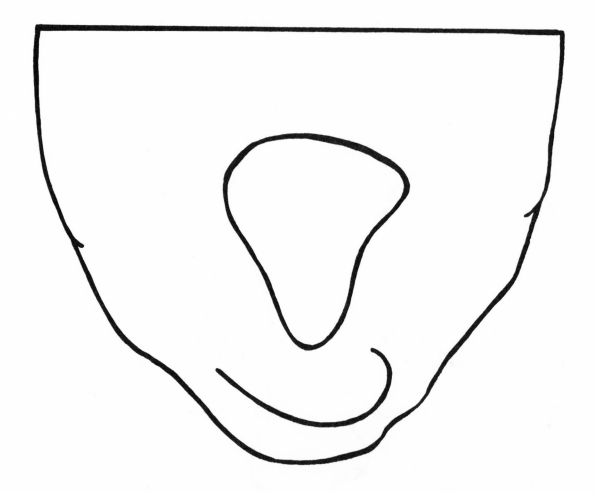

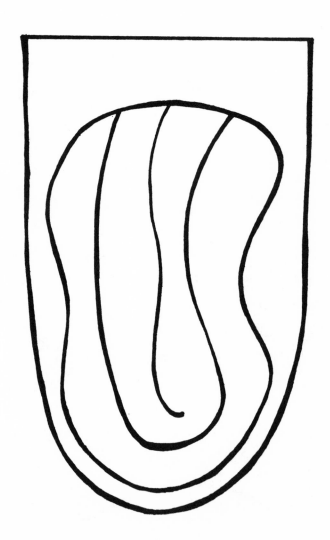

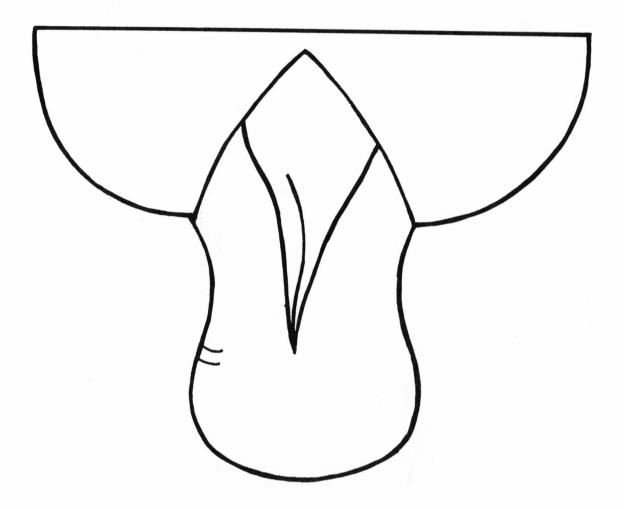

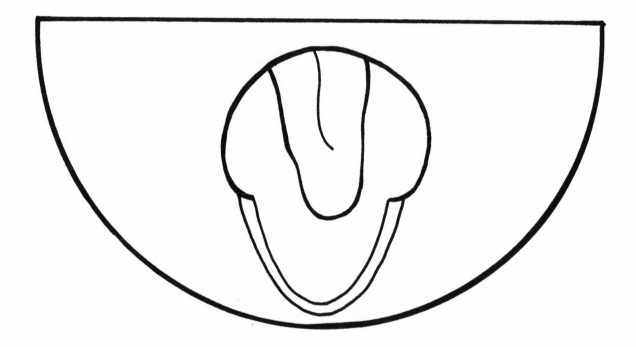

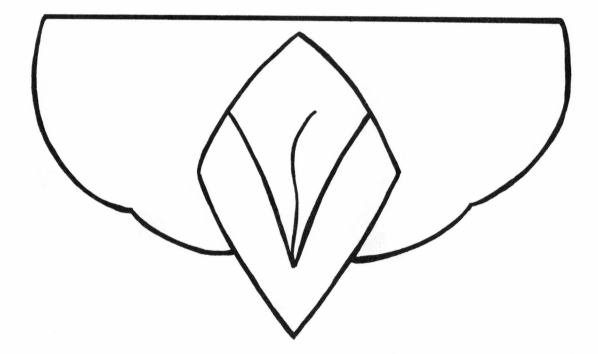

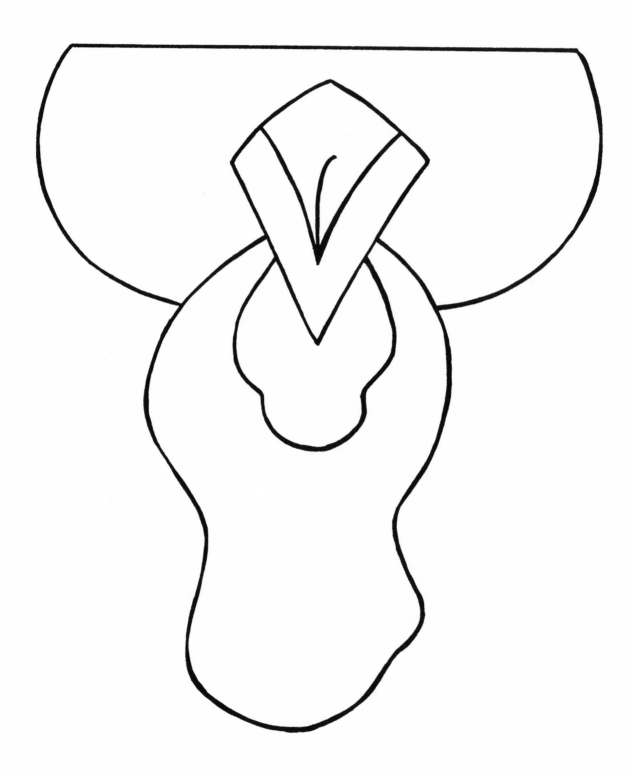

Directions for Old MacDonald
Paper Bag Puppets

Use a 4 or 6 inch paper bag.

With tracing paper, trace the heads and mouth pieces of the puppets. Transfer to poster board or heavy construction paper. Color as desired and outline with black felt tip pens or crayons.

Draw features with a black felt tip pen or trace features onto various colored papers and glue in place, i.e., red paper for mouth, white paper and black felt pen for eyes.

Glue the face piece onto the bottom of the bag, centering the face to cover as much of the bag as possible and to extend just below the flap (see A).

Glue the mouth piece under the flap in the bag, placing the mouth so it lines up with the face piece when the bag is folded flat (see B).

You may have to adjust the length of the mouth piece, depending upon the size of your paper bag (see C).

To operate, place your hand inside the bag with your fingers curled over the flap in the bottom of the bag. Simply move your fingers up and down to make the puppet talk (see D).

While a new bag puppet may seem noisy, as you work the paper, the crunching will subside.

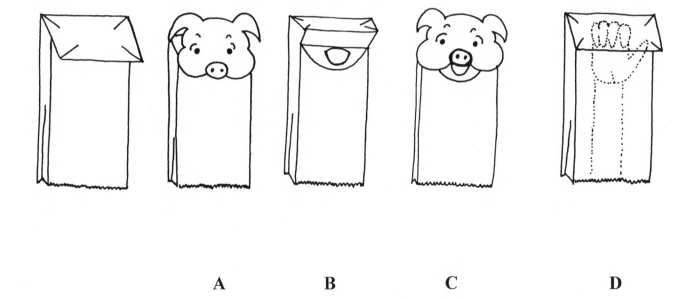

A **B** **C** **D**

The Lion and the Mouse

Cast of Characters: Lion, Mouse

Note on puppets: Because of the flat structure of the mouse puppet, most of his movements will have to be done facing the audience. Turn him slightly to either side to create variety in his movements and to make him a more believable character. The real action will have to be performed by the lion, since he is a flexible puppet with movable arms.

Props: Net; this can be a hair net or fishing net.

Setting: Jungle scene with sun in sky. Suggestion for backdrop: thick grouping of trees. Make a "collage" using pieces of construction paper, colored magazine pictures, wallpaper, and/or cloth. Cut dark colored strips for trunks of trees, and free-form circles of various shades of green to suggest tree tops and bushes. Use yellow circle for sun shining over trees. Overlap the trees to suggest dense jungle.

Puppeteers: Two. Puppeteer A (stage L)—Lion. Puppeteer B (stage R)—Mouse.

(*At rise: Lion is pacing back and forth across stage, as if strolling through the jungle. He continues walking while delivering lines.*)

LION: 'Tis a fine day for a walk through the jungle. (*Stops stage R, looks at audience.*) And a fine day it is, too, to be King of the Beasts. (*Walks across to stage L, stops, holds hand to ear.*) Ah, listen to the birds singing. Truly, it is a lovely day. So lovely, in fact, that I think that I shall lie down right on this very spot and take a nap. Aah . . .

(*Slowly lies down on his side with back to audience, head pointing off stage L.*) (*Mouse enters back, stage R.*)

MOUSE: (*Runs to center stage, then forward.*) Scurry, scurry, my little feet; I must find some food to eat. (*Runs to stage R, stops, looks up at sun, bends slightly backward looking offstage.*) My, but it is a lovely day. (*Turns to audience.*) When the sun is shining so brightly, surely nothing but good luck can come to me. (*Turns stage L, sees Lion, turns back to audience.*) Look at that large yellow hill. I wonder if there is any food on it. I think I'll climb up and see. (*Mouse climbs up the lion's back; do this with the mouse behind the lion, moving the mouse slowly up and across almost to the lion's head. Mouse then starts back down the lion's back. When the mouse is almost off, the lion wakes up and pounces on him; do this by having the lion jump up as the mouse jumps to the side. Then the lion can grab the mouse from behind.*)

LION: (*Roars.*) Who dares to walk on the King of the Beasts? I shall eat you, troublesome mouse, for part of my dinner.

MOUSE: Oh, please, sir, don't eat me. I thought you were a yellow hill. Please don't eat me, I beg you.

LION: Oh, ho! And why shouldn't I eat you, pray tell?

MOUSE: (*Quivers.*) If you do not eat me, sir, perhaps someday I may be of service to you.

LION: (*Moves to left side of the mouse, still hold-*

ing mouse with right hand.) You! You! A tiny, harmless mouse? How can you possibly be of service to me? I am King of the Beasts!

MOUSE: Please, sir. Please. I may be small, but I am useful.

LION: Very well, little mouse. I like your courage. I shall let you go free. But I don't know what you could ever possibly do to help me. (*Frees the mouse.*)

MOUSE: (*Bows slightly.*) Oh, thank you. Thank you, sir, very much. (*Exits stage R.*)

LION: (*Laughs, moves after mouse to center stage.*) How absurd! That silly squeaking mouse thinks he can help the King! (*Laughs, walks stage L, starts offstage, falls in trap; do this by draping net over his head. Lion then backs onto stage.*) Help! Help! (*Roars and struggles.*) I am caught in a trap! Let me out, do you hear? I am King of the Beasts. Help! Somebody help me. (*Roars and struggles to get out of the net.*) (*Enter Mouse stage R.*)

MOUSE: Isn't that King Lion shouting for help? (*Moves to the lion.*) Oh, dear, oh, dear, oh he has fallen into a trap. (*Runs to center.*) What shall I do? I have to help him; I promised him that I would.

(*Runs back to the lion.*) King Lion, sir, I've come to help.

LION: Who's that? You silly little mouse! What could you possibly do? Can't you see I'm caught in this net? (*Struggles.*)

MOUSE: Please, sir, perhaps I can help. Maybe I can gnaw these ropes in two. (*Gnaws; slightly drop mouse behind lion.*) If only I can chew fast enough . . .

LION: The hunters are coming. I can smell them!

MOUSE: (*Pops head up to look.*) Oh, dear, I must hurry. (*Gnaws again.*) There's one more. (*Gnaws.*) And another. There. Pull hard, sir, I think you can pull free. (*Lion moves slightly offstage.*)

LION: (*Pulls.*) Uhh...uhh...oh! (*Pull net off lion.*) Whew! At last! (*Roars.*) Little mouse, thank you very much for saving my life.

MOUSE: It was nothing, sir. I promised that I would help you because you once spared me.

LION: I am sorry that I made fun of your small size. (*Puts hand on mouse's shoulder.*) Come, Friend Mouse, let us go for a walk through the jungle. (*Both exit stage L.*)

—C. S. Peterson and M. B. Hall

Directions for Styrofoam Lion Puppet

HEAD: Use a large styrofoam ball, 6 inches in diameter. Carve a hole in the bottom to fit your index finger and puppet body. Paint the head with yellow or orange spray paint (optional).

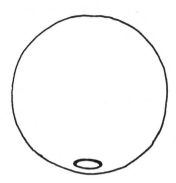

EARS: Make ears according to the following pattern from yellow or orange felt and locate them about 2 inches forward on the head of the lion. Stiffen ear and flap. Mix half white glue and water and paint solution on the ear; let dry. This will allow you to crease the flap and keep the ears standing upright. Fold ear flap toward the back of the head and glue in place. Draw the inner ear line with a black felt tip pen.

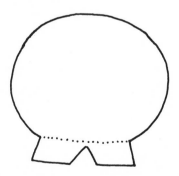

MANE: Make loops of yellow or orange yarn, about 2 inches long. Cut at one end, leaving about six 2 inch strips of yarn. Repeat loops as needed to make a thick mane.

BACK OF HEAD: Make more loops of yarn, but increase the length to 4 inches. Snip one end and glue loops to the head in several layers until the head is well covered.

Draw circle of glue about 2 inches inward on the lion's face. This marks the line for attaching the mane. Using plenty of glue, start placing loops of yarn on the head. Overlap as needed.

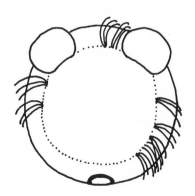

Finish the face by gluing features in place. Start with the eyes at the center of the face.

EYES: Use felt, cutting two sets each (making left and right eyelids). Glue eyelids on outer eye. Glue white below eyelid. Center pupil on white. Center eyes on face and glue.

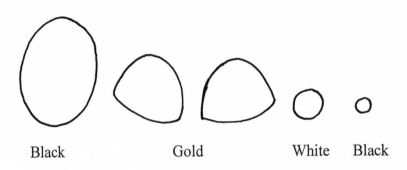

Black   Gold   White   Black

NOSE: Cut one from black felt and glue in place.

WHISKERS: Use toothpicks or pipe cleaners. Glue in place.

EYEBROWS: Cut two from felt and glue above eyes.

PAWS: Add paws by gluing in place on hands.

MOUTH: Cut one from black or red felt and glue in place.

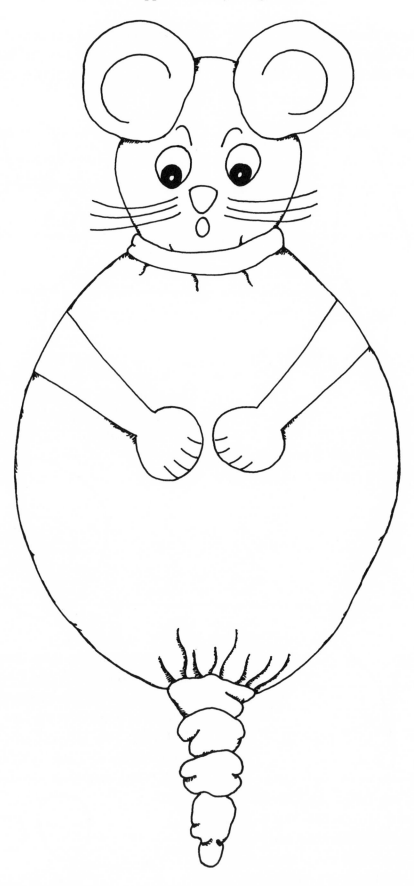

Directions for Mouse Hanger Puppet

For the mouse hanger puppet, use a fairly firm coat hanger. Stretch the hanger out, keeping the handle at the bottom.

When the head and body are formed, stretch an old nylon stocking over the frame. You can cut off half of the handle with wire cutters if you wish.

Pinch "end tips" as straight as possible. Shape the head as a small circle, making it about 2 1/2 by 2 1/2 inches.

Wrap excess stocking around the handle and secure in place with rubber bands. Tie a strip of felt or ribbon at the neck to pull the stocking in around the head.

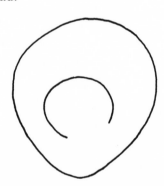

EARS: Cut two from brown felt. Draw inner ear with black felt tip pen. Glue ears in place at the side of the mouse's head, bringing almost one-third of the way down over the face.

EYES: Use felt, cut two sets of each. Glue white circles on outer eye and center pupil over white. Glue eyes in place, about the center of the face.

Continue stretching hanger to form the body, another circle about 6 by 6 inches. You will have to work back and forth between the body and the head to form the circles. Pinch in at the bottom of the body, leaving a handle about 8 inches long.

Black   White   Black

NOSE: Cut from pink felt and glue in place.

ARMS: Cut two from brown felt. Draw hand with black felt tip pen. Glue the mouse arms on the body.

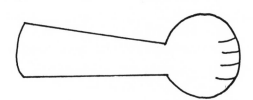

MOUTH: Cut from red or black felt and glue in place.

TO OPERATE: Grasp by the handle, keeping the handle below the stage level as you move the puppet across the stage.

WHISKERS: Use pipe cleaners or tooth picks and glue at sides of the face.

EYEBROWS: Cut two from felt and glue above eyes.

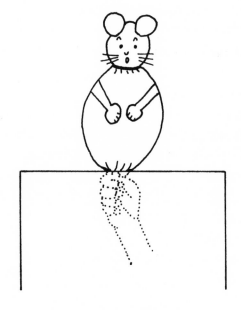

Primary Level Puppets

The Bear Went Over the Mountain

The bear went over the mountain,
The bear went over the mountain,
The bear went over the mountain,
To see what he could see.

And all that he did see,
And all that he did see,
Was the other side of the mountain,
The other side of the mountain,
The other side of the mountain,
Was all that he could see.

So the bear went down the mountain,
The bear went down the mountain,
The bear went down the mountain,
Very happily.

FABRIC: Choose brown or black fake fur for the body or an old brown or black washcloth. Use brown or black felt for the ears.

Place right sides of the fabric together and pin pattern in place. Cut out. Mark ●'s for sewing line around the neck and the ear placement at the top of the head. Cut two ears from the felt, mark the ●'s. Remove the pattern pieces.

Place the front piece over the back piece, placing right sides of the fabric together. Pin at the sides and the arms.

Pull front of the head back to allow you to place the ears at ●'s, as shown. Carefully fold the front over the back of the head, keeping the ears in place at ●'s. Pin the head pieces together, so the ears are securely in place.

Directions for Bear Puppet

Trace the top and bottom pieces of the pattern included on pages 148-149. Include marking the ●'s. Cut out. Overlap top and bottom pieces, matching solid lines. Tape together forming the whole puppet pattern. Trace the ear pattern (appearing on the same page as the top of the puppet) and cut out.

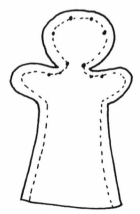

Sew around sides and top allowing 5/8 inch seam allowance. (Use a very fine stitch around curves to make smooth, straight seam.) Following marking ●'s to maintain 5/8 inch seam at neckline. Pivot at large ■'s to form head.

Trim all curved seams close to the stitching line; clip almost to the seam at large ■'s.

Turn the right sides out; pull the ears up, and press the seams lightly.

Stuff the head slightly with an old nylon stockings. Cut features and glue in place.

EYES: Cut two sets each. Glue white over black outer eye, center black pupil on white. Glue in place at center of face.

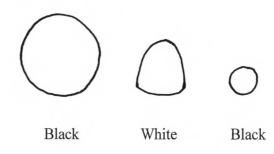

Black   White   Black

NOSE: Cut from black felt and glue in place.

MOUTH: Cut small smile from red felt and glue in place.

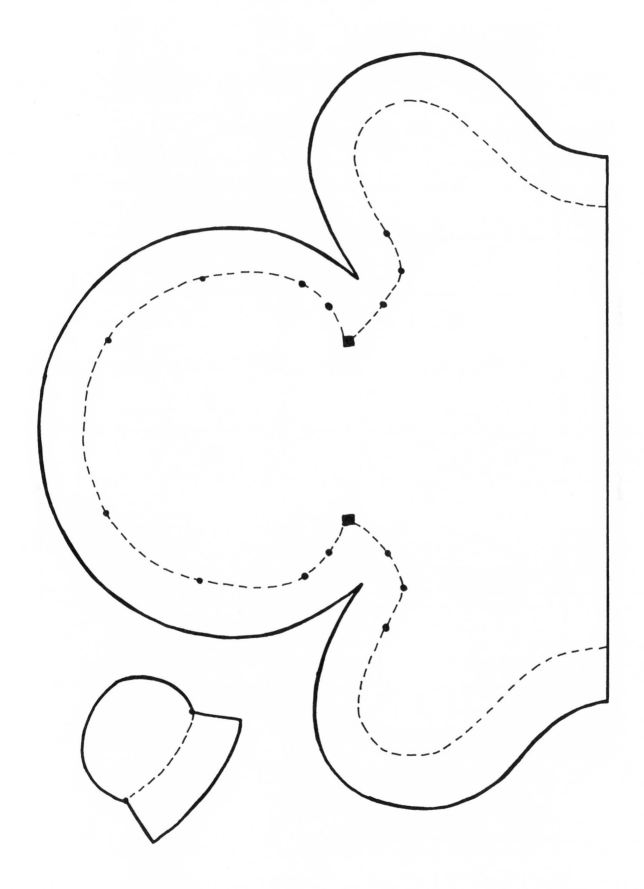

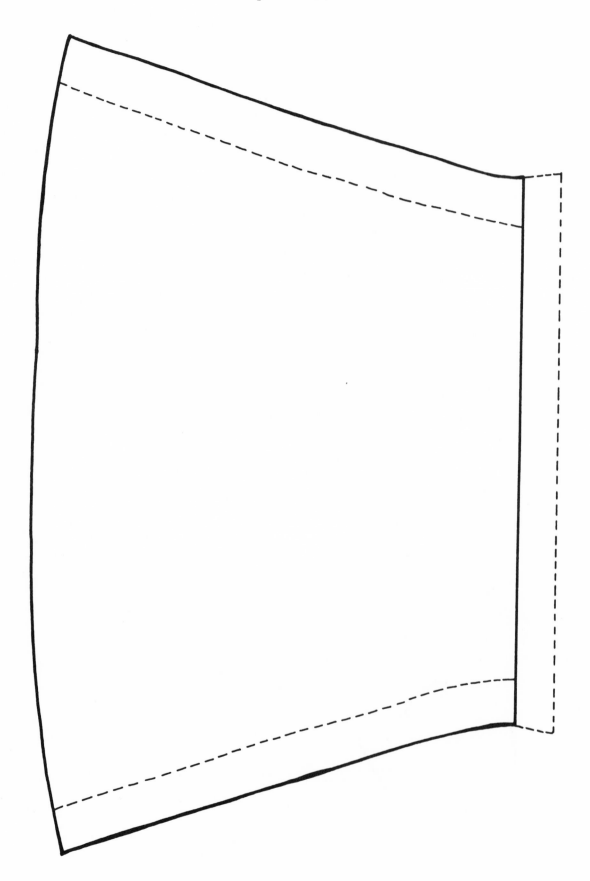

The Shoemaker and the Elves

Cast of Characters: One Narrator, Shoemaker, his Wife, two Elves, a Gentleman, a Lady, a Nobleman.

Props: Broom: use a thin dowel stick, cut several pieces of straw from a real broom and fasten on the stick with a rubber band. Workbench. Window (on backdrop, stage R). Shoes and elves' new clothes are imaginary.

Setting: Shoemaker's shop, sparsely furnished to show poverty. Workbench at center stage, window on backdrop at stage R. Suggestions for backdrop: to create effect of poor shop, use dull, white, or gray paper for walls. Include outline of window with ragged drapes at stage R. Can also have small table and chairs at stage L. A collage effect can be used to make these pieces. Draw window with felt tip pens, make drapes from fabric and glue in place. Table can be cut from colored magazine pictures, construction paper, etc. Add details with felt tip pens.

Puppeteers: Two. Puppeteer A (stage L)— Shoemaker (right hand), Wife (left hand). Puppeteer B (stage R)—First elf (left hand), Second elf (right hand); change puppets—Gentleman (right hand) for each Lady (left hand) appearance, Nobleman (right hand).

Note: If a third puppeteer is available, he or she should operate the Shoemaker or the Wife.

(*At rise: Shoemaker and Wife are standing at workbench. Both search around bench for leather. Shoemaker finds leather, turns to Wife, begins dialogue.* **Note:** *Shoemaker will be at center stage, Wife on his left.*)

NARRATOR: Once upon a time there was a shoemaker who made very fine shoes. In fact, the shoes that he made were of such fine quality that they hardly would wear out. Although the shoemaker was honest and hardworking, he and his wife became poorer and poorer, for bad luck seemed to haunt them every day.

SHOEMAKER: Oh, dear, oh, dear, whatever shall we do? Wife, do you realize that this piece of leather is all the leather that we have? And it will only be enough to make one pair of shoes.

WIFE: (*Goes to husband, puts hand on shoulder to comfort him.*) Don't worry, Husband. Everything will be all right. Why don't you go to bed and in the morning you can make that last piece of leather into shoes.

SHOEMAKER: That's a fine idea. But before I go to bed, I shall cut out the pair of shoes. Then when I get up early in the morning, I can begin at once to sew them. (*Wife nods in agreement, exits stage L. Shoemaker cuts out shoes at workbench, then exits stage L. Clock strikes midnight. Enter Elves stage R, look around room.*)

FIRST ELF: (*Goes to workbench.*) Well, well, well, what's this I see? Here is a pair of shoes all cut out and ready to be sewn.

SECOND ELF: (*Goes to workbench.*) Come, brother, let's get to work. This pair of shoes will not get sewn if we only dance and talk. (Elves busily make shoes.)

FIRST ELF: Aha! All finished!

SECOND ELF: Splendid! Now we must hurry. (*Exit stage R.*)

SHOEMAKER: (*Enter stage L.*) Now where did I leave that leather? I cut it out and laid it on the workbench. (*Goes to workbench, sees shoes.*) What! Wife! Wife! Come quickly!

WIFE: (*Enters stage L, carrying broom.*) Whatever is the matter, Husband?

SHOEMAKER: Never have I seen such beautiful shoes! (*Wife goes to workbench.*) Last night I left the pieces of leather on the workbench and this morning, what do I find? A pair of perfectly made shoes! I simply cannot believe my eyes.

WIFE: Let us put them in the window. Surely someone will want to buy such beautiful shoes as these. (*Shoemaker puts shoes in window.*) Now, Husband, let us tidy up the room while we wait for a customer. (*They work about room. Enter Gentleman stage R.*)

SHOEMAKER: (*Turns to Gentleman.*) Good morning, sir. May I please be of service to you?

GENTLEMAN: Oh, indeed, yes. Those shoes in the window are surely splendid. I should like to try them on.

SHOEMAKER: Of course. (*Goes to window, gets shoes; returns and bends down to help Gentleman try on shoes.*)

GENTLEMAN: A perfect fit! These shoes are so fine that I shall pay you more than the usual price for them. Here, my good fellow, is a handful of gold pieces. (*Exits stage R.*)

SHOEMAKER: Oh, my dear wife! Just look at all of the gold pieces.

WIFE: (*Goes to him, stage R.*) Hurry out and buy some more leather. That should buy enough to make two pairs of shoes. (*Shoemaker exits, stage R; Wife sweeps floor at stage R.*)

NARRATOR: And sure enough, the shoemaker had enough money to buy leather to make two pairs of shoes. (*Shoemaker enters stage R, Wife goes to him, both move to workbench, he cuts out shoes.*) He hurried home with his leather and at once sat down to cut out the shoes.

SHOEMAKER: There. The last piece is cut out. When I get up in the morning, I shall sew together both pairs of shoes.

WIFE: Come now. You have worked so hard today that you must get some rest. (*Both exit, stage L. Enter Elves, stage R, go to workbench.*)

FIRST ELF: What, ho! A workbench full of leather.

SECOND ELF: There is surely enough leather cut out for two pairs of shoes.

FIRST ELF: Then that is one pair for you and one pair for me.

SECOND ELF: You spend so much time talking! I shall be finished making my pair of shoes before you are finished making yours.

FIRST ELF: So it is a race, eh? Well, we shall see who can sew the faster. (*Both Elves work on shoes.*)

ELVES: Finished!

SECOND ELF: A tie! We have finished at the same time.

FIRST ELF: And only just in time. Now we must hurry away. (*Elves exit, stage R. Enter Shoemaker and Wife stage L; both go to workbench.*)

SHOEMAKER: Oh, can it be true? Here where I left pieces of leather I find two lovely pairs of shoes.

WIFE: Two perfect pairs of shoes! Let us put them in the window; surely they will be sold as quickly as the pair yesterday. (*Shoemaker puts shoes in window, returns to workbench. Both straighten up workbench. Enter Nobleman and Lady, stage R.*)

NOBLEMAN: Good sir.

SHOEMAKER: Good day, sir, and is it some shoes you would like?

NOBLEMAN: We were just driving through the village and my lady noticed the shoes in your window. Nothing must do but we stop and inquire about them.

SHOEMAKER: By all means, sir. And would the lady care to try on the shoes?

LADY: Indeed, I would like to try them on. They are the most beautiful pair of shoes that I have ever seen and I must have them. (*Shoemaker goes to window, gets shoes, helps her try them on.*) Perfect!

NOBLEMAN: (*Steps forward, Lady steps back.*) Here, shoemaker. Since the shoes please the lady so much, I am paying you dearly for them. (*Moves back beside Lady.*)

LADY: (*Turns to Nobleman.*) But, my dear, wouldn't you like to try on the other pair of shoes? They would look so splendid on you.

NOBLEMAN: Very well. Shoemaker, I would like to try on the other pair of shoes. (*Shoemaker nods, gets shoes, helps Nobleman try on shoes. Shoemaker returns to center stage. During this action, Lady will have to move backstage.*)

LADY: See there how fine they look.

NOBLEMAN: You are surely right. (*Moves to Shoemaker.*) Here, my friend, are some more gold coins. Good day to you. (*Lady and Nobleman exit, stage R.*)

NARRATOR: And so the shoemaker and his wife received enough money to buy leather to make four pairs of shoes. The shoemaker cut out the shoes before he went to bed, and sure enough, when he got up the next morning, he found four pairs of shoes waiting on his workbench.

And so it went. Every day the shoemaker and his wife would sell the shoes, buy more leather, cut out new shoes, and go to bed. And every morning they found on the workbench perfectly made shoes. People came from all over the kingdom to buy shoes and the shoemaker became quite well-to-do. But one day . . .

(*During narrator's speech the Shoemaker cuts leather at the workbench and the Wife goes to get the broom, returns and sweeps the floor.*)

SHOEMAKER: Wife, I would surely like to know who it is who has been so kind to us and has made all these shoes.

WIFE: (*Goes to Shoemaker.*) Yes, if we knew who the mysterious person is, we could repay his kindness.

SHOEMAKER: Let us hide tonight and see who it is that comes to visit us. (*Both hide at stage L, heads just showing from behind curtain.*)

NARRATOR: So the shoemaker and his wife hid and as the clock struck midnight, (*Elves, enter, go to workbench, sew shoes.*) they could hardly believe their eyes to see two ragged little elves climb up on the workbench, rapidly sew together all of the shoes, (*Elves exit.*) and disappear as quickly as they had come.

SHOEMAKER: (*Shoemaker and Wife enter, stage L, go to workbench.*) So these are the little men who have helped us to become rich.

WIFE: But the poor little fellows! All the time that they have been helping us, they have been going around in rags.

SHOEMAKER: You have given me an idea. Let's make them each an outfit of clothes.

WIFE: Oh, yes. You must make them each a pair of boots and I will make them coats and pants and hats.

NARRATOR: All that day the shoemaker and his wife did nothing but sew for the elves. When at last they had finished all of the clothes, they spread them out on the workbench. Then the two of them hid and waited. (*During the narrator's speech, Shoemaker and Wife sew clothes at work-* bench, *then hide as before. Enter Elves, stage R.*)

FIRST ELF: To work, brother. Tonight I shall sew together more pairs of shoes than you.

SECOND ELF: Another contest! Good. But I think that I can work faster than you.

FIRST ELF: Well, let's begin. (*Both move to workbench.*) Wait! What is this?

SECOND ELF: Clothes! For us!

FIRST ELF: In such fine clothes we will surely be gentlemen.

SECOND ELF: And gentlemen never make shoes, so we shall never again be shoemakers! (*Elves hold hands and dance around; go to workbench, gather clothes, exit stage R.*)

NARRATOR: The two tiny elves gathered up their new clothes, danced away, and were never again seen by the shoemaker and his wife. But as for the noble shoemaker, he and his wife lived happily and good luck thereafter hovered over their little shop.

—C. S. Peterson and M. B. Hall

Directions for Shoemaker Styrofoam Ball Puppet

HEAD: Use a 3 inch styrofoam ball for the Shoemaker's head. Carve a hole in the bottom of the ball to fit your finger.

HAIR: Use thick gray yarn and cut in strips about 2 inches long. For the top of the head, imagine a side part and a balding hairline. Glue strips across the top, bringing down the sides. Fill sides in with strips, overlapping and twisting the yarn to give a rather disorderly appearance.

For the back side of the Shoemaker's head, use 3 inch strips and fill in, again overlapping and twisting the yarn to give a disorderly appearance.

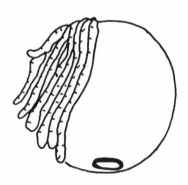

FACE: Cut the Shoemaker's features from felt. Glue his features in place; eyes in the middle of the face, mouth slightly below, and eyebrows above the eyes. You can make his glasses from pipe cleaners, covered with aluminum foil. Glue these in place.

EYES: Cut two small white circles and two smaller black circles. Glue the black pupil over the white.

MOUTH: Cut from red felt in the shape of a smile.

EYEBROWS: Cut two from black felt.

BODY: See directions for the hand puppet with shirt and pants. Choose dark colored fabric for the pants and white fabric for the shirt.

COLLAR: Cut long white cotton rectangle about 2 by 12 inches. Wrap around the neck, overlapping in the front to make "falling collar." Tack in place at the front.

APRON: Trace the pattern on page 183. Choose striped or dark fabric. Pin pattern on fabric and cut out one. Zig-zag edges on a sewing machine (optional).

Cut two strips of fabric about 7 inches long for his shoulder straps. Cut one strip of fabric about 12 inches long for the waistband. Sew or glue the shoulder straps at the top corners.

TO FIT APRON: Put the puppet on your hand and locate the apron at the puppet's waistline. Pin in place. Remove puppet and tack corners of the waistline to the puppet body.

Locate the waistband across the front of the apron. Tack or glue to the apron. Wrap the waistband around the puppet, pulling at the waist slightly.

Overlap the ends of the waistband in the back and tack ends together. Criss-cross the shoulder straps across the puppet's back. Trim excess strap and tuck ends behind waistband. Tack straps to waistband.

POCKET: Cut a square of fabric and glue in place on the apron (optional).

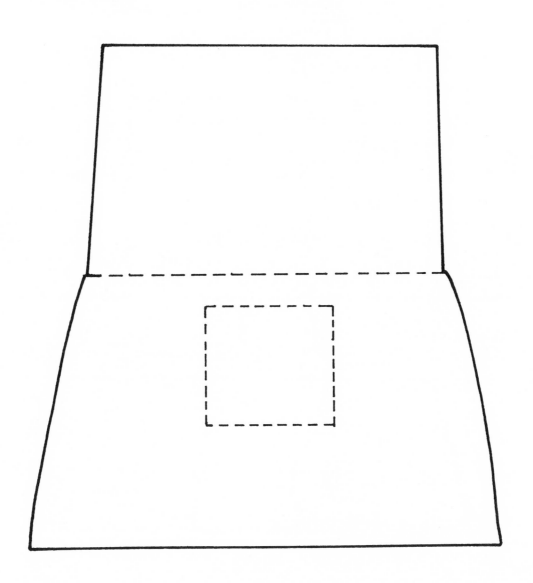

Directions for the Shoemaker's Wife
Styrofoam Puppet

HEAD: For the Shoemaker's Wife's head, also use a 3 inch styrofoam ball. Once again, carve a hole in the bottom to fit your finger.

HAIR: Use thick gray yarn. Cut several strips, about 10 inches long, to wrap around her head. Imagine a center part at the top of her head. Start about a third of the way down on her forehead, making line of white glue around the entire head to establish the hairline from the forehead to the back of the neck. Place first strip of yarn on glue and wrap around the head, bringing ends together at forehead.

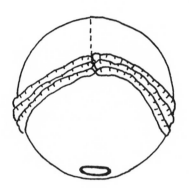

Continue adding strips of yarn to fill in most of the head, leaving circular opening at the back of the head for her bun.

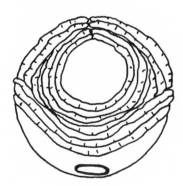

Make 2-3 long braids of yarn, about 20 inches; wrap in a ball to make thick bun. To keep the bun from coming apart, run a needle and thread back and forth through the bun in several places.

Glue the bun in place at the back of the head. For extra hold, stick several straight pins through the bun into the styrofoam ball, unless small children will be using puppets.

FACE: Cut features from felt. Glue features in place; eyes in middle of face, and mouth slightly below.

EYES: Cut two small white circles and two smaller black circles. Glue black pupil on white.

MOUTH: Cut from red felt in the shape of a smile.

GLASSES: Make glasses from pipe cleaners covered with aluminum foil and glue in place.

BODY: Choose light colored fabric and make body as described for hand puppet body.

APRON: Trace the pattern. Use a white cotton fabric. Pin the pattern onto the fabric and cut out one. Cut a narrow strip of fabric, about 20 inches in length, for the waistband.

Make several tucks or gathers across the top (shorter end) of the apron. Sew the waistband to the top of the apron. Tie around puppet's waist and tack to the puppet's body in several places.

SHAWL: Trace the pattern, using smaller version for Shoemaker's Wife, larger for the Lady puppet. Use a lightweight fabric, cotton for the Wife, satin-like for the Lady.

Fold fabric in half and pin pattern in place with shorter edge on fold. Cut out. Zig-zag edges (optional). Trim outside edge of Lady's shawl with lace (optional).

Drape over shoulders, tying a square knot in the front. Tack knot to the front of the puppet's body to keep shawl from slipping.

Directions for Elf Styrofoam Puppets

Make two elves from the same patterns, but change the color of the hair and the jacket on each. For instance, make one elf with red hair and a blue jacket; the other elf with yellow hair and a green jacket.

The elves should appear to be smaller than the other puppets. Use a 2 inch styrofoam ball, and make the body pattern shorter. The body pattern itself will have to stay the same size in order to fit your hand.

HEAD: As before, carve a hole in the bottom of the styrofoam ball to fit your finger.

HAIR: Use thick red or yellow yarn.

For the curls, make 1 1/2-2 inch curls as described for "Mary Had a Little Lamb." Start with the top of the head, gluing about two rows of curls across the top to the sides. These will fit under the hat.

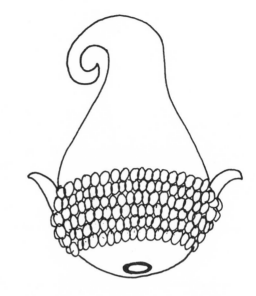

EARS: Trace pattern and cut two from white or tan colored felt. Stiffen ears by mixing half white glue and water. Paint solution on the ears and let them dry. Glue the ears at the sides about in center of the head, leaving pointed extension sticking outward from head.

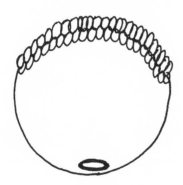

Before completing hair, glue hat and ears in place. Complete the hair by gluing curls across the forehead, back and sides to cover the bottom of the hat and bottom of the ears.

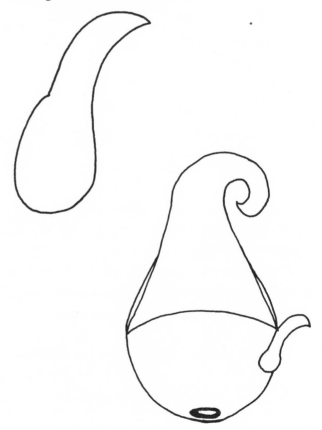

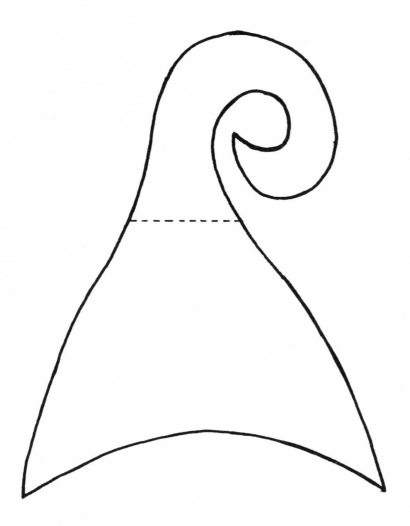

HAT: Trace the pattern and cut two from green or red felt. Glue front and back pieces together above dotted line. To stiffen hat and keep it standing up, mix solution of half white glue and water. Paint solution on the hat and let it dry. Wrap front hat piece across the elf's forehead, gluing in place. Wrap back hat piece around head joining sides together.

EYES: Cut two small white circles and two smaller black circles. Glue the black pupil over the white.

FACE: Cut features from felt. Glue them in place; eyes in the middle of the face, mouth slightly below, eyebrows above eyes, and cheeks at the sides of the mouth.

MOUTH: Cut the mouth from red felt in the shape of a smile.

EYEBROWS: Cut from black felt.

CHEEKS: Cut two small circles from pink felt.

BODY: See directions for hand puppet with shirt and pants. Cut pointed collar for jacket from felt. Put puppet on your hand to locate placement of the collar under the chin. Glue or sew in place. Make buttons out of felt or use real buttons. To suggest "tattered" clothes, cut small patches from fabric and glue on the jacket.

Directions for Gentleman Styrofoam Puppet

HEAD: Use a 3 inch styrofoam ball. Carve hole in the bottom of the ball to fit your finger.

HAIR: Use thick brown yarn. Cut strips about 3 inches in length. For the front, imagine a center part in the hair. Start 1/4 way down on forehead; glue strips from center down to sides, twisting slightly to give wavy hair look. Overlap to give fullness.

Cut 1/2 inch strips of yarn for the sideburns; glue in place along the side, blending under hair. For the back of the head, use 3 inch strips and fill in back, blending with sides and twisting yarn for wavy hair look. Overlap the yarn to give fullness.

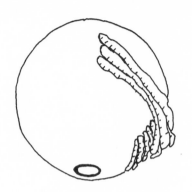

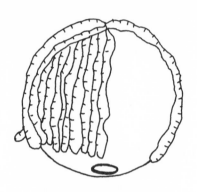

FACE: Cut features from felt. Glue features in place; eyes in middle of face, mouth slightly below, and eyebrows above eyes.

EYES: Cut two small white circles and two smaller black circles. Glue black pupils on white.

MOUTH: Cut from red felt in the shape of a smile.

EYEBROWS: Cut from black felt.

BODY: Choose black fabric for trousers, and white for shirt. See directions for hand puppet with shirt and pants.

CAPE: Choose rich brown fabric and make as described for the King's robe. Tack in front; not necessary to have a button.

COLLAR: Cut a long, white cotton rectangle, about 2 by 18 inches. Wrap this around the neck, tie a square knot in front and drape this over the ends of cape, tacking in place to keep it from slipping.

BELT: Use a strip of brown felt; wrap this around the waistline and glue it in place. Make a buckle from felt or poster board and glue this in place.

Directions for Nobleman Styrofoam Puppet

Make as described for the Gentleman. Omit the sideburns and collar. Use different colored fabric for trousers and cape.

TOP HAT: Trace patterns provided—both the round brim and the hat strip. Transfer the pattern to black poster board or heavy construction paper and cut out. Make a tube from the rectangle, overlapping ends to the dotted line, about 1/2 inch. Glue or tape the ends together, using clear tape.

Center the tube over the hat brim and tape to the brim, using clear tape. Place the hat on the puppet's head and secure by sticking straight pins through hat brim, at edge of tube.

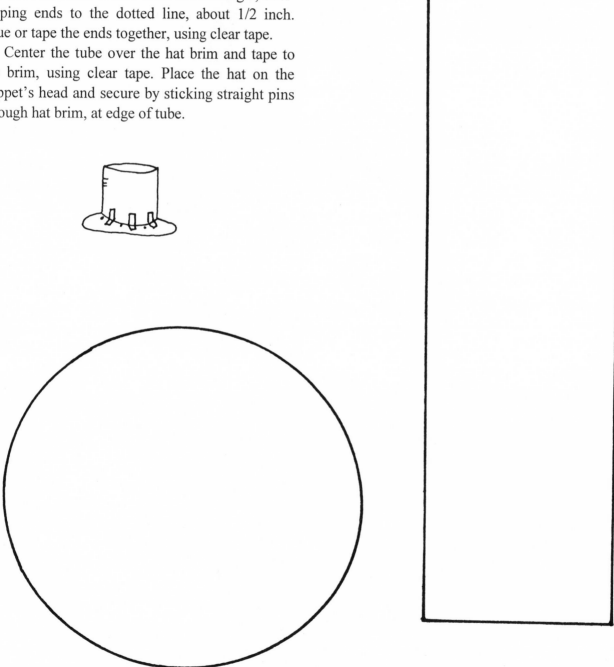

Directions for Lady Styrofoam Puppet

HEAD: Use a 3 inch styrofoam ball. Carve a hole in the bottom to fit your finger.

HAIR: Use thick brown or black yarn. Cover the head with strips of yarn as described for the Shoemaker's Wife. Make a bun as described for the Shoemaker's Wife, increasing the size by using an extra braid. Make three curls, about 1 1/2 - 2 inches long, as described for "Mary Had a Little Lamb." Glue these at the right side of head. Tuck two small feathers into the braid at the top of the Lady's head. Glue or tack this in place with a needle and thread.

FACE: Cut features from felt. Glue features in place; eyes in middle of face, mouth slightly below, and cheeks at sides of mouth.

EYES: Cut two small white circles and two smaller black circles. Glue black "pupil" over white.

MOUTH: Cut from red felt in shape of smile.

CHEEKS: Cut two small circles from pink felt.

BODY: Choose light colored, satin or other fancy material, and make body as described for hand puppet body. Trim neckline with lace for a collar.

SHAWL: See directions for Shoemaker's Wife.

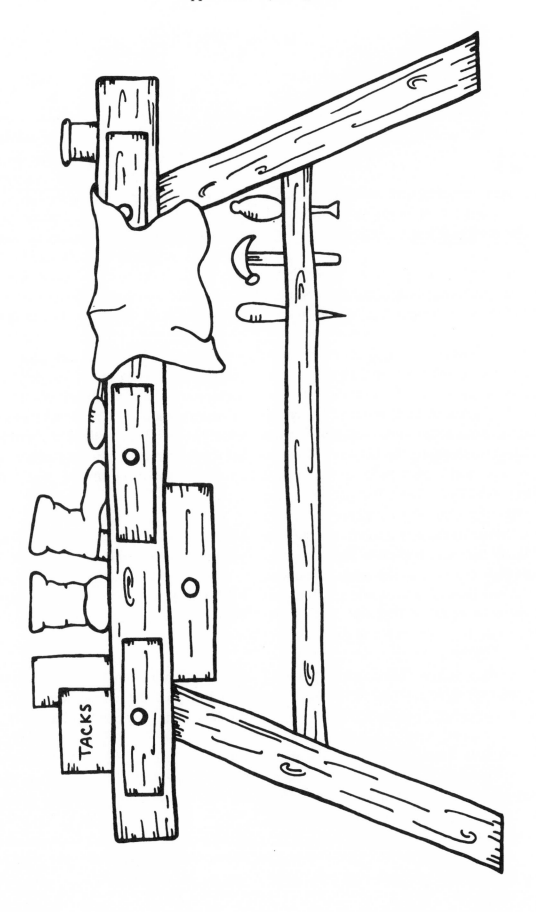

The Frog Prince

Cast of Characters: Princess, Frog, King, Prince

Props: Well, Bed, Table.

Setting: Scene I: garden with well at center stage. Scene II: Princess's room in the castle, with small dinner table at stage R and bed at stage L.

Suggestions for Backdrops: Scene I, trees in the background with row of hedges and flowers in the foreground. Make a "collage" to roughly suggest trees, flowers, etc., using construction paper, colored magazine pictures, wallpaper, and/or cloth. Trees can be dark strips of paper for the trunks, with free-form circles for the treetops. Glue the trees on the backdrop first, about 2/3 way up. Then cut the green hedge forms, and glue them to the backdrop, overlapping the bottom of the tree trunks. Scatter small flower forms in front of the hedges to suggest flower beds. Tape the well to the front of the stage, allowing the puppets to move behind it. Scene II, Princess's room in castle. To create the effect of medieval castle walls, use gray or brown paper, paint, etc., for stone or wooden walls. The bed and the table will be the furniture. Place these at either side of the stage. Make a row of arched windows in the center of the backdrop. Add strips of brown paper running across the top of the backdrop to suggest ceiling beams. You may want to color the table and bed in purples, reds, golds, or blues to brighten up the setting.

Puppeteers: Two. Scene I: Puppeteer A (stage L) —Princess. Puppeteer B (stage R)—Frog. Scene II: Puppeteer A (stage L)—Princess (right hand), King (left hand). Puppeteer B (stage R)—Frog (right hand), Prince (left hand).

Scene I. (*At rise, the Princess is playing with her golden ball stage L near the well. Make motion as if throwing a ball in the air, and catching it. Bring your thumb and finger together in front, then quickly spread them apart as you bend puppet's head upward. Stop while puppet watches ball. Then quickly bring your fingers together again as she catches the ball. On the final throw, move the puppet's head as if watching the ball fall in the well, then quickly run to the well and look in.*)

PRINCESS: It is so cool here by the well. (*Throws the ball.*) I do believe that this is my favorite spot in all of Father's kingdom. (*Throws the ball final time; it drops into the well.*) Oh, no! No! My beautiful golden ball has fallen into the well. I'll never get it out. I'll never see it again. Oh, dear, whatever will I do without my precious golden ball? (*Weeps with her head down, louder and louder.*) (*Enter Frog, stage R, sees Princess, runs to the well.*)

FROG: What is the matter, Princess? Why do you weep as though your heart is broken?

PRINCESS: Oh, it's you, old water-splasher. I weep because my golden ball has fallen into the well.

FROG: Do not weep, Princess. I'm quite sure that I can help you. But tell me, what will you give me if I should bring back your golden ball?

PRINCESS: Dear Frog, I will give you anything that you like—(*Points to each item.*) my clothes, my jewels, my pearls, or even my golden crown.

FROG: I have no use for your clothes, your jewels, or your pearls. And what would I do with your golden crown?

PRINCESS: Then what would you like? Just tell me and please bring back my golden ball.

FROG: It is very lonely being a frog. I will gladly bring back your golden ball if you will be my friend. (*Walks slowly across stage R as he says speech.*) I want to sit beside you at the table and eat with you from your golden plate and drink with you from your golden cup. I want to sleep on your silken bed. (*Turns back to Princess and moves to well again.*) If you will promise these things, I will dive into the well and bring back your golden ball for you.

PRINCESS: (*Clap hands.*) Oh, yes, I promise. Now please hurry and return my golden ball.

FROG: Very well, Princess. (*Dives into the well. To dive, have Frog stand next to well, jump straight up, move over top of well, and down.*)

PRINCESS: (*Turns to audience.*) Imagine that old frog thinking that he can come into the castle and be my friend! (*Looks in well.*) He must live in the water with the other frogs.

FROG: (*Sticks head out of well, facing Princess. Gasps.*) Here, Princess, is your golden ball.

PRINCESS: (*Goes to Frog, takes imaginary ball.*) Oh, my golden ball! I was sure that I had lost it forever! (*Turns, exits stage L.*)

FROG: (*Climbs out of well on left side and runs after Princess. Move Frog out of well in same motion as entered.*) Stop, stop, Princess! Take me with you! I cannot run as fast as you. Wait! Wait! (*Exits after Princess.*)

Scene II. (*In the Princess's room in the castle with table at stage R, bed at stage L. King and Princess are eating dinner, King sits at end of table, center stage, Princess at end, stage R.*)

KING: Well, Daughter, what did you do today?

PRINCESS: I played by the well with my golden ball. (*Off stage is sound of frog feet climbing steps, make sound by slapping your legs with the palm of hands. Sound of knocking on the door.*)

FROG: (*Off stage.*) Princess, Princess, let me in!

PRINCESS: (*Goes to door stage R.*) Oh, no! (*Slams the door when she sees the Frog. Make sound by closing a heavy book. Hurries back to the table.*)

KING: My child, what is the matter? Who was at the door? Was it a giant ready to carry you away?

PRINCESS: No, Father. (*Looks at door.*)

KING: Was it an ugly dwarf?

PRINCESS: (*Shakes head.*) No, no, Father.

KING: Princess, what has frightened you so?

PRINCESS: A horrid old frog.

KING: A frog? What can a frog want of you?

PRINCESS: Oh, Father, while I was playing by the well, I dropped my golden ball and it fell to the bottom of the well. Because I was crying, the frog offered to bring back my golden ball if I would promise to be his friend. I never thought that he would leave the well, but here he is wanting to come into my room. (*Princess points to the door and shudders.*)

FROG: (*Off stage, knocking.*) Princess, Princess, let me in. You promised me that you would be my friend.

KING: What you have promised you must perform. Let the frog in.

PRINCESS: (*Looks at King, then slowly goes to door.*) Come in. (*Returns to her place at table followed by Frog. Frog remains just inside stage R, back away from table.*)

FROG: Princess, put me upon the table.

PRINCESS: (*Looks straight at audience.*) No! I will not have a nasty old frog on the table.

KING: Daughter, do as you promised.

PRINCESS: (*Princess will have to go behind Frog to pick him up. Roughly pulls him to end of table with his face hanging over table; she moves to center.*) There.

FROG: I am hungry after that long walk. Princess, push your golden plate nearer so that we may eat together.

PRINCESS: No! Never! Never will I share my plate with an ugly old frog.

KING: (*Warningly.*) Princess . . .

PRINCESS: Yes, Father. (*Pushes imaginary plate over. Everyone but the Princess eats.*)

FROG: Oh, indeed, that was a lovely meal, but now I have eaten enough. And I am so very tired. (*Looks at Princess.*) Princess, if you will kindly carry me to your silken bed, I would like to go to sleep. (*Princess begins to cry.*)

KING: Daughter, you made a promise to the frog. You must keep it. Now take him to your bed. (*King begins to move stage L.*)

PRINCESS: (*Moves to the King.*) Yes, Father. I shall do as you say.

KING: (*Kisses Princess.*) Good night, Daughter; good night, Frog. (*Exits, stage L.*)

PRINCESS: (*Moves to Frog, picks him up from behind, drops him at foot of bed. Princess backs away behind her bed.*) There. Sleep in that corner, you ugly old frog and leave me alone.

FROG: I am tired and sleepy, and you promised me. Put me upon your bed, or I will tell your father.

PRINCESS: (*Goes to Frog.*) Oh, all right! (*Roughly picks up Frog, moves to the bed with Frog. Frog drops behind the bed and Prince pops up on her right side.*) Now, will you be quiet, you horrid frog?

PRINCESS: (*Jumps back to left end of bed.*) What! What! Who are you?

PRINCE: Oh, Princess. (*Prince backs away to center stage.*) I was a prince, but a wicked witch turned me into a frog. Only a king's daughter could break the spell. I had to remain a frog until a princess would let me eat from her plate and sleep in her bed.

PRINCESS: Oh, you poor thing. (*Moves to the Prince at center stage.*)

PRINCE: Beautiful Princess. (*Takes her right hand.*) You have saved me from years of grief. Will you be my bride?

PRINCESS: Oh, yes, yes! Let's go tell Father. He will be so pleased with my handsome Frog Prince. (*Both exit stage L.*)

—C. S. Peterson and M. B. Hall

Directions for Princess Styrofoam Puppet

HEAD: Use a 3 inch styrofoam ball. Carve hole in the bottom of the ball to fit your finger.

HAIR: Use thick yellow or red yarn. Front of head: cut strips, about 2 inches, to cover the top of the head. Imagine a part in the hair at center of the head. Glue strips from center part to the sides, bringing yarn about 1/3 of the way down over the forehead. Continue adding strips until front of the head is covered.

CURLS: Make 1 1/2 inch curls as described for "Mary Had a Little Lamb." Glue curls around head, starting at sides and continuing around the back.

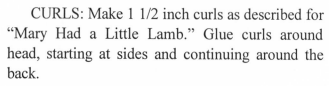

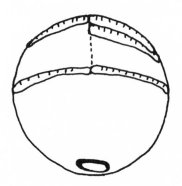

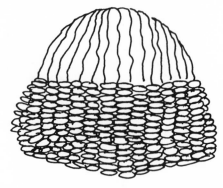

Back of head: use 2 inch strips, glue running downward to midway point on head.

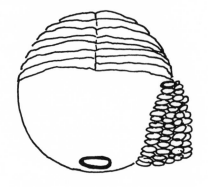

FACE: Cut features from felt. Glue features in place; eyes in middle of face, mouth slightly below, and cheeks at sides of mouth.

EYES: Cut two small white circles and two smaller black circles. Glue black pupils on white.

MOUTH: Cut from red felt in the shape of a smile.

CHEEKS: Cut two small circles from pink felt.

BODY: See directions for hand puppet body. Choose light, rich fabric. Trim with lace at neckline and bows down the front.

CROWN AND VEIL: Fit the crown (pattern on next page) to the head, placing just above the curls and overlapping in the back. Remove and glue crown together at back. Center the veil around the back of the crown and glue to inside edge. While gluing in place, make several small tucks to add fullness.

VEIL: Trace the pattern on this page. Choose nylon netting, chiffon, or similar lacy fabric. Fold fabric in half, pin pattern in place, with the shorter straight edge (across from diagonal edge) on fold in fabric. Cut out and attach veil to crown as described.

CROWNS: The left pattern is for King; right pattern is for Princess and Prince. Trace the patterns. Cut from gold felt (Stiffen felt by mixing a solution of half white glue and half water. Paint this on crown and allow to dry.), gold poster board, or heavy construction paper. Decorate with glitter, sequins, stars, etc.

Fit to puppet's head, overlapping in the back. Remove from head, glue ends together at back. Place on head again and glue in place, or tack with straight pins pushed into the styrofoam.

Put crown on head and glue or tack in place with straight pins.

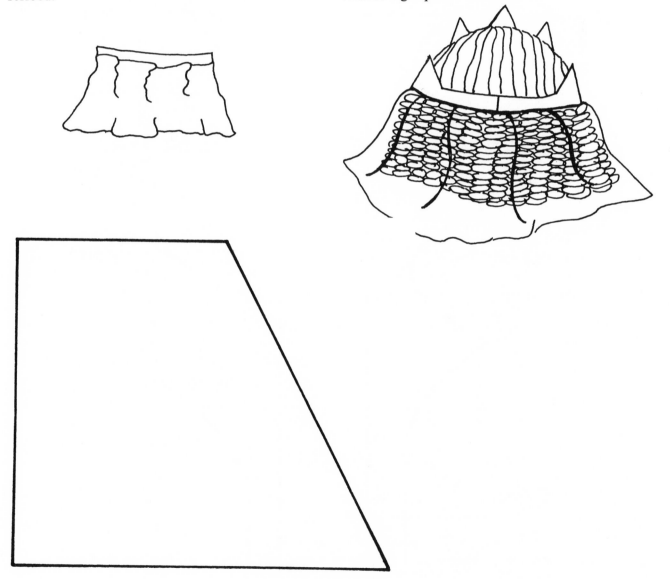

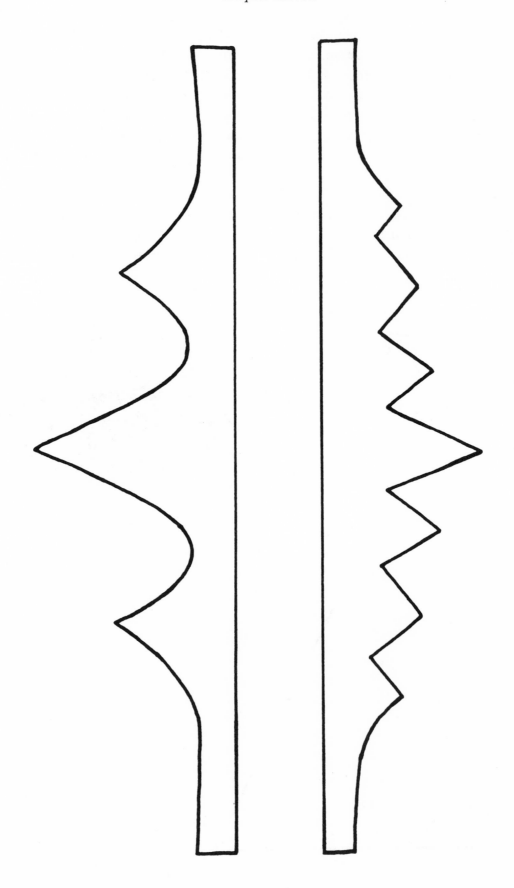

Directions for Frog Paper Plate Puppet

HEAD: Use 6 inch dessert paper plate (heavy weight if possible; if light weight plate, glue two together).

PLATE HEAD: Place the plate on green felt, and trace around the plate, leaving 6 inch circle. Cut out felt circle.

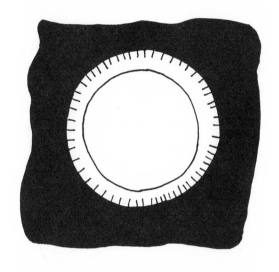

Fold paper plate in half.

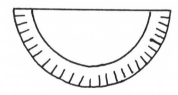

Fold felt in half and cut along fold, leaving two half circles.

Glue felt half circles to top and bottom of folded plate along rounded edges only. Leave straight edge open to form back of frog's head and an opening for your hand to operate puppet. Finish by gluing features in place (see following patterns).

BODY: Use a green or black sock. Cut toe end off. Put sock on arm, pulling up to cover most of your fingers. Tuck raw edges of sock inside puppet's head.

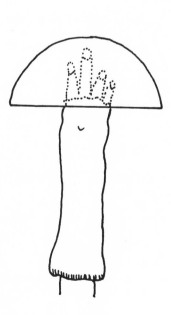

TO OPERATE: To operate movable mouth, place your fingers in the top of the frog's head and your thumb in the bottom. Move your fingers up and down to make the puppet talk.

EYES: Trace pattern and transfer to white poster board and cut two. Make flap for stand-up eyes by folding poster board along heavy dotted line; flap goes to back of head. To make eyes slightly "rounded," gently crease eye along light dotted line.

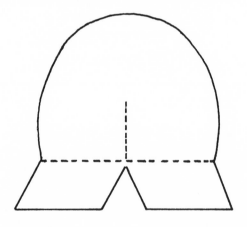

Trace pupil pattern, cut two from black felt or heavy construction paper. Glue in the center of the eye.

Make stand-up eyes by gluing flap to top of frog's head as indicated by the dotted lines:

TONGUE: Trace the pattern and cut two from red felt or heavy construction paper.

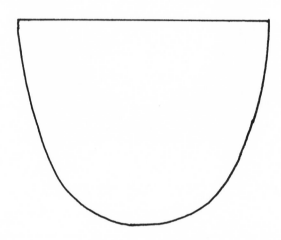

Glue the inside of the frog's mouth top and bottom, placing tongue on the fold in plate.

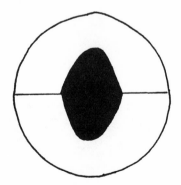

Frog Puppet

Directions for King Styrofoam Puppet

HEAD: Use a 3 inch styrofoam ball. Carve a hole in the bottom to fit your finger. Glue mouth in place, about 1/3 way up from the bottom, using red felt for mouth.

BEARD: Use thick gray or brown yarn. Cut strips of yarn, about 1 or 1 1/2 inches in length. Start at the sides and glue in place covering sides of face and mouth. Make mustache with 1/2 inch strips of yarn.

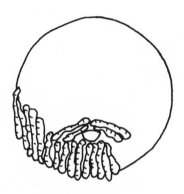

HAIR: Imagine the center part in hair. Glue 2 1/2-3 inch strips around sides from top to jawline. Bring hair on sides of head slightly over beard, blending beard and hair together.

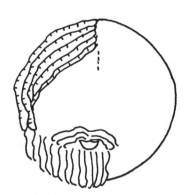

For the back, cut 4 inch strips and glue to cover head from top to neckline.

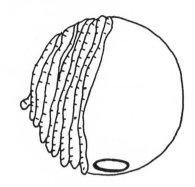

FACE: Cut features from felt. Glue eyes in middle of face; eyebrows slightly above.

EYES: Cut two small white circles, and two smaller black circles. Glue black pupils on white.

EYEBROWS: Cut two from black felt.

CROWN: Make as described in section on Princess.

BODY: See directions for hand puppet with shirt and pants.

BELT: Use a strip of felt, placing belt below normal waistline to give the impression of a fat stomach. Glue to body. Make belt buckle from felt or poster board and glue in place.

ROBE: Trace pattern that follows. Use the shorter version for the Prince (cut along dotted line). For fabric, choose satin, velvet, or similar rich texture. Fold fabric in half, pin pattern in place, with straight edge of pattern on fold. Cut out and zig-zag edges on sewing machine (optional). Decorate with trim, ribbon, etc. Wrap robe around puppet's neck, with tabs closing in front (best to put puppet on your hand for fitting). Pin in place, remove puppet and tack front tabs together with needle and thread. Cover tack with button, sequins, etc.

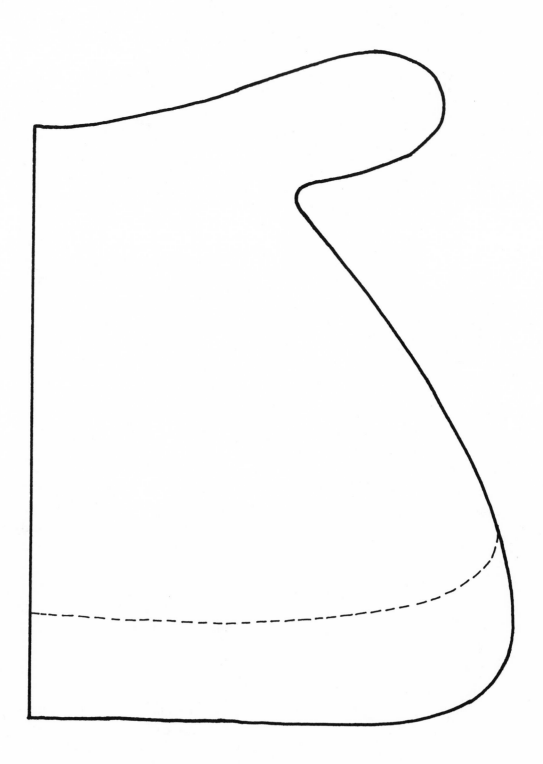

Directions for Prince Styrofoam Puppet

HEAD: Use a 3 inch styrofoam ball. Carve hole in the bottom to fit your finger.

HAIR: Use thick brown or black yarn. For the front, cut strips about 2 and 3 inches. Make bangs with the 2 inch strips, gluing in place from the top of the head to cover the forehead.

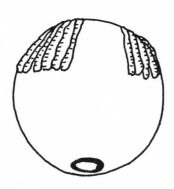

For the sides, use 3 inch strips. Glue from the top of the head over the sides, bringing slightly forward on face.

On back, cut 4 inch strips and glue to cover the head from top to neckline. Be sure to use enough yarn, overlapping where necessary to make thick, full hair.

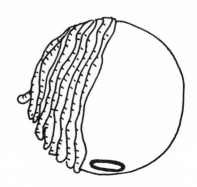

FACE: Cut features from felt. Glue features in place; eyes in middle, mouth slightly below, and eyebrows above eyes.

EYES: Cut two small white circles, and two smaller black circles. Glue black pupil on white.

MOUTH: Cut from red felt in the shape of a smile.

EYEBROWS: Cut from black felt.

BODY: See directions for hand puppet with shirt and pants. Add robe and crown.

CROWNS: For the King, use the pattern on left; for Princess and Prince, use the one on the right. Cut from gold felt (stiffen felt by mixing a solution of half white glue and half water; paint this on crown and allow to dry), gold poster board, or heavy construction paper.

Decorate with glitter, sequins, stars, etc.

Fit to puppet's head, overlapping in back.

Remove from head, and glue ends together at back.

Place on head again and glue in place, or tack with straight pins pushed into the styrofoam.

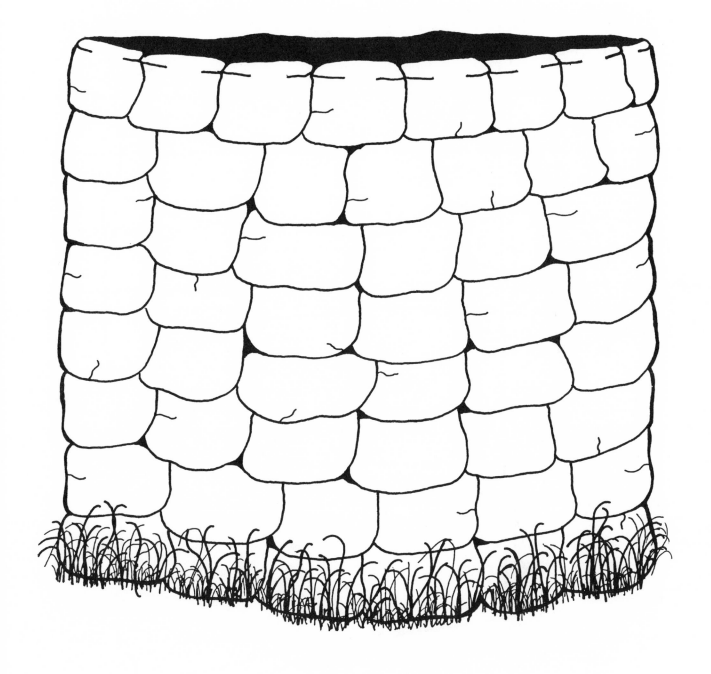

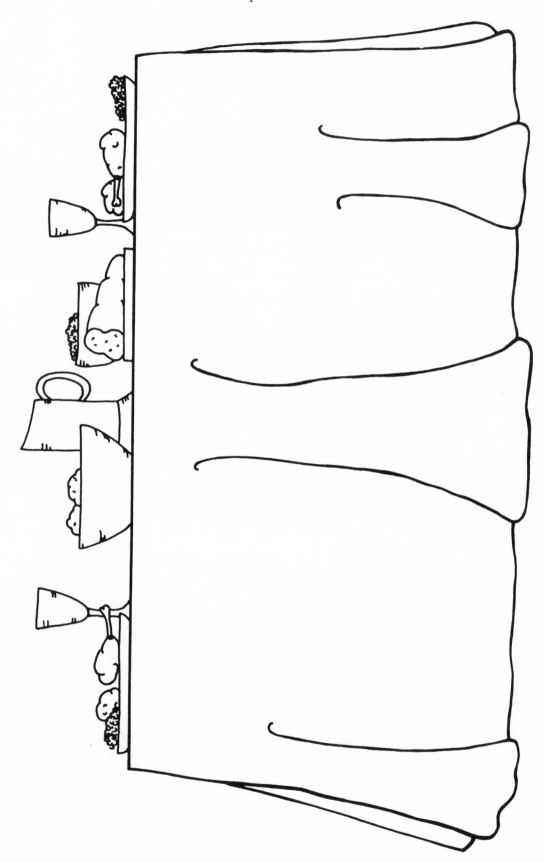

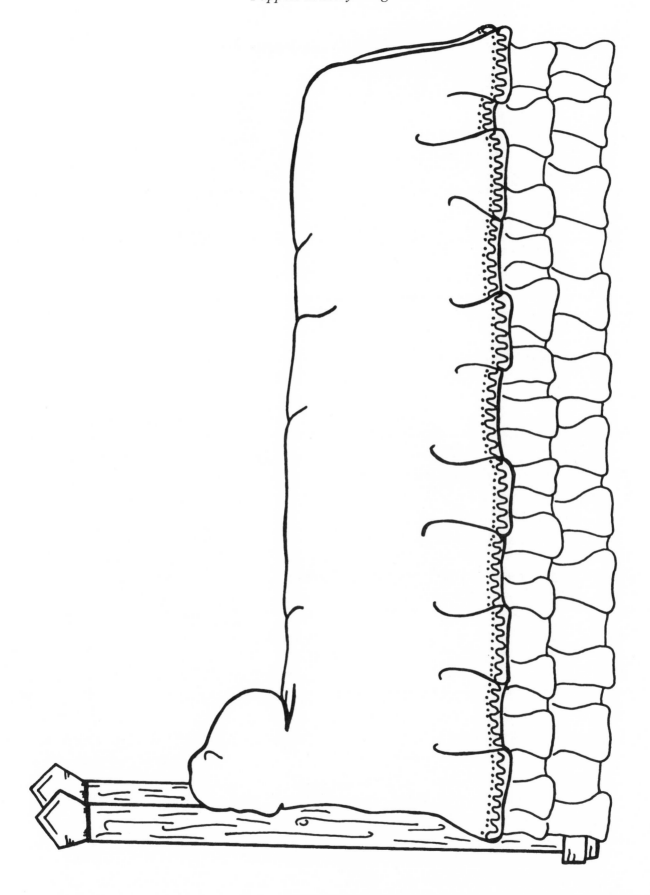

Stories Suitable for Puppet Shows

Aesop	*Hare and the Tortoise*
Aesop	*The Miller, His Son, and Their Donkey*
Anderson	*The Real Princess*
Anderson	*The Ugly Duckling*
Asbjørnsen	*Three Billy Goats Gruff*
Asbjørnsen	*Why the Bear Has a Stumpy Tail*
Bornstein	*Little Gorilla*
Brett	*The First Dog*
Coville	*Aliens Ate My Homework*
De Paola	*Strega Nona*
Elkin	*Six Foolish Fishermen*
Field	*The Gingham Dog and the Calico Cat*
Freeman	*Corduroy*
Gag	*Millions of Cats*
Galdone	*Goldilocks and the Three Bears*
Grimm	*The Bremen Town Musicians*
Grimm	*Frog Prince*
Grimm	*Hansel and Gretel*
Grimm	*Little Red Riding Hood*
Grimm	*Rumpelstiltskin*
Grimm	*The Shoemaker and the Elves*
Grimm	*Rapunzel*
Grimm	*Brave Little Tailor*

Harper	*The Gunniwolf*
Hogrogian	*One Fine Day*
Hutchins	*Happy Birthday, Sam*
Hutchins	*Good-Night Owl*
Ireson	*Gingerbread Man*
Jacobs	*Lazy Jack*
La Fontaine	*The Lion and the Rat*
Langstaff	*Frog Went a-Courtin'*
Lionni	*Swimmy*
Lipkind	*Finder's Keeper's*
Litzinger	*The Old Woman and Her Pig*
Lobel	*Frog and Toad are Friends*
Lobel	*The Pancake*
McGovern	*Too Much Noise*
Meddaugh	*Martha Speaks*
Morgan	*The Turnip*
Mosel	*Tikki Tikki Tembo*
Potter	*Tale of Peter Rabbit*
Rose	*Sorcerer's Apprentice*
Rutherford	*Little Red Hen*
Rutherford	*Three Little Pigs*
Seeger	*Abiyoyo*
Williams	*The Little Old Lady Who Was Not Afraid of Anything*

CHAPTER TWELVE

Storytelling

I'll tell you a story about Jack-a-Nory
And now my story's begun;
I'll tell you another about his brother
And now my story is done.

Storytelling is an ancient oral tradition, currently enjoying a remarkable renaissance. Part of the reason for this revival stems from our innate human desire to connect with others in ways and on levels that are both appropriate and reassuring, and in places that are safe for ourselves and our children.

Storytelling dates back to earliest man. As a form of communication, storytelling was the only system available, before written language, to relate daily experiences and family history. As a form of entertainment, storytelling was the primary mode of fictional discourse. As such, storytelling has proven to be the precursor of theatrical performance. Our very nature as human beings is inexorably tied to storytelling and to the shared experience that it represents.

Some might say that the ancient tradition of storytelling is more alive today than ever before. As modern man expands his technological world, so too does he expand the methods by which he records, learns, and tells stories. As all the peoples of the planet become more connected through that technology, story once again becomes the primary mode of communication.

Think about it. No other art form can do so much with so little. In actuality, storytelling is the process by which a few words that are strung together in some sort of order are spoken aloud for others to hear and enjoy. The power of story, whether personal, political, fantastical, or familial, is in its ability to make us *feel* the events rather than merely witness them.

Why Tell Stories?

The act of telling stories, whether they are true family history or fictional creations, is important for innumerable reasons. Not only is storytelling a way to pass on values from one generation to the next, but it also serves to help develop literary and oral skills, aids in emotional and intellectual development, stretches the imagination, and, through its intimate sharing nature, helps listeners to develop a strengthened sense of community.

And if that were not enough, storytelling is also a tremendous amount of fun—for the listener and the teller. Storytelling is both an excellent educational tool and a rewarding entertainment experience. Story has the ability to wrap its message in sugar and spice thereby making the most undigestible ideas and emotions palatable and even delicious.

Storytelling is a nurturing experience, elevating all those involved to a heightened level of awareness. As a group experience, it offers a gift of time, energy, and caring. As a group experience for children, storytelling does all these things plus encourages reading and the art of listening, gives practice in creative visualization, and offers insight into patterns of human behavior.

For infants and toddlers, storytelling primarily takes the form of simple rhymes, fingerplays, and songs. Since storytelling requires the ability to listen and follow a sequence of events without interruption or disinterest, this ancient tradition is only suitable in its truest form for the more developmentally advanced child (preschooler and above).

Since preschoolers enjoy variety, told stories may be mixed with other forms (such as flannel board, puppetry, and creative dramatics) to create a fulfilling story program. Told stories for this age group may include participation stories, simple folk and fairy tales, and animal fables.

Primary level children, especially, enjoy a told story, and in fact, most eight- to eleven-year-olds prefer it over storytelling with props such as the flannel board and puppetry. For this age group, fairy and folk tales, tall tales, wisdom tales, humorous tales, animal fables, ghost stories, hero tales, myths, legends, literary tales, and personal stories are appropriate.

Finding Stories

There are only two ways to find a story to tell—either you hear one or you read one. Unless it is your habit to attend story programs or festivals, you may not have much exposure to listening to stories being told. If your local library or music store is large enough, however, you will find a rich collection of told stories on cassette tape, CD, and video. Other than this, the best way to find a story is to read a great deal.

You might find a great story to tell from a children's picture book, a collection of children's stories or folk tales, or from local folklore sources. Which ever way you go, one overriding rule must accompany you on your search for the perfect story: it must appeal to you. Never tell a story

you do not like. Only then will you have the energy and desire to commit to learning it, shaping it, and telling it to others.

Choosing the right tellable tale for your personality and taste can prove to be a challenge. A tellable tale is one that has a single well-defined theme, a well-developed plot, dramatic appeal, and is appropriate for the age group you have in mind. You may find that while they aren't quite tellable in the format that you find them, some stories have potential—that is, they may be adaptable into a told story with a few minor alterations—and you should not dismiss them out of hand.

Wherever you find your stories, both those with potential or those perfect the way they are, be sure to take note of their source and keep a copy of their text. You may feel that you are amassing too large a collection of potential stories as you go on this journey, but it is very important that you continue this process of story collection, no matter how many there eventually may be.

It is recommended that you start with a simple folk tale. They are the easiest to learn and retain because of their repetitious structure and your own familiarity with them. Stories such as "The Three Billy Goats Gruff," "The Three Bears," "The Great Big Enormous Turnip," or "The Three Little Pigs" work well in this regard. Simple folk tales are like little blueprints, offering you untold ways of expressing the wonder, joy, and entertainment value present in them. Section six of this book offers sources to assist you in your story selection search.

Learning a Story

There are dozens of ways to learn a story, but each method begins with the same first step: reading the story over and over and over. During this phase of story learning, you are paying particular attention to details such as story sequence, character, plot devices, mood changes, key phrases, and the story's opening and closing moments. You may elect to plot all this out on a chart or think it through in your mind. Either way, you must get to know your story as if you had written it yourself.

Visualize the story as it progresses, making note of suggestions in the tale itself and those that you invent along the way. Picture the details of the setting, what the characters look like, how they move and gesture. Listen to how the characters speak and how the voice of the storyteller rings in your ears.

From this point on, how you learn the story is entirely up to your own tastes and ways of taking in information. If you are a visual learner, you might storyboard the tale, depicting each major event in sequence, almost like a comic book. Or you might mind map the story, letting your own creative juices flow as you weave the web in your thoughts and memory. If you are an aural person, you could tape yourself reading the story and repeatedly play the tape (in your car or while jogging) until you come to truly know it. Or, if you learn by owning the words, perhaps you might write out the story in long hand several times and get it into you that way.

If you have previously told stories with the flannel board or with puppets, it is a very simple step to tell the same story without these props. In fact, some of your first told stories may come to you in this way.

There should never be a need to memorize an entire story word for word unless it is a literary tale and to paraphrase it would destroy the intent or mood of the work. Literary tales, such as the *Rootabaga Stories* by Carl Sandburg or anything by Dr. Seuss, Farjeon, Kipling, Milne, Poe, or the short stories of Margaret Mahey, contain such beautiful language that they need to be read aloud to be appreciated fully.

The only sequences that you should commit to memory are those portions of the story that are purposely repetitious (like "run, run, run, as fast as you can, you can't catch me, I'm the Gingerbread Man," or "Fee, fie, foe, fum, I smell the blood of an English Man") as well as the opening and closing sentences of the story. This memorization is done to assist you in structuring the story in your mind and securing the story to some sort of permanent spot in your long-term memory.

Practicing a story can be a great deal of fun. Various methods include self-appraisal (standing in front of mirror and observing yourself as you tell or video taping for playback), partner-coaching (using a best friend, co-worker, or family member as your pretend audience), and imaginative-visualization (picturing your telling in your head).

After you have learned the story, focus your practice sessions on details of gesture, movement, facial expression, and vocal variety, making them all as natural and integral to the characters and the spirit of the story as you possibly can. As you move farther along in your practice phase, remember to time your story so that you can most effectively judge how and when to use your tale in your story program.

Telling the Story

We all tell stories. If you share the details of a television show, book, or movie you are telling stories. If you repeat jokes or anecdotes that you have heard, you are telling stories. If you tell your child about what it was like when you were a kid, how you had to walk five miles in the snow to school, you are telling stories. If you gossip, you are telling stories. And in the most extreme sense, if you lie, you are telling stories. Everyone on this planet tells stories, every day. Only the lucky few of us get paid to do it for a living.

There is no wrong way to tell a story. In fact, there are as many ways to tell a story as there are people telling them. Everyone has their own style; their own way about them. If you are a dramatic or flamboyant person, tell stories that way. If you are soft-spoken and demure, tell stories this way. Tell stories in a way that is comfortable for you.

No matter how you tell stories, you should keep a few basic considerations in mind. They include: enthusiasm, eye contact, vocal control, vocal variety, sincerity, appropriate gestures and facial expressions, and pacing. There are many good sources available to assist you in honing your performance, and several are listed in section six.

If you experience some stage fright while you are telling, there are a few tricks that you can call upon to help you through your anxiety.

- First, try breathing. It is amazing just how one can forget to breathe in a time of crisis. Take a few deep breaths to clear you head of scary self-defeating thoughts and loosen your limbs. This simple act will do wonders to get you back on track and telling like the professional that you are.

- Visualize yourself doing well. This helps you to refocus on the task at hand and forget about those worrying "what ifs" that plague us sometimes.

- Let the moment go. Don't dwell on your mistake and even pretend to yourself and your audience that you meant to do it that way! No one will know that you didn't if you don't let on.

- Forgive yourself immediately. Everyone makes mistakes and, most likely, no one will ever even know that you have flubbed but you.

- If you say the wrong thing, correct yourself, but do not apologize to your audience. Instead, have a sense of humor about it and try to laugh at yourself. This simple act will endear you to your audience instead of spreading the discomfort you feel onto them.

Above all, remember that you can only truly learn to tell a story by telling. You will find that you will learn to make adjustments to your story depending on your audience and your own mood at the time. So many things go into the story process that to presume to be able to address all of those elements is absurd.

You may even discover that, each time you tell your story, slight modifications magically evolve. This is a good thing! If this happens, it means you are truly in the story, connected to the moment of telling, going with your group, expanding your story's potential, and enlivening the experience for all.

Preschool Stories for Telling

The King's Prized Possession

This is a circular participation tale that ends where it begins. It is a variant of the classic Chinese tale "The Stonecutter." The silly notion of a king continually changing his cat's name, as he discovers new powerful natural elements, appeals to both preschool children and adults.

There are only two characters in this story. I'll be one of them and you the other. I am the king, and you are the most important character in the tale—you are the king's prized possession, his cat. What does a cat say? "Meow." Great. Now you are ready for the story.

This is a story about a king. A good king. A noble king. A handsome king. A just king. A wise king. This king was beloved by all the people in the land. But this king had a problem. The king had a cat—now that wasn't the problem. The king loved his cat. The problem was the cat had no name! All things that are loved have a name. So this is a very big deal for this king.

And he made his problem worse. See, he didn't want to name his cat just any name. Oh, no. This king decided that since he was the king, that his cat had to be named after the most powerful thing in the entire universe. But the king could not figure out what that was. So he thought, and he thought, and he thought, until his thinker got sore.

The king decided to take a break from thinking and take a walk in his royal garden and smell his royal roses. As he was walking along, enjoying the day, he just happened to look up into the sky and said, "Oh! I have found the most powerful thing in the entire universe!"

Now what do you suppose he saw when he looked up into the sky? (*ask the group for suggestions, until,*) Yes, he saw the sun. "The sun is the most powerful thing in the entire universe because

it gives light to the entire earth. From now on, cat, your name will be Sun." And the cat said, "Meow."

Now the king was very happy with this name. He liked it very much. And after all, the sun is the most powerful thing in the universe.

And then the king happened to notice something. It was starting to get dark, but it wasn't yet night time. Hmmm. What could cause such a thing? (*ask the group for suggestions, until,*) Yes, a cloud. A dark cloud had moved in front of the sun and was blocking the light.

And the king said, "Oh, I have made a terrible mistake. The sun is not the most powerful thing in the universe. The cloud is the most powerful thing in the entire universe because it can block the light of the sun! Oh, now I must change your name. So sorry. From now on, your name will be Cloud." And the cat said, "Meow."

Now the king liked this name even better. He thought of a cloud as a fluffy thing and his cat as a fluffy thing. And after all, the cloud is the most powerful thing in the universe!

And then the king happened to notice something. He felt something brush against his cheek. It was invisible. He heard something in his ear. And when the king looked up into the sky, he saw the clouds being pushed across the sky. What pushes clouds across the sky? (*ask the group for suggestions, until,*) Yes, the wind.

"Oh, I have made a terrible mistake. The cloud

is not the most powerful thing in the universe. The wind is the most powerful thing in the entire universe because it can push clouds across the sky! Oh, now I must again change your name. So very sorry. From now on, your name is Wind." And the cat said, "Meow."

Now, believe it or not, the king liked this name even better. He loved this name. He thought of the wind as fleet and swift and so was his cat. And after all, the wind was the most powerful thing in the entire universe!

The king was so happy with this name that he went inside of his kingly castle and sat down on his kingly throne and got a great big kingly grin on his face.

And then, the king happened to notice something. He could no longer feel the wind against his cheek. He could no longer hear the wind in his ear. Although when he looked outside his window, he could still see the leaves moving on the trees. What stopped the wind from coming into the castle? (*ask the group for suggestions, until,*) Yes, the wall. The wall had blocked the wind.

"Oh, I have made a terrible mistake. The wind is not the most powerful thing in the universe. The wall is the most powerful thing because the wall can block the wind from coming into my castle. Oh, so sorry, but I have to change your name again. From now on, your name will be Wall." And the cat said, "Meow."

Now the king did not like this name at all. "Wall? Wall? Ooohhh. Oh well," said the king. "Since the wall is the most powerful thing in the universe, so be it."

Then the king happened to notice something. He heard a small noise. "SCRATCH, SCRATCH, SCRATCH." The king looked, and there, peeking his head through a hole in the wall that it had nibbled was a teeny, tiny, mouse!

"Oh!" said the king. "I have made a terrible mistake. The wall is not the most powerful thing in the universe. The most powerful thing is a mouse, because it can eat its way through a wall. Oh, I have to change your name once again," said the king. "From now on, your name will be Mouse." And the cat said, "Meow."

Now the king thought this was a very strange name for a cat. But, since the mouse was clearly the most powerful thing in the entire universe, well, so be it.

But then, the king happened to notice something. He saw the mouse running across the floor, being chased by the cat!

"Oh," said the king. "I have made a terrible mistake. The mouse is not the most powerful thing in the universe. The most powerful thing in the entire universe is a cat, because it can chase mice across the floor. I must change your name again. From now on cat, your name is Cat." And the cat said, "Meow."

And ever since that day, the cat has indeed been called Cat. Because, after all, as everyone who is owned by a cat knows, the cat is the most powerful thing in the universe.

—adapted by Stefani Koorey

Peace and Quiet

A variant of the classic Yiddish story, this version is perfect for group participation. It is easily adaptable to the flannel board or presented as puppet theater.

Once upon a time, a little old farmer lived in a little old house on a little farm near a little village. While his farm was small, he had lots of animals. What kind of animals live on a farm? Cows? Yes. And what do cows say? "MOOOO." Pigs? Yes. And what do pigs say? "OINK OINK OINK." Horses? Yes. And what do horses say? "NEIGH NEIGH." And chickens? Yes. And what do chickens say? "CLUCK CLUCK CLUCK."

The old farmer was very unhappy because he could never, ever get any peace and quiet. You see, his house was so old that it made all kinds of noise. The door in his little house creaked. Can you make a creaking door with me? CRREEE AAAK! His floor squeaked. Can you make a squeaking floor with me? SQUUEEEKKK! And his windows rattled all night long. Can you make a window rattle with me? RATTLE RATTLE RATTLE RATTLE!

With all that creaking and squeaking and rattling, the man could not get any sleep. So he decided to visit the Wise Woman in the village and ask for her advice.

He knocked on her door. KNOCK KNOCK KNOCK. "Wise Woman, Wise Woman, can you help me? I'm not getting any sleep. All night long my house makes too much noise! All night long the doors creak. CRREEEAAAK! The floors squeak. SQUUEEEEEKKK! And the windows rattle. RATTLE RATTLE RATTLE RATTLE! What do I do?"

The Wise Woman thought, and thought, and thought. Finally she said, "Do you have any chickens on that farm?"

"Yes, I have many chickens," the man answered.

"When you go home tonight, I want you to bring a chicken into the house," advised the Wise Woman.

"A chicken? Into my house? Oh, have you ever smelled a chicken before? P-U! Oh, well," said the man, "I did ask for your advice. I shall do as you say. But this better work!"

The man went home and took a chicken from his barn and put it into his house. That night, he laid down and tried to get some sleep. But the door creaked, CRREEEAAAK! The floor squeaked, SQUUEEEEEKKK! The windows rattled, RATTLE RATTLE RATTLE RATTLE! And the chicken clucked, "CLUCK CLUCK CLUCK." The man got even less sleep than before!

So the next day, he went once again to see the Wise Woman. "Oh, Wise Woman," he moaned, "I did what you told me. I took a chicken into my house, and I'm still not getting any sleep. What do I do?"

The Wise Woman thought, and thought, and thought. Finally she said, "Do you have any pigs on that farm?"

"Yes, I have many pigs," the man answered.

"When you go home tonight, I want you to bring a pig from the barn and put it into your house," advised the Wise Woman.

"A pig? In my house? Oh, have you ever smelled a pig before? PP-UU! Oh, well," said the man, "I did ask for your advice. I shall do as you say. But this better work!"

The man went home and took a big fat pig from his barn and put it into his house. That night, he laid down and tried to get some sleep. But the door creaked, CRREEEAAAK! The floor squeaked, SQUUEEEEEKKK! The windows rattled, RATTLE RATTLE RATTLE RATTLE! The chicken clucked, "CLUCK CLUCK CLUCK." And the pig oinked, "OINK OINK OINK." The man got even less sleep than before!

So the next day, he went once again to see the Wise Woman. "Oh, Wise Woman," he moaned, "I did what you told me. I have a chicken and a pig living in my house, and I'm still not getting any sleep. What do I do?"

The Wise Woman thought, and thought, and thought. Finally she said, "Do you have any cows on that farm?"

"Yes, I have many cows," the man answered.

"When you go home tonight, I want you to bring a cow from the barn and put it into your house," advised the Wise Woman.

"A cow? In my house? Oh, have you ever smelled a cow before? PPP-UUU! Oh, well," said the man, "I did ask for your advice. I shall do as you say. But this better work!"

The man went home and took a cow from his barn and put it into his house. That night, he laid down and tried to get some sleep. But the door creaked, CRREEEAAAK! The floor squeaked, SQUUEEEEEKKK! The windows rattled, RATTLE RATTLE RATTLE RATTLE! The chicken clucked, "CLUCK CLUCK CLUCK." The pig oinked, "OINK OINK OINK." And the cow mooed, "MOOOOOOOO." The man got even less sleep than before!

So the next day, he went once again to see the Wise Woman. "Oh, Wise Woman," he moaned, "I did what you told me. I have a chicken and a pig and a cow living in my house, and I'm still not getting any sleep. What do I do?"

The Wise Woman thought, and thought, and thought. Finally she said, "Do you have any horses on that farm?"

"Yes, I have many horses," the man answered.

"When you go home tonight, I want you to bring a horse from the barn and put it into your house," advised the Wise Woman.

"A horse? In my house? Oh, have you ever smelled a horse before? PPPP-UUUU! Oh, well," said the man, "I did ask for your advice. I shall do as you say. But this better work!"

The man went home and took a horse from his barn and put it into his house. That night, he laid down and tried to get some sleep. But the door creaked, CRREEEAAAK! The floor squeaked, SQUUEEEEEKKK! The windows rattled, RATTLE RATTLE RATTLE RATTLE! The chicken clucked, "CLUCK CLUCK CLUCK." The pig oinked, "OINK OINK OINK." The cow mooed. "MOOOOOOOO." And the horse neighed, "NEIGH NEIGH!" The man got even less sleep than before!

So the next day, he went once again to see the Wise Woman. "Oh, Wise Woman," he moaned, "I did what you told me. I have a chicken and a pig and a cow and a horse living in my house, and I'm still not getting any sleep. And if a man cannot sleep, he cannot live. What do I do?"

The Wise Woman thought, and thought, and thought. Finally she said, "I think that it is time to kick all those noisy animals out of your house."

Wearily, the man trudged home, and happily he put the horse, the cow, the pig, and the chicken back in the barn where they belonged. Then he lay down and fell asleep. The door creaked, but he did not wake up. The floorboards squeaked, but he did not wake up. The windows rattled, but he did not wake up. He slept all night long. When he woke up in the morning, he was refreshed and rested.

"Ahhhhh," he sighed. "Peace and quiet at last!"

—adapted by Stefani Koorey

The Three Wishes

This tale works great as either a told or flannel board story. The image of the sausage attached to the end of the woodsman's nose makes this a popular and funny story.

Once upon a time there was a woodsman. You could tell he was a woodsman because he carried an axe. Do you know what a woodsman does for a living? (*Ask for suggestions from your audience.*) Well, he takes that axe into the woods every day and he chops down trees like this: "Whack, whack, whack." And the tree falls: "Tim-ber!" And then, he takes his axe and chops the tree into smaller pieces, like this: "Chop, chop, chop." And then, he sells the tree for firewood. That's how he makes his living.

This woodsman lived with his wife in a very small house at the edge of the woods. This particular woodsman was really very smart. You see, this particular woodsman decided one day that, instead of chopping down twenty trees a day and coming home with sore arms and a sore back and sore shoulders, he would try and find just one great big tree to cut down. That way, he would only have to chop down one tree and he would still have the same amount of firewood. Pretty smart, huh?

On this particular morning, the woodsman started out on his search for the biggest tree he could find. But, before he left, he kissed his wife goodbye (*pucker kissy sound*). Then he began his search. He looked high. Everybody look high. He looked low. Everybody look low. He looked left. Everybody look left. He looked right. Everybody look right. He looked up. Everybody look up. He looked down. Everybody look down. And when he looked back up again, OH MY (*gasp*), he had found the biggest, most amazingly enormous tree he had ever, ever seen.

And he said, "Hot diggity dog, that's the tree for me!" And so he raised his axe and brought it

down against the tree. (*Raise your imaginary axe.*) "Whack, whack, whack, whack." When all at once he heard, "Hey, cut that out." (*Use a pixie kind of voice for the gnome.*)

Well, the woodsman stopped chopping and looked around at who said that. He looked all around: behind the tree, in the knothole of the tree, up into the tree. Nothing. "Hmmm," thought the woodsman. "I wonder what that noise was." And then he heard, "grrrooowwwlll." (*Hold your stomach each time it growls.*) "Oh," said the woodsman, "It's my stomach making all that noise. I forgot to eat my breakfast this morning and now my insides are wantin' food. Next time I'll remember to eat before I start choppin' trees. But now, I gotta go back to work."

And so the woodsman raised his axe again and brought it down against the tree. "Whack, whack, whack, whack." Again he heard the voice, a little bit louder, "Hey, I said, cut that out!" The woodsman stopped chopping and this time looked all around the tree, and up into the tree, and thumped his head a bit, and still couldn't find out where that voice was a comin' from. And then he heard, "grrrroooowwwwlll." "Oh," said the woodsman, "There goes my stomach again. I'm hungrier than I thought I was. I should hurry up and finish this job and get home for a great big lunch."

For the third time, the woodsman raised his axe and brought it down against the tree. "Whack, whack, whack, whack." And for a third time, the woodsman heard a little voice, a little bit louder, say, "HEY, I SAID, CUT THAT OUT! I'M DOWN HERE AT YOUR FEET, YOU NINNY."

The woodsman looked down at his feet, and there was a teeny tiny itsy bitsy little man! The woodsman looked at the little man and the little man looked at the woodsman. Finally, the woodsman spoke. "Well, what do you want, little fellow?"

"I live in this tree! My whole little family lives in this tree! I want you to go find another tree to chop down, and leave my home alone!"

The woodsman tugged on his chin a bit. And then he said, "If I'da known this was your home, I never would have laid my axe to it. Yes, I'll go find another tree to chop down." And with that, the woodsman started to walk away.

"Hey, wait a minute!" said the little man. "Since you've been so nice about this, and I didn't even have to ask you twice, I'm going to grant you three wishes. Now be careful what you wish for." And with that, the little man disappeared, lickety-split.

The woodsman could hardly believe his eyes and ears. Three wishes! Oh boy! Three wishes! "Hot diggety dog," said the woodsman. "Why, with one of those wishes, I could wish for a brand new house. And with one of those wishes, I could wish for brand new clothes. And with one of those wishes, I could wish for lots and lots of money!"

So he ran all the way home and met his wife at the door and gave her a great big kiss (*pucker kissy sound*).

"What are you doing home so early?" his wife inquired.

"Oh, you won't believe it!" And then the woodsman told his wife what had happened. And you know what? He was right. She didn't believe him. But he told her again that it was true. At last it sunk into the wife that they had indeed three whole wishes! "Hot diggety dog!" she said. "Three wishes! Why, with one of those wishes, we could wish for a brand new house. And with one of those wishes, we could wish for brand new clothes. And with one of those wishes, we could wish for lots and lots of money! What shall we wish for first?"

The woodsman started to speak. "Well, I think

that we should . . ." and with that his stomach growled. He tried again. "Well, I think that we should . . ." and with that his stomach growled even louder. "I think that I had better eat first. I can't wish on an empty stomach. First we eat, then we'll wish!"

"Oh," said his wife. "That would be a good idea, only there isn't any food left in the house. Not even a crumb of bread."

"Oh," said the woodsman, holding his stomach. "I've got to eat something. I can't think. I can't do anything. Oh, I can only think about food. Oh, and my favorite food is sausage. Oh, I wish I had me a great big old sausage right now. Uh-oh."

And with that, a great big sausage came out of the chimney and flew across the room and landed on the table.

"I did say I was hungry! Let's eat, we still have two more wishes," said the woodsman.

"Just one minute. Just one cotton-pickin' ever-lovin' minute! You know what you did? You used one of our wishes and wished for a sausage!! You are a foolish, foolish man! Why, I wish that sausage was attached to the end of your nose. Uh-oh!"

And with that, the sausage flew up off the table, flew around the room and landed, zoooop, right on the end of the woodsman nose!

"Oh, no!" said the woodsman. "I hab a dauddige on my dose! I hab a dauddige on my dose!"

"Oh, oh, oh," said the wife. "I'll think of something. Let's see. How about I try and pull it off." She grabbed hold of the sausage and pulled hard.

"OH, dop dat! Dat hurt! Now get dis dauddige off my dose!"

"Oh, my," said the wife. "Let's see. I could take your axe and chop it off!"

"Oh, no you don't. You might dop off my dose and I'm no doing dru life wid no dose on my face! You doe what you have do do."

"Oh," said the wife. "How about we take that last wish and wish for lots and lots of money and take a little bit of that money and go to Wal-Mart and buy some ribbons and bows and decorate that sausage on the end of your nose!"

"NO! You doe what you have do do."

"Oh, all right." said the wife. "I wish the sausage was off your nose." And with that, the sausage flew off the woodsman's nose and flew around the room and landed PLOP right between the woodsman and his wife.

The woodsman looked at his wife. The wife looked at the woodsman. They both realized that that morning they had three whole wishes.

With one of those wishes they could have wished for a brand new house; with one of those wishes, they could have wished for brand new clothes; with one of those wishes they could have wished for lots and lots of money. But they didn't. And all they had to show for their three wishes was a sausage and an argument.

But this story still ends happily every after because they still had (*pucker kissy sound*) each other!

—adapted by Stefani Koorey

Why Dogs Hate Cats

This is a very easy and fun story to learn. Consider using different voices for the dog and the cat, and ask your audience to join in on the "My Ham" and "Our Ham" songs. Invent your own tune for both songs.

Once upon a time, not your time, nor my time, but one time, the dog and the cat spoke the same language. Believe it or not, they also used to be best friends. They loved to do everything together. They played together, they sang together, they worked together. But their most favorite thing to do was to eat together. And their favorite food was ham. Oooh-weeee! Did they love ham. Nice thick slabs of juicy ham. Since ham was their favorite food, every chance they had, they'd buy some ham.

One day, Mr. Dog turned to Mr. Cat and said, "I got a little extra money, and you've got a little extra money. Now, if we put your money and my money together, we'll have enough money to get a whole ham. What do you think?"

Mr. Cat said, "Let's do it, let's do it, let's do it, let's do it!"

So they went to town and bought themselves a whole ham. Have you ever seen a whole ham? Well, they are really big. They are really heavy. There's this big piece of meat with a big ole bone sticking out of it—called a ham bone. Well, they bought that ham but it was so big and so heavy that they had to take turns carrying it home. The dog carried it first and as he walked down the road, he sang a little song. The song he sang went like this: "Our ham! Our ham! Our ham!" When it got too heavy, Mr. Dog set the ham down. That meant it was Mr. Cat's turn to carry it.

The cat picked up the ham and slung it over his little cat shoulder. As he went along he sang a song too. But the cat's song went like this: "My ham! My ham! My ham!" The dog heard what the cat was singing, but he didn't say anything. Since they were best friends and all, dog decided to give cat the benefit of the doubt. He thought it would be best to teach his friend a lesson by example.

So dog picked up the ham, slung it over his shoulder, and a little louder this time, sang, "Our ham! Our ham! Our ham!" Then he set it down and waited to see what the cat would do.

Well, the cat picked up the ham, like he was supposed to, and looked right at the dog and sang, "My ham! My ham! My ham!""

The dog had had about enough of this, so he said to the cat, "Tell me, Mr. Cat, why do you sing, 'My ham?' It is our ham. I put up half the money and you put up half the money and share is share alike. Why are you singing, 'My ham?'"

That cat didn't say a word. You know cats will do that. You ask them a question, but instead of answering you, they ignore you. Well that's just what this cat did. There wasn't anything that the dog could do except pick up the ham, sling it over his shoulder, and really loudly this time, sing, "OUR HAM. OUR HAM. OUR HAM." Then he set it down.

Well, that cat picked up that ham, slung it over his cat shoulder and looked right at the dog and sang, "My ham! My ham! My ham!" They were almost home when all of a sudden that cat ran up a big oak tree, sat down on a limb of that tree, and proceeded to eat the whole ham!

That dog was so angry, he was fit to be tied. There was steam coming out of his ears he was so mad. He was sitting down at the foot of that tree and he barked and jumped and growled and snarled. But he couldn't climb the tree, so there was nothing he could do. He looked up just in time to see that cat fling out a little cat claw and use it like a toothpick to pick the last little bit of ham from between his little cat teeth.

Mr. Dog raised his fist at the cat and yelled, "I can't get you now, Mr. Cat, but just you wait. When you come down out of that tree, and I know you will, I'm going to chase you til you drop."

And that's why, to this very day, whenever a dog sees a cat, he chases him. Because that cat ate the whole ham.

—adapted by Charlie Hoeck

Primary Level Stories for Telling

Bear That Ate Them Up

A variant of "Sody Sallyrytus," this tales takes place in the mountains of Tennessee. Introduce the story by explaining how in that part of the country, they don't call them "bears" but call them "bars"—not like "candy bars" but "grizzly bars." Once the children get the hang of the rhythm of the story, they will join in without coaxing.

Way back in the hills, way way back, there lived a little old man and a little old woman and a little boy and a little girl. They lived in a little house at the edge of the woods.

One day, the old lady said, "Little old man, will you go down the road apiece and get me some nice fresh baked bread from the bakery? You know how I like fresh baked bread to go with my supper. Would you do that for me please?"

The little old man said, "I'd be happy to." So he went a-walkin down the road, and a-walkin down the road, and a-walkin down the road. And there, in the middle of the road, stood a great big bear! And the bear said, "I done drank a barrel of water, I done ate a hunk of cheese, and now I'm a-gonna eat you too!" And sure enough, just like that, the bear ate the little old man up. Whole, in one bite.

Well, now, that little old lady was still waitin' on her bread. And she didn't know what happened to the little old man. So she said to the little girl, "Little girl, little girl, will you go down the road apiece and get me some nice fresh baked bread from the bakery? You know how I like fresh baked bread to go with my supper. Would you do that for me please?"

The little girl said, "I'd be happy to." So she went a-walkin down the road, and a-walkin down the road, and a-walkin down the road. And there, in the middle of the road, stood a great big bear!

And the bear said, "I done drank a barrel of water, I done ate a hunk of cheese, and I ate me a little old man, and now I'm a-gonna eat you too!" And sure enough, just like that, the bear ate the little girl up. Whole, in one bite.

Well, now, that little old lady was STILL waitin' on her bread. And she didn't know what happened to the little old man or the little girl. So she said to the little boy, "Little boy, little boy, will you go down the road apiece and get me some nice fresh baked bread from the bakery? You know how I like fresh baked bread to go with my supper. Would you do that for me please?"

The little boy said, "I'd be happy to." So he went a-walkin down the road, and a-walkin down the road, and a-walkin down the road. And there, in the middle of the road, stood a great big bear! And the bear said, "I done drank a barrel of water, I done ate a hunk of cheese, and I ate me a little old man, and I ate me a little girl, and now I'm a-gonna eat you too!" And sure enough, just like that, the bear ate the little boy up. Whole, in one bite.

Well, now, that little old lady was STILL waitin' on her bread. And she didn't know what happened to the little old man, the little girl, or the little boy. But she figured, "If you want something done right, you has to do it yourself!"

So that little old lady went a-walkin down the road, and a-walkin down the road, and a-walkin down the road. And there, in the middle of the road, stood a great big bear! And the bear said, "I done drank a barrel of water, I done ate a hunk of cheese, and I ate me a little old man, I ate me a little girl, and I ate me a little boy, and now I'm a-gonna eat you too!" And sure enough, just like that, the bear ate the little old lady up. Whole, in one bite.

Now as you can imagine, from eatin' all those people, that bear was big and fat. And he was a-waddlin' down the road, and a-waddlin' down the road, and a-waddlin' down the road. And there in the middle of the road was a squirrel.

And the bear said, "I done drank a barrel of water, I done ate a hunk of cheese, and I ate me an old man, I ate me a little girl, I ate me a little boy, and I ate me an old woman, and now I'm a-gonna eat you too!"

But the squirrel said, "Oh, no, you aren't!" and he ran up a tree. Well, there was the bear, looking up into that tree. And he said, "I'm gonna come and get you squirrel, cuz' bears can climb trees!" And with that, the bear started a-climbin' that tree, and a-climbin' that tree, and a-climbin' that tree. He got to the very top and he looked around for that squirrel. He looked and looked. And there, out on the longest limb of that tree was that squirrel.

So that bear started walking out on that limb. He got about half way out and then, SNAP, that limb broke out from under him and he fell, AAAA-HHHHHHH!, down to the ground, where he hit real hard, and busted right open.

And out jumped the old man, and he said, "Goody, goody, I got out!" Out jumped the little girl, and she said, "Goody, goody, I got out!" Out jumped the little boy, and he said, "Goody, goody, I got out!" And out jumped the old woman, and she said, "Goody, goody, I got out!" And way up in that tree, the squirrel was a-lookin down at that bear and said, "Goody, goody, I didn't get in!" And that's the end of the story.

But it's not the end of the tale. See, that old woman is really very smart. Know why she's so smart? Well, she goes to the library every week and checks out books. And when she's done reading them, she brings 'em back and checks out more. So that little old lady knew just what to do.

She went home and got herself a needle and thread. And she came back to that bear who was a-lyin' all split open underneath that tree. And she said, "All right, Mr. Bear, I'll do you a deal. If you promise not to eat anymore of my kinfolk, and stick strictly to berries and nuts, I'll sew you back up again. How about them apples?"

There was nothing else the bear could do but agree to the deal. So the little old lady sewed that bear up and sent him on his way. Now that's the end of the tale.

—adapted by Stefani Koorey

The Boy Who Loved to Fish

Eerie scary tale for older children. It teaches youth not to disrespect their mamas and that selfishness is a dangerous trait to possess.

Once there was a boy named Ben who lived way out in the country in a little town called Pahokee with his mother and younger brother and sister.

Now Ben and his family were poor, and Ben didn't like it one bit. Every day after school, Ben would have to go out into the fields and work until the sun went down because he had to help his mother with the bills. He'd even have to work all day Saturday. Ben hated that.

So Sunday was his only day off and that was the day that Ben would go down to Lazy Day Creek and do his fishing. Oh, Ben just loved to fish! Not too many people in Pahokee could fish better than Ben.

Sometimes he'd catch so many fish that his mother would have to give some away. Oh, how Ben wished that he could fish every day. But he couldn't because he had to work and help his mother.

So Ben was mad at the world. He showed nobody respect, even his own mother. Whenever she asked him to go down to Mr. Green's Country Store for her, he'd stomp his feet. Whenever she asked him to wash dishes or take out the trash, he'd get angry and yell, "Don't I do enough around here?!! I hate this place!" And whenever she asked him to go to church, he would just ignore her. He refused to go to church.

One Sunday morning Ben's mother was sick. She was so sick that she could not go to church. She called Ben into her room and said, "Ben, I don't want you to go fishing today. I want you to take your brother and sister to church for me. Then I want you to come home and prepare dinner for the family. I'm feeling a might poorly today."

Well, Ben went into a rage. "What!? You expect me to go to church and not go fishing?" he yelled. "You know how much I love to fish! How dare you ask me that!? This is my only day off to fish and that's exactly what I'm gonna do, I'm going fishing!!"

He packed himself a lunch, grabbed his fishing gear and stormed out of the door. He stopped by Mr. Green's Country Store and bought a 50-cent container of worms and then headed on down to Lazy Day Creek.

When he got there, he walked over to his favorite spot, sat down, baited his hook, threw his line in the water, and waited. As he waited for the fish to begin biting, he reached into his sack, pulled out a peanut butter sandwich and started to take a bite, when he felt a tug at his line. "Oh, I've got a catch already," he said.

So he began pulling on his line, but it was hard to pull. Ben put down his sandwich and, using both hands, he began to pull a little harder. But the line was still hard to pull. Ben started pulling with all his strength but the line just wouldn't budge.

Then, all of a sudden, the line started pulling him. Well Ben kept on pulling with all his might, but the line kept pulling him. Pretty soon, he found himself at the edge of the water.

At this point, Ben decided to drop his pole and get out of there! He didn't want to see what was at the other end of that line. But before he could even take five steps, a haunting voice came from the middle of the creek and said, "STOOOOPPPP!!!"

Ben froze dead in his tracks. He wanted to run but he couldn't take another a step. Then the voice said, "TUUUURRRRNNNN ARROOUUND!!"

Ben tried not to turn but a force slowly pulled

him around. Ben closed his eyes as tight as he could. Then the voice said, "AAAAKKKKK!"

Ben didn't want to go back to that lake, he wanted to go home to his mother, but his legs began to move. As if they had a life of their own and he couldn't control them. He wanted to cry, but he couldn't, his body was being controlled by that voice, he just kept walking toward the creek.

When he got to the edge of the water, the voice said, "STTOOOOPPPP!" Ben stopped. Then the voice said, "Ohppen your eyes!" He tried to keep his eyes shut tight, but they slowly began to open. "AAAAAAGGH!"

There standing before Ben was a creature that made Ben want to faint! The creature's left leg was made of seaweed and sticks with bugs crawling out. His right leg was made of mud with blood oozing out. His chest looked like fish scales with snake heads slithering out, their tongues were flailing and their fangs were showing. The evil creature smiled, maggots and worms came pouring out of his mouth. And his eyes burned red like fire.

Then the creature said, "LOOOOK DOOO-WWWWWN!!"

Ben looked down, and, and, and, his left leg turned into seaweed and sticks with bugs crawling out and his right leg turned into mud and started bleeding. His chest turned into fish scales with snake heads slithering out. Then maggots and worms began pouring out of his mouth and his eyes felt like they were on fire!!! The creature said, "Since you love fishing so much, you come with me to live among the fish."

From that day on, Ben's mother never saw him again and nobody ever knew what happened to him and nobody ever went to Lazy Day Creek to fish again.

—adapted by Crystal Sullivan

Why the Sky Is Far Away

This is a story of the Bini people of Nigeria. It is estimated to be at least five hundred years old. For such an old tale, it bears a remarkable connection to modern times and concerns.

A great while ago, when the world was full of wonders, the sky was very close to the earth. In fact, it was within reach of all the people of the planet. Best of all, the sky was food!

At that time, the people did not have to work for food. They did not have to plant crops or harvest them. They did not have to prepare food for eating. They did not have to worry about food at all. If anyone was hungry, all they would have to do is reach up to the sky and take a piece of it and eat it.

Sometimes it tasted just like pizza. Sometimes it tasted like marshmallows. Sometimes it tasted like blue cotton candy. You see, it could taste like whatever you wanted it to taste like.

Since the people did not have to spend their days working for food, they had lots of free time. Every day was like summer vacation. They could spend all of their time doing whatever they wanted to do. They could weave, and carve, play sports, sing and dance, or tell stories all day long.

The ruler of this wonderful place was named King Oba. On special occasions, when the great king wanted to give a party, his servants would cut out pieces of the sky and shape them into wonderful forms—monkeys, diamonds, hearts, or butterflies.

But as time went on, the sky grew angry. See, the people forgot to appreciate the sky. They took their food for granted, and they became wasteful. They cut far more sky than they needed and threw what they didn't use onto the garbage heap.

One morning, the sky grew very dark. Thick black clouds moved quickly through the sky. Thunder rumbled and lightning flashed. The wind blew loudly. The people were frightened.

"Oba!" the Sky God boomed. "Your people are wasting my gifts. They are throwing away my food. If you continue to waste the food, if you continue to throw the food onto garbage heaps, the sky is going to move far, far away and you will have to fend for yourselves!"

The people were terrified. King Oba was terrified. He made the people promise not to waste the sky any longer. "Take only what you need," he warned. "The sky is angry because of our greed. Stop wasting the sky, we won't have any sky left to eat."

The people were very, very careful. They took only what they needed from the sky. If they were hungry, they only took a little bit instead of a great big piece. And the people ate all they took. Nothing was thrown away. Nothing was wasted.

Now, once every year there was a great festival in Oba's kingdom. At the festival, the people danced, and ate, and played sports, and ate, and told stories, and ate. Oh, they ate a lot! And they had a wonderful time.

Everyone was very tired early that day from all the festivities. So, the people went to their homes and went to bed early, with full tummies and smiles on their faces.

All except one, that is. This one woman did not go home and go to bed like everyone else. This one woman was never satisfied. She always wanted more of everything. More dancing, more stories, more food.

She realized that she was still hungry, so while everyone else was sleeping soundly, she reached up into the sky, meaning to take a small piece of the sky for a snack, and accidentally took an entire handful!

"Oh, no," she said. "I have taken too much of the sky. I am not this hungry. And I cannot throw any away. What shall I do?"

Then she had an idea. She ran into her house and woke her husband. "Oh, husband," she begged. "I accidentally took too much of the sky. I cannot finish this and I need your help. Please finish off this piece of the sky."

Her husband, groggy from too much food and drink, said, "I am not hungry. I could not eat another bite. Go wake the children, they are always hungry." And with that, he went back to sleep.

The woman went into her children's room and woke up her two little ones. "Oh, children," she begged. "I have accidentally taken too much of the sky. I cannot finish this and I need your help. Please finish off this piece of the sky."

Her children, groggy from too much sport and too much food said, "Oh mother, we couldn't eat another bite! We are as full as full can be. Sorry." And with that, they fell back asleep in their beds.

The woman was desperate. She did not want to be the one who displeased the Sky God and brought down his wrath. She thought and thought and thought. At last she said, "I have it!"

She crept very quietly outside, making sure she was as silent as she could be. She crept around her house to the back yard and dug a small hole. She looked around to make sure no one could see her, and ever so gently, she buried the piece of the sky in the earth.

She looked around again to make sure none had seen her do this, and then quietly and carefully she went back into her house and went to bed.

Well, the Sky God had not seen her do this. But the God of the Earth had. And the God of the Earth woke the God of the Sky and told him what this woman had done.

The next morning, the sky grew very dark. Thick black clouds moved quickly through the sky. Thunder rumbled and lightning flashed. The wind blew loudly. The people were frightened.

"Oba!" the Sky God boomed. "Your people have wasted my gifts for the last time! They have thrown away my food for the final time. I told you what would happen. Now the sky is going to move far, far away and you will have to fend for yourselves!"

And at that, the sky went up and up and up and up and up. The people could not reach it. It was gone. The people tried to reach the sky. They stood on each other's shoulders, but still it was out of reach. They climbed to the top of the tallest buildings, but still the sky was out of their reach. They stood on each other's shoulders on top of the tallest buildings, and still they could not reach the sky. The sky was gone. The people were going to have to learn to fend for themselves.

And ever since that day, that was indeed the case. The people had to work for their food. They had to learn how to plant crops and harvest them. They had to learn how to prepare food for eating. They had to worry about food all the time. And all that free time that the people had? Well, that was gone forever. All because the people wasted the sky and the sky went far away.

—adapted by Stefani Koorey

Anansi and Tiger

This is one of many stories that attempts to explain how all stories became known as Anansi Tales. It contains a more complicated plot than the other stories in this chapter and is intended for older primary level children.

Long, long ago when animals could talk and understand each other very well, the most important animal was not Anansi the spider. Nothing at all was named for him. In those days, it was Tiger who was thought the greatest of all animals.

"This will never do," Anansi said. "I cannot, will not, should not, could not, would not stay a nobody. Not me! Not Anansi!"

And so Anansi the spider went walking, walking, walking through the forest to Tiger's house. Tiger was sitting on his front porch. Ever so politely, Anansi said, "Oh, Mighty One, I have a favor to ask of you."

Tiger yawned, showing off his razor sharp fangs. And tiger stretched, showing off his razor sharp claws. And Tiger spoke, showing off his loud voice, "What would you ask of me, little spider man?"

"Oh, Magnificent One," said Anansi. "Many things are named after you because you are such a powerful beast. Tiger butter, tiger beetle, tiger butterfly, tiger eye, tiger fish, tiger frog, tiger maple, tiger mosquito, tiger lily, tiger moth, tiger nut, tiger pear, tiger shark . . ."

"Yes, yes, yes," bellowed Tiger. "You bore me. Get to the point."

"Oh, Majestic One," said Anansi. "I would like something named after me too!"

"And what, little spider man, would that be?" Tiger asked, flicking his tail impatiently.

"Oh, Marvelous One, I would like something very small, very unimportant, insignificant, trivial, worthless, minuscule, irrelevant. I would like to have stories named after me."

"Stories? How silly," said Tiger, laughing. "How very weak and small and silly! Just as weak and small and silly as a spider! Very well," Tiger said. "But, before I grant you this favor, you must do me two favors in exchange."

"What are they, Oh Munificent One?" asked Anansi.

"First, you must bring me a gourd full of live bees. Nye, nye, nye," laughed the Tiger, who was sure that Anansi the little spider man would shake with fear at the very thought of so difficult a task.

But Anansi only bowed very low and said, "Your wish is my command, Oh Merciful One!"

And off went Anansi, walking, walking, walking before Tiger could change his mind.

He snatched up a hollow gourd, one with only one small opening, and went straight to where a swarm of bees lived in a hollow tree.

"Alas, oh alas. Oh, woe is me," sighed Anansi.

"Buzz, Buzz, why all the buzz moaning, Anansi?" asked the bees, buzzing around Anansi's head.

"Why, I made a bet with Tiger. And now I think that I'm going to lose it."

"Buzz. What type of buzz bet was that?" the bees asked.

"I bet the Tiger," explained Anansi, "that I could tell him how many bees this gourd can hold. But now I see that I can't possibly know such a thing. Since you are bees, do you, perhaps, know the answer?"

"Buzz. No. We don't know such a thing either," said the bees.

"Well, I am very curious about it," Anansi told them slyly. "Aren't you?"

"Yes, yes, we are now very curious too! Buzz, buzz, buzz."

"We could easily solve this problem." Anansi held up the gourd so that the bees could see the opening. "If you fly in, one by one, I can count how many of you fit in here."

"Very buzz well," said the bees. "Since we are as curious about the answer as you."

So the bees flew in, one by one, until the gourd was full. Anansi quickly plugged the hole and went walking, walking, walking back to Tiger.

Anansi presented the gourd to Tiger. "Here you are, Oh Masterful One. Here is your gourd full of bees."

Tiger roared. How had Anansi done this task? How had such a weak, small, silly spider done it?

"Very well," Tiger grumbled at last. "You have brought me the bees. But now you must do me a second favor. You must bring me rattlesnake and you must bring him to me ALIVE! Nye, nye, nye."

Tiger was sure that Anansi would shake with fear at the very thought at so difficult a thing.

But Anansi only bowed very low and said, "Your wish is my command, Oh Majestic One."

And off Anansi went, walking, walking, walking before Tiger could change his mind.

Anansi knew that snake followed the same path every day when he went to the stream to drink. Anansi decided to set a trap for snake.

He made a noose out of a vine. In the center of the noose, Anansi placed a nice, ripe, tasty banana. As soon as snake slithered into the noose, Anansi planned to pull it tight.

Sure enough, snake came slithering, wasawoosu, wasawoosu, wasawoosu, down the path. Snake saw the banana and pounced on it.

Anansi tried to pull the noose tight. But snake was much too strong for the vine. He easily broke the noose without even realizing it was there and slithered, wasawoosu, wasawoosu, wasawoosu, on his way.

"Ohhh. That trap was not big enough," Anansi

told himself. "This one will be better!"

So Anansi dug a hole. At the bottom he put a nice, ripe avocado pear, then greased the sides of the pit. "Once snake slithered into this hole," said Anansi, "he won't be able to climb out again!"

But snake wrapped his tail about a branch, reached down into the hole, snatched up the tasty avocado pear without even touching the slippery sides of the pit, and slithered, wasawoosu, wasawoosu, wasawoosu, on his way.

"Ohhh. That trap was not clever enough!" Anansi told himself. "This one will be better."

So Anansi bent down one of the flexible, strong bamboos on the ground and tied a noose to it. Inside the noose, Anansi placed an egg.

"As soon as snake touches the noose," Anansi said, "it will release the bamboo, and, TWARP, hang up the snake so I can take him alive to Tiger."

Snake slithered by, wasawoosu, wasawoosu, wasawoosu, saw the egg, and with his mouth watering, licked his lips. Snake picked the egg neatly out of the noose without disturbing it at all.

"That is three traps," Anansi told himself, "and not one has worked. They are just not strong, big, or clever enough."

So Anansi tried another tactic. Anansi walked up to snake as though he was very troubled. "Alas, alas, oh woe is me," sighed Anansi.

Snake sat up. "What is wrong with you, spider man?" snake asked. "You sound sooooo discontented."

"Oh," said Anansi. "I made a foolish bet with Tiger, and now I don't know how I am ever going to win it."

"What bet is this?" asked snake.

"I told Tiger that you are the longest thing in the world."

"And so I am," snake boasted.

"But," said Anansi, "Tiger says something else. Tiger says that the bamboo tree is taller than you are long. And now that I look at you, I think that Tiger might be right."

"That is nonsense!" snake cried. "Anyone can

plainly see that I am longer than a bamboo tree! Cut down that bamboo and measure it against me. I know you will win this bet."

So Anansi cut down the longest bamboo he could find, and put it down next to snake.

"Hmmm." Anansi scratched his head. "How are we going to do this? If I start measuring your head, your tail may slither up, and if I start measuring your tail, your head may slither down. How can we possibly get an accurate measurement?"

Snake hissed. "Silly spider man. All you need to do is tie my tail to the end of the bamboo. Then I will stretch all the way out, and you will see how much longer I am than the stupid bamboo!"

"Ahh," said Anansi. "An excellent idea!" Anansi tied snake's tail firmly to the end of the bamboo. Snake stretched himself out. "I'm sorry, snake," Anansi said. "The bamboo is still longer than you."

"Then tie my middle to the bamboo and I will stretch my head further," said snake.

So Anansi tied the middle of snake to the bamboo. "Now stretch snake! Stretch as far as you can!" said Anansi. Snake stretched and stretched. "I am sorry, snake," said Anansi. "The bamboo is still longer than you!"

"Oh, I am much longer than bamboo. Tie my neck to the bamboo and I will stretch my head farther."

Snake stretched and stretched as far as he could. Anansi quickly tied his neck to the bamboo.

"Yes," said Anansi. "You are right. You are indeed longer than the bamboo. You are also good and caught."

Anansi carried the bamboo, with snake tied to it, and presented it to Tiger. "Here you are, Oh Melodious One," said Anansi. "Here is your snake, and very much alive."

Tiger roared. How had Anansi done this task? How had such a weak, small, silly spider done it?

"Very well," Tiger grumbled at last. "You have completed both favors. From now on, stories will be known as Anansi tales."

And that is why, to this very day, all trickster stories are called Anansi Tales—because Anansi the little spider man tricked the bees, tricked the snake, but most of all, tricked the Magnificent, Mighty, Marvelous, Munificent, Merciful, Masterful, Melodious Tiger.

—adapted by Stefani Koorey

Ordinary Red Beans

This is an audience participation story. Instruct the group that their part is to sing the following: "We're just ordinary red beans" and jump around when the teller's back is turned. Be sure to explain the difference between ordinary red beans and Mexican jumping beans before beginning.

For many years, my friend (*let audience pick name: ex. John*) was working in a grocery store (*let audience choose the store: ex. Winn Dixie*). In all those years he worked there, John had never missed a day of work. Now why did he never miss a day of work? So he could take a long vacation to his favorite place in the whole world, Mexico!

Finally, the day arrived. John packed his bags and went to the airport to get on a plane to Mexico.

When he got to Mexico, he drove to his hotel, unpacked his bags and did all of his favorite things: swimming, walking on the beach, eating, (*let audience choose some activities*), and shopping. While he was shopping, John found some Mexican jumping beans. Oooh, they were so neat, jumping around the jar like that, all by themselves, that he decided to take them home with him.

He got on the plane, went back to his house, unpacked, and put the jumping beans on the windowsill in the kitchen. He crawled into bed, exhausted, ready for a good night's sleep. (*Stretch and yawn with the audience.*) But before he could go to sleep, he heard some noise in the kitchen. It was those beans jumping around in the jar! (*Make jumping beans noises: weee, hee-hee, yahoo, yipee, etc.*) They were so loud that John couldn't sleep a wink all night.

The next day, he packaged up those Mexican jumping beans and put them for sale in the Winn Dixie, but nobody bought them. So the next day, John put a new label on them, "Ordinary Red Beans." It just so happened that an old woman (*if the teller is a man, an old man*) walked by and saw those "Ordinary Red Beans" and decided to buy them. "I just love ordinary red beans," she said. "I can't wait to take them home and cook them up to eat!"

The old woman took them home and put them next to the stove and started to boil the water. "Yummy, yummy!" she said. "I can't wait to eat those beans. But this water is taking so long to boil, I'll just go up to my room and clean out my closet." (*At this point, the teller explains to the audience that this is where their part comes in, as explained in the beginning, and turns his/her back on the audience, pantomiming cleaning. Speak to yourself about cleaning, then mention the beans. Most likely the kids will be too loud at this point to hear you anyway, and whip around to face the au-*

dience. Look mad. The audience should be chant-ing, "We're just ordinary red beans." If not, coach them.)

"Did I hear something down here? Huh, maybe not. I'll just go back to my cleaning." (*Turn back around and "clean." Repeat above and whip back around to the audience, who should be chanting when you turn around.*)

"I thought I heard something down here, but I guess not. I'm just going to get back to my cleaning!" (*Turn back to audience, repeat above. Have fun with the kids and pretend to turn around before doing so.*)

"No, no! I did hear something! These are defin-itely not ordinary red beans!" the old woman shouted, and she took the beans back to the store.

When she saw John, she gave them back say-ing, "These are NOT ordinary red beans!" Well, now John had the beans again. He couldn't take them home again, what should he do?

(*Ask the audience for their suggestions and try to incorporate as many as possible into the ending. Examples: John threw the beans away and set the dumpster on fire; John flushed all the beans down the toilet; or John mailed the beans back to Mexico. The audience will "tell" you how to end this story.*)

—adapted by Reba R. Gordon

CHAPTER THIRTEEN

Creative Dramatics

Creative dramatics in the story program allows children to express themselves and simultaneously gain insight into others. It is an appropriate means of helping children relate to and understand literature by capitalizing on children's innate inclination toward dramatic play.

Dramatic play is a natural part of growing up for all children, regardless of cultural origin. During unstructured play time, children may pretend to be airplanes, cars, dogs, parents, or cowboys. By this kind of experimentation, they gain some understanding of the persons or things that they are dramatizing.

In story programs, you have a perfect situation in which to structure children's dramatic play. By asking them to dramatize certain portions of stories, you are offering the youngsters a formal opportunity to interpret with their minds and bodies. Two- and three-year-old children will imitate action and emotions suggested by you or by pictures relating to the story. They are more likely to "be" cats than to consider how cats might react. Four- and five-year-olds are beginning to understand emotions, and with simple guidelines can portray feelings expressed by story characters. Children age six to eight years are quite capable of creative interpretation. With a little assistance from you, they will delight in dramatizing the moods and emotions of others.

The prime goal of creative dramatics is to stimulate children to interpret the action of a story using their own thoughts, experiences, and imaginations. You are not creating a play, but rather giving the children a situation or emotion that they can portray through facial expressions and some gestures.

Remember that there is no right or wrong interpretation. One child may use an unconventional interpretation, but as long as that child is participating, he or she is using their imagination and creating. Do not try to force a particular expression or gesture, but try to help the children understand the situation and then let them do whatever they feel. For instance, if the situation was one in which the children would feel sad, ask them what they would look like if they were sad, and what they would do with their hands and body, or in other words, what gestures they might make. Ask if they would bow their heads and pout, rub their eyes as if crying, or just frown.

Each child will have a different response depending on his or her own experience. All may need some coaxing or further explanation of the situation to help them react. If they do not understand what it is to be sad, then you might say that if your dog was lost, you would feel sad. Ask the children how they would look, and what they would do. The important thing is to let them decide and react accordingly.

Along with the following stories are some suggestions for the situations you would ask the children to interpret. You may choose to explore other portions of the stories, but just remember to keep it simple.

Read the story aloud first so that the children are familiar with the plot and the characters. Then, go back to the sections you want to interpret and ask for the children's responses. You may choose to reread the section to them or just describe the action of the story. For instance, in "The Three Bears" you might decide to return to the part of the story where Goldilocks is tasting the porridge. Instead of rereading, ask how Goldilocks would look as she tasted each dish. Or, if you want the portion where the bears discover that their house has been invaded to be enacted, ask the children in the group how each bear might respond, including tone of voice and emotional reaction (fear, anger, sadness).

You may give the children in your program several suggestions as to how they might react, but then tell them that each must decide what to do. Once you have discussed the situation, tell the children that they will now be Goldilocks and taste the first bowl of porridge. When they have had enough time, stop them and move on to the next situation, until you have finished the story.

Toddlers and Creative Dramatics

In using creative dramatics with toddlers, you will have to give specific examples for the children to follow. They may have some individual reactions, but generally you have to be more of a leader to this age group than with the older children. The interpretations will mostly be in the nature of physical movements rather than facial expressions or gestures. Whenever possible, show toddler age children pictures to suggest the action of the story.

Dramatic play can easily be structured to fit a story program. Select a dramatic play situation that relates to a story you have read in your program. If you have used "The Three Little Kittens," ask the children to be cats by crawling on all fours and meowing. If you have read *Good Night, Owl* by Hutchins, ask them to be birds by flapping their arms and cheeping. A plane may be interpreted by holding their arms outstretched and rocking back and forth. Other suggestions for dramatic play activities are dogs, cars, ducks, lions, cows, and trains. Keep the situation simple, and use familiar animals and inanimate objects that tie into stories you are using.

Creative Dramatics for Toddlers

Jack Be Nimble

Jack be nimble; Jack be quick;
Jack jumped over the candlestick.

Directions for "Jack Be Nimble"

Tell the children to stand up. Ask them to jump in the air like Jack did when he was jumping over the candlestick. Then recite the rhyme and insert the activity.

Bye, Baby Bunting

Bye, baby bunting,
Daddy's gone a-hunting,
To get a little rabbit skin
To wrap the baby bunting in.

Directions for "Bye, Baby Bunting"

With the children seated, have them wave "bye-bye." Then ask them to fold their arms in front of them and rock back and forth as if cradling a baby. Then recite the rhyme and insert activity.

Row, Row, Row Your Boat

Row, row, row your boat
Gently down the stream.
Merrily, merrily, merrily, merrily,
Life is but a dream.

Directions for "Row, Row, Row Your Boat"

Find a picture of a row boat to show while you sing the song. With the children sitting on the floor, have them make rowing motions with their arms while you sing the song again.

Trot, Trot, to Boston

Trot, trot, to Boston; Trot, trot, to Lynn;
Trot, trot, to Salem; Home, home, again.

Directions for "Trot, Trot, to Boston"

Have the children stand and prance in place as horses, with their hands brought up to their chests, pretending to hold the reins. Then recite the rhyme and insert the activity.

Jack and Jill

Jack and Jill went up the hill,
To fetch a pail of water;
Jack fell down, and broke his crown,
And Jill came tumbling after.

Directions for "Jack and Jill"

Have the children stand up and tell them they are going to be Jack and fall down. Have them drop to the floor. Next tell them they will have to be Jill, and have them roll over as if they are tumbling down the hill. Recite the rhyme and insert activity.

Little Robin Redbreast

Little Robin Redbreast
Sits upon a rail.
Niddle, noddle goes his head,
Wiggle, waggle goes his tail.

Directions for "Little Robin Redbreast"

Ask the children to stand up. First have them nod their heads as the robin did. Then have them wiggle back and forth to wiggle waggle their tails.

Creative Dramatics for Preschoolers

Tom, Tom the Piper's Son

Tom, Tom the Piper's son
Stole a pig and away he run.
The pig got eat,
And Tom got beat,
And he went crying down the street.

Directions for "Tom, Tom the Piper's Son"

Tell the children that they are Tom. How would he feel if he had just been spanked? Would he be sad and sorry for what he did? How would he look if he is crying? Would he open his mouth wide as if crying loudly, or would he drop his head and cover his face with his hands?

Doctor Foster

Doctor Foster went to Gloucester
In a shower of rain;
He stepped in a puddle,
Right up to his middle,
And never went their again.

Directions for "Doctor Foster"

Have the children stand up. Tell them they are Dr. Foster who is wearing a long raincoat. How would he feel when he steps in the deep puddle? Would he be surprised, or mad, or sad? What would he do with his coat to try to keep it out of the water?

Little Jack Horner

Little Jack Horner sat in a corner
Eating his Christmas pie.
He put in his thumb and pulled out a plum
And said, "What a good boy am I!"

Directions for "Little Jack Horner"

Tell the children they are going to be Jack. How would he stick his thumb in a pie and move it around to find a plum? Would he be very slow and careful, or quick and eager? After he finds the plum and pulls it out, how would he look if he felt like a "good boy"? Would he sit up straight and proud and give a great big smile, or would he look all around and show everyone his plum as he smiles? What would he do with his hands to show his plum? Would he eat the plum in the end or put it back in the pie?

Lucy Locket

Lucy Locket lost her pocket.
Kitty Fisher found it.
Not a penny was there in it,
But a ribbon round it.

Directions for "Lucy Locket"

Tell the children that they are first going to be Lucy Locket. She has lost her pocket or purse. How would she feel? Would she be upset and cry? Would she look around for her purse and start to cry? Now have the children be Kitty Fisher. How would she look when she finds the pocket? Would she be surprised and happy? What would she do when she sees that there is not any money in it? Would she be sad and disappointed? Does she take the purse with her or give it back? What does she do in either case (to end the story)?

Are You Sleeping?

Are you sleeping, are you sleeping,
Brother John, Brother John?
Morning bells are ringing,
Morning bells are ringing.
Ding, dong, ding. Ding, dong, ding.

Directions for "Are You Sleeping?"

Sing the song several times so that the children know the words, or are at least familiar with them. Then tell the children that they will be Brother John. How does he look when he is sleeping? Does he fold his arms over as he sleeps? Does he snore? How does he feel when the bells ring and wake him up? Is he surprised and does he wake up quickly, shaking his head? Or is he glad to wake up and does he yawn and stretch? After the children have interpreted the song, sing it again while they repeat their reactions.

One, Two, Three, Four, Five

One, two, three, four, five,
Once I caught a fish alive.
Six, seven, eight, nine, ten,
Then I let it go again.

Why did you let it go?
Because it bit my finger so.
Which finger did it bite?
The little one upon the right.

Directions for "One, Two, Three, Four, Five"

Recite the rhyme several times. Ask them to say it with you. Once they have learned it, ask them if any of them have ever caught a fish, how big was it, and what motion they used to catch the fish. Some may use a rod and reel, some catching the fish with their hands. Ask them what they would do if a fish bit their finger and how quickly they might let the fish go if it did nip them.

Faces

There is only one me. But sometimes I have a happy face and sometimes I have a sad face. It all depends.

When I get dressed all by myself and Mama says that I have my shoes on the right feet, I have a happy face because I feel proud.

When I spill cereal on my shirt at breakfast time, I have a sad face because I feel like I am bad.

When I build a tall building with my blocks, I have a happy face because I did a good job.

When my baby brother knocks down my building, I have a mad face because I feel angry.

When I hit the baby and he cries, I have a sad face because I feel ashamed.

When I pick up my blocks without being told, I have a happy face because I feel grown-up.

When Mama holds the baby and rocks him, I have a sad face because I feel jealous.

When Mama puts the baby to bed, then holds ME on her lap and tells me that I am her super big child, I have a happy face because I feel loved.

So you see, while there is only one me, I sometimes have a happy face and sometimes a sad face. That's because I have different kinds of feelings. Don't you have different kinds of feelings, too?

—C. S. Peterson

Directions for "Faces"

Read the story, then tell the children you are going to read it again. Ask them to be the person in the story and make a happy or sad face as you read. Keep the interpretation simple, pausing after each section to encourage them to feel the emotions and make an appropriate face. For instance, in the section when they feel proud, encourage them to sit up straight and tall and give a big grin. They may change in the next section to hanging their heads, pouting, or frowning. The interpretations will probably be quite similar, but the children should be able to express the different emotions and may show some variety.

The Playground

One warm sunny day, Daddy said to Amy and Jeffrey, "I have a surprise for you. Guess where we are going today!"

"To Grandma's house!" guessed Amy.

"No," said Daddy.

"To the grocery store!" guessed Jeffrey.

"No," said Daddy.

"To watch the airplanes?" asked Amy.

"No," said Daddy.

"To Aunt Jean's farm?" asked Jeffrey.

"No," said Daddy, "we are going to the playground."

"Hurray! Hurray!" shouted the children.

So Daddy and Amy and Jeffrey went to the playground. Oh! So many things to do!

"Daddy," said Amy, "will you please push me on the swings?"

"Oh, yes, Daddy, please," begged Jeffrey.

So Daddy pushed the children in the swings. First he pushed Amy three times. Then he pushed Jeffrey three times.

Jeffrey said, "Look, Amy, do you see the slide? Daddy, can we go on the slide now?"

"Yes," said Daddy, "If you will be very careful."

Amy and Jeffrey ran to the slide. First Jeffrey climbed up the ladder. Up the steps he climbed. One, two, three, four, five, six steps. How high in the air he was! Then Amy climbed up the ladder. Up the steps she climbed. One, two, three, four, five, six steps. How high in the air she was! Then she sat down and slid, whoosh! down the slide.

"Ooh," said Amy "I see a see-saw. Jeffrey, let's go on the see-saw. May we, Daddy, please?"

So Daddy helped the children on the see-saw. Jeffrey sat on one end of the see-saw. Then Daddy pulled down the other end of the see-saw for Amy to sit on. Up and down they went. Up and down, up and down. "Whee!" shouted the children, "this is fun!"

"Look," said Daddy. "Over there is the merry-go-round."

"Oh, boy, the merry-go-round," said Jeffrey.

"May we ride it? Please, may we ride it, Daddy?" pleaded Amy.

Daddy laughed. "Of course you may ride the merry-go-round. Hop on and I will push it for you."

Amy and Jeffrey hopped on the merry-go-round and held on tight. Daddy pushed them around and around, faster and faster. At last the merry-go-round stopped.

"I'm dizzy," said Amy.

"So am I," said Jeffrey.

"I think it is time for us to go home," said Daddy.

"May we come back again sometime?" asked Amy.

"Of course you may," said Daddy.

Daddy and Amy and Jeffrey all held hands as they went home.

—C. S. Peterson

Directions for "The Playground"

After you have read the story, tell the children that they will be Amy and Jeffrey. How do Amy and Jeffrey feel as they are trying to guess where they are going? Are they puzzled and confused? Do they close their eyes tightly to think what it might be, or do they hold their heads in their hands as they try to think? How do Amy and Jeffrey feel when they find out they are going to the playground? Are they happy and excited? Do they clap their hands as they shout, "Hurray"?

Now Amy and Jeffrey are at the playground, so ask the children to stand up and pretend they are going on the different rides. How would Amy and Jeffrey go on the swings? Suggest to the children that they sway their arms up and down to show they are swinging. Would Amy and Jeffrey smile and laugh as they swing? Would they start out slowly and then go up high on the third push?

How do Amy and Jeffrey climb up the six steps on the ladder of the slide? Do they go up slowly or quickly? When they reach the top, how do they feel when they see how high up they are? Are they a little bit afraid? How do they go down the slide? Have the children stand on their tiptoes and then drop to the floor. Do Amy and Jeffrey go very fast as they "whoosh"?

How do Amy and Jeffrey go on the see-saw? Have the children stand up and then squat down several times. Ask them if the children in the story go up and down slowly or quickly? How do they look as they shout "whee"?

Finally, how do Amy and Jeffrey go on the merry-go-round? Have the children stand and turn around in circles. When Amy and Jeffrey stop, what do they do if they are dizzy? Do they drop to the ground, or do they stand up and hold their heads to try and stop the dizzy feeling? Are they glad they came to the playground as they hold hands and go home?

Little Bo Peep

Little Bo Peep has lost her sheep
And can't tell where to find them;
Leave them alone, and they'll come home,
Wagging their tails behind them.

Directions for "Little Bo Peep"

Tell the children that they are Little Bo Peep. What does she do to look for the sheep? Does she try to call them, does she strain to look in the distance, or does she start walking around trying to find them? She knows the sheep are lost. How does she feel: angry, scared, or sad? How does she feel when the sheep come back? Is she happy and relieved? What does she do to welcome the sheep home? Does she hug them or scold them not to wander away again?

Be careful not to venture into the personal with this rhyme. For instance, do not ask the children if they can recall a time when their own animals were lost and did not come home. You may stir up some sad memories and that is not the objective of creative play.

Creative Dramatics for Primary Level Children

There Was an Old Woman

There was an old woman who lived in a shoe;
She had so many cockroaches,
She didn't know what to do;
She caught fifteen bugs,
And chopped off their heads,
And dipped them in chocolate
And ate them instead.

Directions for "There Was an Old Woman"

Since all of the primary level children will have already heard the story of the old woman who lived in the shoe, introduce some humor by altering the rhyme. You may alter it in any fashion you choose, as it is a simple rhyme to rewrite.

The children will be the Old Woman. How does she feel to live in a shoe? What kind of shoe is it—a loafer or a sneeker or a boot? Is it a tight fit or is it an extra wide size? How does she feel to have an infestation of cockroaches? Are they the kind that fly? Remind the children that in some cultures, chocolate covered bugs are a delicacy. How would it taste? Would it crunch as you chewed it? What other ways could the Old Woman have reduced her cockroach population?

If you elect to do this rhyme with the traditional words, have the children first be the Old Woman and then the children. How does the Old Woman feel with so many children? Is she angry, confused, or frustrated? What does she do to show this? Does she give a big sigh and put her hands on her hips, or does she throw her hands in the air as if to say "I give up"?

Now tell the group that they will be the children. Do they like having broth without any bread? How does it taste? How do they feel when they are spanked and sent to bed? What would they do?

The Queen of Hearts

The Queen of Hearts
She made some tarts
All on a summer's day.
The Knave of Hearts,
He stole the tarts
And took them clean away.

The King of Hearts,
Called for the tarts
And beat the Knave full sore.
The Knave of Hearts,
Brought back the tarts
And vowed he'd steal no more.

Directions for "The Queen of Hearts"

You can divide the group into three parts to be the Queen, the Knave, and the King. For the Queen, how would she feel when she has finished making her tarts? Is she tired, or very proud of her work? What does she do when she discovers the tarts are stolen? Does she feel surprised and look all around for them, and then feel sad and angry? Does she sit and cry, or call for the King?

How does the Knave feel after he has stolen the tarts? Is he glad and pleased with his success, or is he afraid of what might happen to him? Does he eat one of the tarts or does he try to hide them and save them for later?

How does the King feel when he calls for the tarts and the Knave? Hoe does he tell the Knave to never steal again? Does he shake a finger at him, or cross his arms in front of him to scold the Knave?

How does the Knave feel when he has been beaten? Is he sorry for what he did, or is he upset and mad at the King? How does he show his feelings?

The Hare and the Tortoise

Once long ago there lived a hare who was always boasting about how fast he could run. All of the other animals became quite disgusted with the hare. But it was true. He could run faster than any of them.

One day the animals had gathered for a picnic. Everyone was eating and having a fine time when the hare began bragging that he could run faster than anyone because of his fine strong legs.

Although the tortoise was usually a very patient creature, on this day he simply could not bear the hare's boasting. With a long sigh he challenged the hare to a race.

Now the hare was more than surprised that the incredibly slow tortoise would offer to race him. Though the hare laughed and jeered, however, the tortoise steadfastly insisted that he could beat the hare in a fair race. So the hare at last agreed.

All the animals became very excited and began at once to plan the race. They decided that the race should begin at the fallen log and end at the old dead stump. The hare and the tortoise agreed and lined up by the fallen log.

The hare looked haughtily at the tortoise, but the tortoise just waited quietly at the starting line. The sparrow and the blue jay flew down to the old dead stump to judge the winner, and the frog agreed to start the race. "On your mark! Get set! Go!" he croaked.

Both the hare and the tortoise dashed from the starting line. That is, the hare dashed. The tortoise moved very, very slowly, and the hare was quickly far ahead. The hare, prancing along, said to himself, "That foolish Tortoise! Surely he doesn't think that he can outrun me. Why, I'm so far ahead that I'll just stop and nibble some grass."

After he had eaten, the hare looked back at the tortoise, who was far, far behind. "I am so far ahead of the tortoise," said the hare, "that I think that I shall take a little nap. I will have plenty of time to beat that slow-poke." So saying, the hare snuggled down in the tall grass and was soon fast asleep.

Meanwhile, the tortoise plodded on. Slowly, slowly, step by step, closer and closer to the finish line he inched. Slowly, slowly, step by step, he passed the sleeping hare. Slowly, slowly, step by step, at last he was only a few paces from the old dead stump.

The hare woke up, yawned, and stretched. "I wonder where old slow-poke Tortoise is," he mused. He looked far behind him, but, of course, he could not see the tortoise. In disbelief he looked toward the old dead stump and sure enough there was the tortoise only steps away from it. The hare ran fast, faster than he had ever run in his life. But before he reached the finish line, he heard cheering and shouting.

The sparrow and the blue jay shrieked and chattered, "Tortoise has won the race! Tortoise is the winner! Hurray for Tortoise!"

The hare arrived at the old dead stump just in time to hear the tortoise tell the other animals how he outran the hare by plodding slowly and steadily along. And from that day to this, the hare has never again boasted about his speed.

—retold by C. S. Peterson

Directions for "The Hare and the Tortoise"

After you have finished the story, have the children stand up and tell them that they will be the hare. How would he boast to the other animals? Would he stand straight and tall, puff out his chest, and smile at himself? Or would he pace back and forth with his nose in the air?

When the tortoise challenges the hare to a race, what would the hare do? Would he point at the tortoise and laugh softly to himself thinking it would be a silly race? Or would he slap his leg and laugh out loud at the tortoise?

After the race has started, what does the hare do while he nibbles the grass? Does he grab a few handfuls, eat quickly, laugh to himself, and shake his head at the the idea that the tortoise even thinks he stands a chance against the hare? Or does he flop on the ground and slowly eat as he yawns and looks back for the tortoise? How does he take a little nap? Does he stretch out flat on his back or curl up on his side? Is he comfortable on the grass or is it wet with dew?

When he wakes up and stretches, what does he do when he realizes the tortoise is almost at the finish line? Does he open his eyes wide and shake his head to make sure he is not dreaming? Or does he jump to his feet, and slap the side of his face in shock?

As the hare arrives at the finish line and finds out he has lost, how does he feel? Is he mad at himself and ashamed? Does he hang his head and slowly turn away? Or does he sit down on the ground, put his head in his hands, and give a big sigh?

The Boy Who Cried Wolf

Once long ago in a far off kingdom there lived a lad called Hans. Now Hans was a shepherd boy whose lonely job it was to take the sheep far up the hillside each day to graze. While Hans loved the sheep and was proud to be doing a grown-up job, he sometimes felt very much alone up on the high hillside. It helped none at all that he could see the good people of the village down below busy at their daily tasks. What Hans wanted was someone to talk to and to share his meager lunch of cheese and bread.

One day as the sheep grazed lazily nearby, Hans sat in the green grass under a tree feeling even lonelier than usual. "If only I had someone to talk to," he said sadly to himself as he watched the lively village down below him. "If only I had someone to talk to, but no one ever climbs up into the hills except me and my sheep." As he sat pulling blades of grass and feeling sorry for himself, he suddenly had an idea. Jumping up and running a ways down the hill, Hans shouted, "Wolf! Wolf! A wolf is after the sheep!"

Down below in the village, the people heard Hans' cry for help. Grabbing tools and sticks, they rushed up the hillside to help rescue the sheep. As

they arrived breathless at the top of the hill, they saw Hans laughing and laughing. "It's only a joke," he said. The villagers grumbled angrily as they trudged down the hill to go back to their work.

It was but a day or so later when Hans was again feeling lonely. "I wonder," he said to himself. "It worked before. Will it work again?" With that he ran down the hillside calling, "Wolf! Wolf! A wolf is after the sheep!"

As before the villagers armed themselves with sticks and hoes and rushed up the hillside to aid Hans and the sheep. And as before when they reached the top, there they found Hans sprawled in the grass. "It's only a joke," he laughed. Once again the angry villagers trudged downhill to return to their work.

Now before many days had passed, Hans was again sitting in the grass under the tree watching the villagers down below. Hearing a slight rustle in the bushes, he turned to look. There in front of him with eyes gleaming wickedly, was a huge, shaggy wolf. Hans was terrified. He was so frightened that he could only shiver and stare at the snarling wolf. At last Hans found his voice and screamed, "Wolf! Wolf! Wolf! A wolf is after the sheep!"

Down below in the village the people hardly looked up from their work. "It is only Hans," they said to each other. "It is only Hans trying to trick us again."

Hans screamed again even louder than before. "Wolf! Wolf! A wolf is after the sheep!" But no one came to his aid.

Bravely, Hans tried to chase away the wolf. But the huge wolf was not afraid of one small boy. Although Hans did his best, the wolf killed many of the sheep and the others ran bleating into the deep forest.

Hans made his way alone down the hillside to the village. When he told what had happened to the sheep, the people shook their heads in sorrow and reminded him that no one believes a liar.

—retold by C. S. Peterson

Directions for "The Boy Who Cried Wolf"

After you have read the story, tell the children that they will be Hans. They first will be sitting in the green grass feeling lonely. How would he look as he sits pulling blades of grass? Would he pout and sigh? Would he frown and look sadly at the village below, and then back at the grass?

What does Hans do when he suddenly gets an idea? Does he break into a great big smile and jump to his feet, or does he snap his fingers and smile slowly as if to say "That's a great idea," and then jump to his feet? Does he wave his arms frantically as he calls for help, or does he put his hands to his mouth to make himself heard in the village below?

When the villagers arrive at the top of the hill, how is Hans laughing at them? Is he slapping his knees and pointing at the villagers? Or is he doubled over and holding his stomach and then falling to the ground because he is laughing so hard? What does his laugh sound like?

What does Hans do when he sees the real wolf? Does he sit with his eyes and mouth wide open as he shivers in fright, or does he jump to his feet and point at the wolf as he slowly backs away and shivers? What should you do if you see a wolf?

In the end, what does Hans do when he tells the villagers about his sheep? Is he sorry and ashamed of his lies and angry with himself? Does he hang his head low and speak softly? Does he wipe a tear from his eye and look back up the hill where his sheep were lost? Does he promise never to play tricks again? Do the villagers forgive Hans for his trickery and hope he has learned his lesson?

The Three Bears

Once upon a time in a small house deep in the woods there lived three bears: the great big Papa Bear, the middle-sized Mama Bear, and the teeny tiny Baby Bear.

One day just as the bears were ready to eat their porridge, they found that it was so hot that it burned their mouths. So Mama Bear said, "Come, let's go for a walk in the woods. When we return, the porridge will be just right for eating."

So the three bears went for a walk in the woods.

Meanwhile, a little girl with golden curls who was called Goldilocks came skipping down the path through the woods. When she saw the Bears' house, she stopped and peeped around a tree. "What a dear little house!" she exclaimed. "I wonder who lives there." She walked up to the door and knocked timidly. After she waited for a moment she knocked firmly. When still there was no answer, she pushed the door open just a tiny crack and called, "Is anyone home?"

When she received no answer, she tiptoed quietly into the bears' house. "Oh!" she said delightedly, "what a darling house! Why, look! There is food on the table. And I'm so hungry after my long walk. Perhaps if I take just a little bite . . ."

She picked up Papa Bear's spoon and tasted a bite of the porridge in his great big bowl. "Oh, that's much too hot," she cried. She tasted a bite of the porridge in Mama Bear's middle-sized bowl. "Ooh, that's much too cold," she said. She tasted just a bite of the porridge in Baby Bear's teeny tiny bowl. "Mmm, delicious!" she murmured. "Maybe I'll just have another little taste. And another. And another." And Goldilocks ate taste after taste until Baby Bear's porridge was all gone.

Goldilocks, feeling refreshed with a tummyful of warm porridge, looked around the Bears' house. At once she spied the Bears' chairs in the living room, and being curious, decided to try them out.

First she sat down in Papa Bear's great big chair. "My," she said, "this chair is much too hard." So saying, she climbed down from Papa Bear's great big chair and slipped into Mama Bear's middle-sized chair.

After a moment, she said, "This chair is much too soft." Just then she spotted Baby Bear's teeny tiny chair and ran to it. "This chair is just right!" she declared. She sat and rocked and rocked and sat. But Goldilocks was too heavy for the teeny tiny chair, and sure enough, it broke all to pieces.

Goldilocks felt bad about the broken chair. But not for long. There in front of her was a staircase leading to the upstairs bedroom. And of course the curious little girl went up to look.

First she saw Papa Bear's great big bed. "What a big bed!" she cried as she lay down upon it, "but it is much too hard." She looked at Mama Bear's middle-sized bed. "This is a nice looking bed," she said lying down upon it, "but it is much too soft." Then Goldilocks saw Baby Bear's teeny tiny bed.

"Oh," she said lying down and pulling up the covers, "this is a perfect bed." And being very tired from her day's adventure, she was soon fast asleep.

Now just at this moment the three bears finished their walk and burst into the kitchen, hungry for their porridge. Papa Bear said in his great big voice, "Someone has been eating my porridge." Mama Bear said in her middle-sized voice, "Someone has been eating my porridge." Baby Bear said in his teeny tiny voice, "Someone has been eating my porridge and has eaten it all up."

The bears went into their living room. "Someone has been sitting in my chair!" said Papa Bear in his great big voice. "Someone has been sitting in my chair!" said Mama Bear in her middle-sized voice. "Someone has been sitting in my chair," said Baby Bear in his teeny tiny voice, "and has broken it all to pieces."

The bears went upstairs to their bedroom. "Someone has been sleeping in my bed!" said Papa Bear in his great big voice. "Someone has been sleeping in my bed!" said Mama Bear in her middle-sized voice. "Someone has been sleeping in my bed," said Baby Bear in his teeny tiny voice, "and here she is!"

Suddenly, Goldilocks woke up. Opening her eyes, she saw the three bears all staring down at her. Goldilocks sprang from her bed, ran down the staircase, out the door, and through the woods. And never again did she visit the house of the three bears.

—retold by C. S. Peterson

Directions for "The Three Bears"

After you have read the story, tell the children that they will be Goldilocks. To begin, tell the children that Goldilocks has just discovered the bowls of porridge. How does she pick up Papa Bear's great big spoon to taste his porridge? Is it so heavy that she has to use two hands, or can she just barely hold it with one hand? How does she look when she finds that it is too hot? Is she shocked? Does it burn her mouth, so that she waves her hand in front of her mouth to cool it off? Or does she take deep breaths to cool her mouth?

How does Goldilocks look when she tastes Mama Bear's porridge? Does she wrinkle her face up as if it were almost bitter tasting, or does she shake her head as if to say "Yuck, that will never do"?

How does she feel when she tastes Baby Bear's porridge? Is she glad she finally found something good to eat? Does she pat her stomach and grin? Or does she open her eyes wide and smile broadly? After she has had several tastes, does she eat it all up quickly? Or does she continue to take just one more taste until it is finally gone?

Now she decides to try out the chairs. How would she climb up into Papa Bear's chair? How would she sit on a very hard chair? Is she disappointed and mad when she finds it is too hard? How would she slip into Mama Bear's chair? Would she sink right down into the chair, or would she slowly slide lower and lower?

How does she feel when she spots Baby Bear's chair? Is she delighted to see the little chair because she is sure it will be just right? Or is she somewhat doubtful, but willing to try it anyway? After she has sat and rocked for a minute, what does she do when the chair breaks all to pieces? Does she fall to the floor? Does she sit there in shock, or does she jump right up again when she realizes what she has done?

When she sees the staircase, how would she look since she is such a curious girl? Would she be somewhat cautious as she thinks about going upstairs, or would she be very brave and march right up?

After she has tried Papa and Mama Bear's beds, what does she do when she sees Baby Bear's bed? Does she smile happily and jump in quickly, or does she carefully and slowly climb in and then snuggle under the covers?

Now the bears have come home and they finally discover Goldilocks in Baby Bear's bed. When she wakes up, how does she feel? Is she shocked and afraid? Does she lie there and look at all three bears with her eyes wide open? Or does she sit right up, shake her head and gasp before she springs from the bed and dashes out of the house?

PART FOUR

PARTICIPATION
ACTIVITIES
AND
WIGGLEBREAKS

CHAPTER FOURTEEN

Fingerplays

Fingerplays are a part of our folk heritage, for many have been passed orally from one generation to another. For literally hundreds of years, children have delighted in the action, repetition, rhythm, and dramatization of these little games. To children, each fingerplay tells a story and offers them a chance to participate in the telling.

Fingerplays help to train the memory, teach number concepts, increase vocabulary, improve listening habits, give practice in following directions, assist in hearing specific sounds and rhymes, and develop manual dexterity. As a part of the story program, fingerplays can be used successfully to introduce the program or a picture book or merely to gain the attention of all the children.

Repeat each fingerplay you do several times for best effect and to give the children a chance to learn the accompanying actions. In the toddler story program, parents and caregivers should be assisting their children to copy the storyteller's movements. If you see a child who can't seem to get the idea and the adult is not helping out, make some eye contact with the grown up and silently indicate the necessary motions. They should, if they are at all conscious, get the drift of your plea.

You will want to take special care in the selection of fingerplays to use with the various age groups. Remember, toddlers have very limited finger dexterity and can master only the simplest of maneuvers such as those required in "Two Little Blackbirds" and "My Turtle."

Preschoolers enjoy counting fingerplays such as "Five Little Kittens" and "Five Soldiers." Although most preschoolers enjoy the rollicking good fun of "Thumbkin," only the more mature ones can handle its difficult actions.

Fingerplays will generally be unacceptable for use with primary level children. This age group, however, will respond enthusiastically to action stories, which are sophisticated cousins to fingerplays. Some popular actions stories include "Just Like Brownie" and "The Spaceman in the Rocket Ship" by Bernice Wells Carson. Action stories, used in moderation, can provide necessary stretching exercises midway in the story program.

As you master this chapter on fingerplays and the succeeding chapters on songs and singing activities, and physical activities and games, you will have a repertoire that will serve you adequately for most story programs. Try using a quiet fingerplay to calm your listeners before a picture book, a participation song or action story midway through the session to accommodate necessary large muscle movement. Experiment with any number of combinations of story program elements, discovering your own techniques for maximizing their contribution to your story program and to your audiences.

Fingerplays for Toddlers

My Turtle

This is my turtle
   (*make fist; extend thumb*)
He lives in a shell.
   (*hide thumb in fist*)
He likes his home very well.
He pokes his head out when he wants to eat.
   (*extend thumb*)
And pulls it back in when he wants to sleep.
   (*hide thumb in fist*)

Hands on Shoulders

Hands on shoulders, hands on knees,
   (*follow action as rhyme indicates*)
Hands behind you, if you please;
Touch your shoulders, now your nose,
Now your hair and now your toes;
Hands up high in the air,
Down at your sides and touch your hair;
Hands up high as before,
Now clap your hands, one, two, three, four.

Two Little Blackbirds

Two little blackbirds sitting on a hill;
   (*make two fists, thumbs up*)
One named Jack, the other named Jill.
   (*raise one hand, then the other*)
Fly away, Jack; fly away, Jill.
   (*left thumb flies behind back, then right*)
Come back, Jack; come back, Jill.
   (*left hand, then right hand to original positions*)

Little Jack Horner

Little Jack Horner sat in a corner
Eating his Christmas pie.
   (*extend left hand, palm upright*)
He put in his thumb,
   (*stick thumb in palm*)
And pulled out a plum,
   (*hold up thumb*)
And said, "What a good boy am I."

Hickory, Dickory, Dock

Hickory, dickory, dock.
   (*bend arm at elbow, holding up lower part for clock, palm open*)
The mouse ran up the clock;
   (*forefinger and middle finger of left hand for mouse*)
The clock struck one, the mouse ran down.
   (*clap hands for strike, then mouse runs down arm*)
Hickory, dickory, dock.

Five Fingers

Five fingers on this hand, (*hold up one hand*)
Five fingers on that; (*hold up other hand*)
A dear little nose, (*point to nose*)
A mouth like a rose, (*point to mouth*)
Two cheeks so tiny and fat. (*point to each cheek*)
Two eyes, two ears, (*point to each*)
And ten little toes; (*point to toes*)
That's the way the baby grows.

Jack-in-the-Box

Jack-in-the-box
Sits so still.
    (*make fist, thumb inside*)
Won't you come out?
"Yes! I will!"
    (*thumb jumps out*)

Mr. Bullfrog

Here's Mr. Bullfrog sitting on a rock;
    (*left hand closed, thumb upright at frog*)
Along comes a little boy;
    (*index and third fingers of right hand walk*)
Mr. Bullfrog jumps! Kerflop!
    (*thumb dives as if into water*)

The Family

First is the father, who brings us our bread;
    (*touch each finger in turn, beginning with thumb*)
Then comes the mother, who puts us to bed;
Next comes the brother, who plays with his ball;
And this is the sister, who cuddles her doll;
But this is our baby, the last of all.

Right Hand, Left Hand

This is my right hand,
    (*follow indicated instructions*)
I'll raise it up high.
This is my left hand.
I'll touch the sky.
Right hand, left hand.
Roll them around.
Left hand, right hand,
Pound, pound, pound.

Choo, Choo, Choo

Choo, choo, choo,
    (*slide hands together*)
The train comes down the track.
    (*run fingers down arm*)
Choo, choo, choo,
    (*slide hands together*)
And then it runs right back.
    (*run fingers up arm*)

Little Bunny Rabbits

Little bunny rabbit goes hopping, hopping by.
    (*hold up forefinger and middle finger of right hand to make ears; make hand hop*)
He meets another bunny who says with a sigh,
    (*hold up forefinger and middle finger of left hand to make ears*)
"Will you be my friend?" And the first one says, "I'll say!"
    (*wiggle ears of left hand; wiggle ears of right hand*)
So they hop off together to the meadow to play.
    (*make both hands hop side by side*)

—C. S. Peterson

Here's a Cup

Here's a cup, and here's a cup,
    (*make circle with thumb and forefinger of one hand; extend arm, and repeat*)
And here's a pot of tea.
    (*make fist with other hand and extend thumb for spout*)
Pour a cup, and pour a cup,
    (*tip fist to pour*)
And have a drink with me.
    (*make drinking motions*)

Open Your Hands

Open your hands; close your hands;
  (*follow indicated instructions*)
Give your hands a clap.
Open your hands; close your hands;
And lay them in your lap.

Five Little Kittens

Five little kittens in the yard by their house.
  (*hold up fingers*)
This little kitten chases a mouse.
  (*point to thumb*)
This little kitten catches her tail.
  (*point to forefinger*)
This little kitten stalks a brown snail.
  (*point to middle finger*)
This little kitten has yarn in a heap.
  (*point to ring finger*)
This little kitten is fast asleep.
  (*point to little finger*)
Mother Cat says, "There's milk to eat."
And scat! go the kittens after their treat.
  (*clap hands*)

—C. S. Peterson

Clap Your Hands

Clap your hands, clap your hands,
Clap them just like me.
  (*follow indicated instructions*)
Touch your shoulders, touch your shoulders,
Touch them just like me.
Tap your knees, tap your knees,
Tap them just like me.
Shake your head, shake your head,
Shake it just like me.
Clap your hands, clap your hands,
Now let them silent be.

One, Two, Three, Four, Five

One, two, three, four, five,
  (*hold up hand, count off fingers*)
I caught a fish alive!
  (*catch a fish with both hands*)
Six, seven, eight, nine, ten,
  (*hold up other hand, count off fingers*)
I let him go again.
  (*let the fish go back into the water*)
Why did you let it go?
  (*hold up hands to shoulder shrug, palms up*)
Because it bit my finger so.
  (*hands on hips*)
Which finger did it bite?
The little one upon the right.
  (*hold out pinky of one hand*)

Once I Saw a Little Bird

Once I saw a little bird go hop, hop, hop.
  (*hold one palm out flat while two fingers of the
  other hand hop across it*)
And I cried, "Little bird,
Will you stop, stop, stop?"
I was going to the window to say
"How do you do?"
But he shook his little tail,
And far away he flew.
  (*shake your tail and flap your wings*)

Space Ship

Inside the rocket ship
  (*scrunch down, hands in front with tips of
  fingers touching to form tip of the rocket*)
Just enough room
Here comes the countdown:
10, 9, 8, 7, 6, 5, 4, 3, 2, 1, 0, ZOOM!
  (*jump up and raise arms with rocket tip high
  into the air as if blasting off*)

I Saw a Little Rabbit

I saw a little rabbit go hop, hop, hop.
   (*make rabbit ears with index and middle
      finger of right or left hand, then hop the
      fingers*)
I saw his little ears go flop, flop, flop.
   (*bend the fingers down and then up for flops*)
I saw his little nose go bink, bink, bink.
   (*point to nose three times*)
I saw his little eyes go wink, wink, wink.
   (*blink both eyes three times*)
I said, "Little rabbit, won't you stay?"
   (*turn rabbit ears towards your face*)
Rabbit looked at me and he hopped away!
   (*hop the rabbit away from you*)

Grandma's Spectacles

Here are Grandma's spectacles
   (*make circles around eyes with thumb
      and index finger*)
And here is Grandma's hat;
   (*join both hands at fingertip and put on
      top of head to make a hat*)
And here's the way she folds her hands
   (*place one hand over the other*)
And puts them in her lap.
   (*lay both folded hands in lap*)

The Apple Tree

Away up high in the apple tree,
   (*point up to a tall tree*)
Two red apples smiled at me.
   (*make apples from tightened fists*)
I shook that tree as hard as I could;
   (*pretend to grab tree and shake it*)
Down came the apples,
Mmmmm, were they good!
   (*rub tummy in circular motion*)

Touch Your Nose
(*follow indicated instructions*)

Touch your nose
Touch your chin
That's the way the game begins.
Touch your eyes
Touch your knees
Now pretend you're going to sneeze.
Touch your hair
Touch one ear
Touch your two red lips right here.
Touch your elbows
Where they bend
That's the way the touch game ends.

This Is My Family

This is the father, short and stout.
   (*hold up thumb*)
This is the mother, with children about.
   (*hold up index finger*)
This is the brother, tall you see.
   (*hold up middle finger*)
This is the sister, with a toy on her knee.
   (*hold up ring finger*)
This is the baby sure to grow.
   (*hold up pinky*)
And here is the family all in a row.
   (*hold up all five fingers*)
1-2-3-4-5. (*count the five fingers*)

I Wiggle
(*follow indicated instructions*)

I wiggle my fingers,
I wiggle my toes,
I wiggle my legs,
I wiggle my nose.
Now no more wiggles are left in me.
So I will be quiet and still as can be.

Five Little Ducks

Five little ducks that I once knew
    (*hold up five fingers of either hand*)
Big ones, little ones, skinny ones too.
    (*wiggle fingers*)
But the one little duck with a feather on his back,
    (*hold up one finger*)
All he could do was quack, quack, quack.
    (*put hands together to make a beak and move
    the beak as if to quack it*)

Down to the river they would go,
    (*waddle like a duck would*)
Waddling, waddling, to and fro.
But the one little duck with a feather on his back,
    (*hold up one finger as before*)
All he could do is quack, quack, quack.
    (*motion repeated as before*)

Up from the river they would come,
    (*waddle like a duck*)
With a ho, ho, ho and and hum, hum, hum.
But the one little duck with a feather on his back,
    (*motion as before*)
All he could do is quack, quack, quack.
    (*motion as before*)

Ten Little Ducklings

Ten little ducklings
    (*move hands as if to waddle*)
Dash, dash, dash.
Jumped in the pond
    (*make jumping motion with hands*)
Splash, splash, splash.
When mother duck called them,
"Quack, quack, quack,"
Ten little ducklings
Swam right back.
    (*move hands as if to swim*)

The Beehive

Here is the beehive.
    (*hold hand in a closed fist*)
Where are the bees?
They're hidden away,
Where nobody sees.
Let's count them as they come out of their hive.
    (*open the hand, one finger at a time*)
1-2-3-4-5, they're alive!
    (*fingers fly around as the bees escape*)

Tiny Little Mouse

In a tiny little hole, lives a tiny little mouse.
    (*make a circle with one hand*)
"To you, it is a hole," he says,
"To me, it is a house."
    (*point to self, make house with steepled fingers*)

Houses

Here is a nest for a robin;
    (*cup both hands*)
Here is a hive for a bee;
    (*fit hands together*)
Here is a hole for a bunny;
    (*make circle with finger and thumb*)
And here is a house for ME.
    (*fingertips together to make roof*)

Here Are Mother's Knives and Forks

Here are Mother's knives and forks;
    (*interlock fingers, palms up*)
Here is Mother's table;
    (*interlock fingers, palms down*)
Here is Mother's looking glass;
    (*make peak of two forefingers*)
And here is Baby's cradle.
    (*interlock fingers and rock back and forth*)

Fingerplays for Preschoolers

Five Little Squirrels

Five little squirrels were sitting in a tree,
   (*touch each finger in turn, beginning with
   thumb*)
The first one said, "What do I see?"
The second one said, "I smell a gun."
The third one said, "Let's all run."
The fourth one said, "Let's hide in the shade."
The fifth one said, "I'm not afraid."
BANG went the gun.
   (*clap hands loudly*)
And away they all run.
   (*put hands behind you*)

Dig a Little Hole

Dig a little hole
   (*dig a small hole with your finger in the palm of
   your other hand*)
Plant a little seed
   (*drop a seed into the hole*)
Pour a little water
   (*sprinkle water over seed*)
Pull a little weed
   (*pull weeds and toss over shoulder*)
Chase a little bug
   (*shooing motion with your free hand*)
Heigh-ho, there he goes!
   (*shade eyes and watch it fly away*)
Give a little sunshine
   (*lift up hand to the sun*)
Grow a little rose.
   (*use other hand and raise it up behind the
   other to indicate a growing thing, then
   take a big sniff, eyes closed, smiling*)

My Flower Garden

I dig the ground
   (*dig as with a shovel*)
And plant the seeds
   (*plant seeds into hand*)
And very carefully
Pull the weeds.
   (*pull weeds out of hand*)
With help from the rain
   (*wiggle fingers as falling
   raindrops*)
And the bright, warm sun
   (*form circle with fingers*)
My spring flower garden
   (*hold up outstretched fingers as
   flowers*)
Has begun.

—C. S. Peterson

The Squirrel

Whisky, frisky, hoppity, hop,
Up he goes to the tree top.
   (*bend elbow to make tree, hop one finger
   up the arm*)
Whirly, twirly, round and round,
Down he scampers to the ground.
   (*run around and down arm*)
Furly, curly, what a tail!
Tall as a feather, broad as a sail.
   (*put hands together to make a wide tail*)
Where is his supper? In a shell.
   (*cup hands*)
Snappity, crackity, out it fell.
   (*open hands at bottom*)

Ten Little Fingers

I have ten little fingers
And they belong to me.
> (*hold up both hands, and do motions as
> instructed*)
I can make them do things;
Would you like to see?
I can close them up tight,
I can open them up wide,
I can put them together,
I can make them hide,
I can hold them up high,
I can hold them down low,
I can fold them together,
And hold them just so.

Five Soldiers

Five little soldiers standing in a row.
> (*hold up five fingers of right hand*)
Three stood straight and two stood so.
> (*right thumb holds forefinger down, other
> three fingers stand up*)
Along came the captain, and what do you think?
> (*march forefinger of left hand*)
Up jumped those soldiers as quick as a wink.
> (*thumb and forefinger raise up*)

Shh! Little Mouse

Tiptoe . . . tiptoe, little mouse.
> (*creep forefinger and middle finger along
> forearm*)
Tiptoe quietly through our house.
Be very still;
> (*hold creeping fingers still as if listening*)
Don't make a sound.
> (*raise forefinger to lips*)
Shh! little mouse, the cat prowls around.

—C. S. Peterson

Here's a Bunny

Here's a bunny
> (*hold up first and second fingers
> of right hand*)
With ears so funny
> (*bend the two fingers forward*)
And here is his hole in the ground,
> (*make circle with thumb and forefinger
> of left hand*)
When a noise he hears,
He pricks up his ears,
> (*straighten two fingers of right hand*)
And hop, he goes into the ground.
> (*pop right fingers through the circle*)

Three Little Monkeys

Three little monkeys, swinging in the tree,
> (*three fingers, turned upside down, swinging
> to and fro, as if from a tree*)
Teasing Mr. Crocodile, "You can't catch me!"
> (*thumbs of both hands in ears, taunting*)
Along came Mr. Crocodile, as quiet as can be,
> (*two hands, palms together, gliding in water*)
And SNAPPED that monkey right out of that tree.
> (*snap your palms as if you bite*)

Two little monkeys, swinging in the tree,
> (*two fingers, as before*)
Teasing Mr. Crocodile, "You can't catch me!"
> (*repeat motion as before*)
Along came Mr. Crocodile, as quiet as can be,
And SNAPPED that monkey right out of that tree

One little monkey, swinging in the tree,
> (*one finger, as before*)
Teasing Mr. Crocodile, "You can't catch me."
Along came Mr. Crocodile, as quiet as can be,
And, SNAP!
"Naa, naa, you missed me, now you gotta kiss
me!" (*teasing motion, plus stick out your tongue*)

Little Turtle

There was a little turtle
And he lived in a box.
  (*cup your hands*)
He swam in the puddles,
  (*swimming motions*)
And he climbed on the rocks.
  (*finger of one hand climbing onto
  other hand*)
He snapped at the mosquito,
  (*snap fingers of one hand together*)
He snapped at the flea,
  (*repeat*)
He snapped at the minnow,
  (*repeat*)
And he snapped at me.
  (*snap at your nose*)
He caught the mosquito,
  (*catching motion with both hands*)
He caught the flea,
  (*repeat*)
He caught the minnow,
  (*repeat*)
But he couldn't catch me.
  (*wave the forefinger of one hand back and
  forth*)

Five Green and Speckled Frogs

Five green and speckled frogs
Sitting on a speckled log,
  (*left hand palm down, right hand palm vertical
  to left hand, touching at side of left hand*)
Eating a most delicious bug, yum, yum.
  (*rub tummy and smack lips*)
One jumped into the pool
Where it was nice and cool,
  (*right hand leaps over left to dive into water*)
Now there are four green speckled frogs.
  (*hold up four fingers*)

Four green and speckled frogs, etc.
  (*four fingers, motion as before*)

Three green and speckled frogs, etc.
  (*three fingers, motion as before*)

Two green and speckled frogs, etc.
  (*two fingers, motion as before*)

One green and speckled frog
  (*one finger, motion as before*)
Sitting on a speckled log,
Eating a most delicious bug, yum, yum.
He jumped into the pool
Where it was nice and cool,
Now there are no green speckled frogs.
  (*either make a zero with your fingers,
  or else shrug shoulders, palms up*)

Five Little Pumpkins

Five little pumpkins, sitting on the gate;
  (*one hand behind the other, fingers of hand
  that is behind are popped up with tips as
  pumpkins, sitting on the gate of the side of
  other hand*)
The first one said, "My, it's getting late."
  (*wiggle thumb*)
The second one said,
"There are witches in the air."
  (*wiggle index finger*)
The third one said, "But we don't care."
  (*wiggle middle finger*)
The fourth one said, "Let's run, let's run."
  (*wiggle ring finger*)
The fifth one said, "It's just Halloween fun."
  (*wiggle pinky finger*)
"Woooooo-ooooooo," went the wind.
And out went the lights.
And five little pumpkins rolled out of sight.
  (*roll hand one over the other*)

CHAPTER FIFTEEN

Songs and Singing Activities

Many traditional participation songs provide an opportunity for physical activity and offer a bit of variety in the story program. Since children love to sing and to participate, many look forward to rounds, call and response, and motion songs as their favorite segment of the story program.

One of the best things about using music in your story program is that you do not need to be able to read music, have a good voice, or play a musical instrument in order to be successful with it. Children don't care whether you are a Pavarotti or a Raffi—they just enjoy the activity of singing. Remember, if you can, how carefree you felt belting out a tune as a child. Since you didn't care if you couldn't sing well then, don't give it a second thought now. If you absolutely can't sing and feel adding your voice would somehow ruin your program, then use the song in chant form. Bring enthusiasm to your program, and the rest will follow.

For toddlers, a very simple version of "Eensie Weensie Spider" is fun. For a change of pace, sing it first using a black glove on your hand for a spider puppet. Then remove the glove and have the children perform the hand motions as they sing the song.

For preschoolers, that same "Eensie Weensie Spider" can become a new adventure if you would sing it with different sized spiders in the song. For instance, try "The Great Big Spider" followed by "The Teeny Weeny Spider" and you will get a great response from your audience. Invite the pre-schoolers to come up with their own spiders and try it again. There is an endless supply of spider types from which they may choose (sad spiders, happy spiders, grumpy spiders, silly spiders, etc.). Finally, to finish the spider idea, ask your preschoolers to do "Eensie Weensie Spider" one more time, but this time without speaking or singing the words, just doing the hand motions. Both you and your audience will delight in the effect silence has on this well known ditty.

For the preschool group, there are also a number of good participation songs. Favorites include "The Wheels on the Bus," "B-I-N-G-O," "The Farmer in the Dell," "Did You Feed My Cow?" "I Had a Rooster," and "Mr. Sun." Following directions more easily and having greater motor development, preschoolers participate with vigor.

Children in the primary grades relate to participation songs and still enjoy the variety they bring to story programs. Among their favorites are "Keep Moving," "Eddie Coocha Catcha Camma," "Pawpaw Patch," "Mama Mama," "My Aunt Came Back," and the always-frightening "There Was an Old Woman All Skin and Bones." Primary level children and young adults particularly enjoy songs which challenge their wits, especially those with surprise endings.

Remember all those camp songs and girl and boy scout tunes you learned as a youngster? Use them. Remember your favorite skip or jump rope chants? Use them. Remember the songs your own children have tortured you with on long car trips? Use them. You probably know many more songs than you thought you did if you would only think about it.

For those who require more than your memories to create a music catalog, there are dozens of fabulous sources listed in section six from which you may choose. And don't forget the cassette tape, CD, and video collections at your public library. There are so many wonderful songs for children, of all ages, that you certainly have no excuse for not finding something that suits your interests, talent, or programming tastes.

As you grow more confident in your ability to effectively use music in your story program, consider adapting some of your own or add movement to a traditional song that everyone knows. The tune to "Twinkle, Twinkle, Little Star" works well with all sorts of rhymes and poems, as does "Frere Jacques," "The Battle Hymn of the Republic," and "My Bonnie Lies Over the Ocean." Piggy-back your own words to these tunes and, *presto*, you have a new and fun routine to add to your repertoire.

As Naomi Baltuck, in *Crazy Gibberish* (Linnet, 1993), writes, "Be creative, take a few risks, but most of all, have FUN! Let yourself go and you'll be surprised at what you can do!"

Songs and Singing Activities for Toddlers

I'm Growing
(to the tune of the "It's Raining, It's Pouring")

I'm growing, I'm growing,
> *(start low to the ground, bent over, and rise
> as you say "growing")*

I'm growing up all over.
I'm growing here, I'm growing there.
> *(point to various parts of the body)*

I'm just growing everywhere.
> *(extend arms up and around then back to side)*

Head, Shoulders, Knees, and Toes
(to the tune of "Tavern in the Town")

Head, shoulders, knees, and toes, knees and toes.
> *(touch parts of the body as indicated)*

Head, shoulders, knees, and toes, knees and toes,
Eyes, and ears, and mouth, and nose,
Head, shoulders, knees, and toes, knees and toes.
> *(repeat several times, progressively faster
> for greatest fun)*

The Eensie Weensie Spider

The eensie weensie spider went up the water spout.
> *(make climbing motion with fingers, either up forearm or in air)*

Down came the rain and washed the spider out,
> *(flutter fingers down)*

Out came the sun and dried up all the rain,
> *(form circle with fingers or with entire arms)*

And the eensie weensie spider went up the spout again.
> *(make climbing motions once again)*

I'm a Little Teapot

I'm a little teapot, short and stout.
   (*bounce with knees slightly bent*)
Here is my handle,
   (*one hand on hip*)
Here is my spout.
   (*extend arm out at side*)
When I get all steamed up, hear me shout,
"Tip me over and pour me out."
   (*bend at waist sideways to pour out of spout*)

Down by the Station
(*to the tune of "Little Bunny Foo Foo"*)

Down by the station, early in the morning,
   (*group walks in circle, marching beat*)
See the little puffer bellies all in a row.
See the station master pull the little handle.
Chug, chug, toot, toot, off we go.
   (*raise arm, pull handle twice, marching*)

Ring Around the Rosie
(*group moves in circle, motion as indicated*)

Ring around the rosie, a pocket full of posies,
Ashes, ashes, we all fall down.

Here We Go Round the Mulberry Bush
(*group moves in circle, motion as indicated*)

Here we go round the mulberry bush,
The mulberry bush, the mulberry bush.
Here we go round the mulberry bush,
So early in the morning.

This is the way we wash our hands, etc.

This is the way we wash our face, etc.

This is the way we brush our teeth, etc.

This is the way we wash our clothes, etc.

Songs and Singing Activities for Preschoolers

Wheels on the Bus

The wheels on the bus go round and round,
> (*rotate arms in circles*)
Round and round, round and round.
The wheels on the bus go round and round,
All through the town.

The horn on the bus goes beep, beep, beep, etc.
> (*press imaginary horn or nose on your face*)
The money on the bus goes clink, clink, clink, etc.
> (*drop in imaginary coins*)
The people on the bus go up and down, etc.
> (*sit up straight then slouch back down in place*)
The wipers on the bus go swish, swish, swish, etc.
> (*wave hands*)
The babies on the bus go "whaa, whaa, whaa," etc.
> (*hands to eyes for imaginary baby cry*)
The mothers on the bus go "shhh, shhh, shhh," etc.
> (*index finger to lips*)
The daddys on the bus go read, read, read, etc.
> (*pretend to hold up newspaper, move head left to right*)
The windows on the bus go open and shut, etc.
> (*hands up, palms swivel to the face, then away, then back*)
The driver on the bus says, "Move on back," etc.
> (*point behind you with thumb*)
The headlights on the bus go on and off, etc.
> (*start with two fists held out, then open and close hands*)
> (*end song with first stanza repeated*)

Where Is Thumbkin?

Where is Thumbkin? Where is Thumbkin?
    (*put both hand behind back to start*)
Here I am. Here I am.
    (*show one thumb, then the other*)
How are you today, sir?
    (*bend on thumb, as if it is talking*)
Very well, I thank you.
    (*bend other thumb, as if talking*)
Run and play. Run and play.
    (*put thumbs behind back*)

Where is Pointer? Where is Pointer? etc.
    (*repeat as above, use forefinger*)

Where is Tall Man? Where is Tall Man? etc.
    (*repeat as above, use middle finger*)

Where is Ring Man? Where is Ring Man? etc.
    (*repeat as above, use ring finger*)

Where is Tiny? Where is Tiny? etc.
    (*repeat as above, use pinky finger*)

Where is everyone? Where is everyone?
Here we are. Here we are.
    (*show all fingers on one hand, then the other*)
How are you today, sirs?
    (*bend all fingers on one hand*)
Very well, we thank you.
    (*bend all fingers on the other hand*)
Run and play. Run and play.
    (*put hands behind back*)

Row, Row, Row Your Boat
(*try as a round*)

Row, row, row your boat,
Gently down the stream.
Merrily, merrily, merrily, merrily,
Life is but a dream.

Are You Sleeping?
(*try as a round, sung to tune of "Frere Jacques"*)

Are you sleeping? Are you sleeping?
Brother John. Brother John.
Morning bells are ringing, morning bells are ringing.
Ding, dong, ding. Ding, dong, ding.

If You're Happy and You Know It

If you're happy and you know it,
Clap your hands.
    (*clap your hands twice*)
If you're happy and you know it,
Clap your hands.
    (*clap your hands twice*)
If you're happy and you know it,
Then your face will surely show it.
    (*point to big smile on your face*)
If you're happy and you know it,
Clap your hands.
    (*clap your hands twice*)

If you're happy and you know it,
stomp your feet.
    (*stomp your feet twice*), etc.

If you're happy and you know it,
Shout, "Hurray!"
    (*shout hurray while raising arm in air*), etc.

If you're happy and you know it,
Do all three.
    (*clap hands twice, stomp feet twice, shout
    hurray once with arm movement*), etc.

Do Your Ears Hang Low?
(sung to tune of "Turkey in the Straw")

Do your ears hang low?
Do they wobble to and fro?
Can you tie them in a knot?
Can you tie them in a bow?
Can you throw them over your shoulder,
Like a continental soldier?
Do your ears hang low?

Yes, my ears hang low.
Yes, they wobble to and fro.
I can tie them in a knot.
I can tie them in a bow.
I can throw them over my shoulder,
Like a continental soldier.
Yes, my ears hang low.

Do your ears hang high?
Do they reach up to the sky?
Do they stand up when they're wet?
Do they hang down when they're dry?
Can you wave them at your neighbor,
With a minimum of labor?
Do your ears hang high?

Yes, my ears hang high.
Yes, they reach up to the sky.
Yes, they stand up when they're wet.
Yes, they hang down when they're dry.
I can wave them at my neighbor,
With a minimum of labor.
Yes, my ears hang high.

I Had a Little Chicken
(to the tune of "Turkey in the Straw")

Oh, I had a little chicken
And she wouldn't lay an egg,
So I poured hot water
Up and down her leg.

And the little chicken giggled,
And the little chicken begged,
And my poor old chicken
Laid a hard-boiled egg!

Oh, I had a silly chicken
He went scratching in the dirt,
And he scratched so hard
That his feet, they hurt.
So we bandaged them way up
From the thigh bone to his toe.
And you should have seen that chicken
Do a do-si-do!

Oh, I had a silly chicken
Who liked to eat all day,
She'd start with some bird seed,
And she'd end with marmalade.
And she sang a solacing
Which sounded like a ballad,
And my chicken laid a sandwich
Filled with egg and tuna salad.

The Little Skunk Hole
(sung to tune of "Turkey in the Straw")

Oh, I stuck my head
In the little skunk's hole,
And the little skunk said,
"Well, bless my soul!
Take it out! Take it out!
Remove it!"

Oh, I didn't take it out,
And the little skunk said,
"If you don't take it out,
You'll wish you were dead,
Take it out! Take it out!"
P-U! I removed it!

Baby Bumble Bee
(*traditional*)

Oh, I'm bringing home a baby bumble bee,
Won't my mommy be so proud of me?
I'm bringing home a baby bumble bee,
"Ouch! It stung me!" (*spoken*)

Oh, I'm squishing up the baby bumble bee,
Won't my mommy be so proud of me?
I'm squishing up the baby bumble bee,
"Ohh! It's yucky!" (*spoken*)

Oh, I'm wiping off the baby bumble bee,
Won't my mommy be so proud of me?
I'm wiping off the baby bumble bee,
"Now my mommy won't be mad at me." (*spoken*)

VARIANTS:

Oh, I'm bringing home a little baby turtle,
Won't my mommy really pop her girdle?
I'm bringing home a little baby turtle,
Snappy, snappy, snappy,
"Ohh! It bit me!" (*spoken*)

Oh, I'm bringing home a baby rattlesnake,
Won't my mommy shudder and shake?
I'm bringing home a baby rattlesnake,
Rattle, rattle, rattle,
"Ohh! It bit me!" (*spoken*)

Oh, I'm bringing home a baby crocodile,
Won't my mommy run about a mile?
I'm bringing home a baby crocodile,
Snappy, snappy, snappy,
"Ohh! It bit me!" (*spoken*)

Oh, I'm bringing home a baby dinosaur,
Won't my mommy fall right through the floor?
I'm bringing home a baby dinosaur,
Gobble, gobble, gobble,
"Ohh! it ate me!" (*spoken*)

It Ain't Gonna Rain No More
(*traditional*)

(*chorus*)
It ain't gonna rain no more, no more,
It ain't gonna rain no more.
So how in the heck
Can you wash your neck,
If it ain't gonna rain no more?

Oh, a peanut sat on a railroad track.
It's heart was all a flutter.
Along came the 9:05—
Oops, peanut butter!

There ain't no flies on me, on me,
There ain't no flies on me,
There may be flies
On some of you guys,
But there ain't no flies on me.

A boy stood on a burning deck.
His feet were full of blisters.
He tore his pants on a rusty nail,
And now he wears his sister's.

I woke up in the morning.
I glanced upon the wall.
The roaches and the bedbugs
Were having a game of ball.
The score was six to nothing.
The roaches were ahead.
A bedbug hit a home run
And knocked me out of bed.

Miss Lucy had a baby,
She named him Tiny Tim.
She put him in the bathtub,
To see if he could swim.
He drank up all the water,
He ate up all the soap.
He tried to eat the ducky,
But it wouldn't go down his throat.

Songs and Singing Activities for Primary Level Children

The Noble Duke of York

The noble Duke of York,
He had ten thousand men;
He marched them up to the top of the hill,
   (*stand up*)
And marched them down again.
   (*squat down*)
And when you're up, you're up.
   (*stand up*)
And when you're down, you're down.
   (*squat down*)
And when you're only half-way up,
   (*squat, half-way*)
You're neither up
   (*stand up*)
Nor down.
   (*squat down*)

Note:

There are other ways of performing this song. If you want your audience to remain seated, you can offer this activity variant: the first time singing the song, you leave a blank space every time the word "up" appears; in the second round, omit the word "down"; and the third time around, leave blank spaces for both "up" and "down." This can be a difficult, but hilarious, participation activity that will take some practice on your part before you introduce to your audience.

Pink Pajamas
(to the tune of "Battle Hymn of the Republic")

I wear my pink pajamas
in the summer when it's hot.
I wear my flannel nighties
in the winter when it's not.
And sometimes in the springtime
and sometimes in the fall,
I jump right in between the sheets
with nothing on at all.

Glory, glory, hallelujah;
Glory, glory, what's it to ya.
Balmy breezes blowing through ya.
With nothing on at all.

Mama Mama
(call and response, chanted in cadence)

Leader: Mama mama have you heard?
Group: (Mama mama have your heard?)
Leader: Papa's gonna buy me a mockingbird
Group: (Papa's gonna buy me a mockingbird)
Leader: And if that mockingbird don't sing
      (group repeats all lines as above)
   Papa's gonna buy me a diamond ring
   And if that diamond ring don't shine
   Papa's gonna buy me a fishin' line
   And if that fishin' line gets broke
   Papa's gonna buy me a billy goat
   And if that billy goat runs away
   Papa's gonna spank my boomsyay
   And if my boomsyay gets sore
   Papa's gonna buy me a grocery store
   And if that grocery store burns down
   Papa's gonna buy me an evening gown
   And if that evening gown don't fit
   Papa's gonna say, "I quit! I quit!"

Polly Wolly Doodle
(traditional)

Oh, I went down South for to see my Sal
Sing Polly wolly doodle all the day
My Sal, she is a spunky gal
Sing Polly wolly doodle all the day

(chorus to be repeated between sections)
Fare thee well, fare thee well,
Fare thee well my fairy fay
For I'm going to Louisiana for to see my
   Susyanna
Sing Polly wolly doodle all the day

Oh, my Sal, she is a maiden fair
Sing Polly wolly doodle all the day
With curly eyes and laughing hair
Sing Polly wolly doodle all the day

Behind the barn, down on my knees
Sing Polly wolly doodle all the day
I thought I heard a chicken sneeze
Sing Polly wolly doodle all the day

He sneezed so hard with the whooping cough
Sing Polly wolly doodle all the day
He sneezed his head and the tail right off
Sing Polly wolly doodle all the day

Oh, a grasshopper sittin' on a railroad track
Sing Polly wolly doodle all the day
A-pickin' his teeth with a carpet tack
Sing Polly wolly doodle all the day

Oh, I went to bed but it wasn't any use
Sing Polly wolly doodle all the day
My feet stuck out like a chicken roost
Sing Polly wolly doodle all the day.

I Went Into the Water

(to the tune of "Battle Hymn of the Republic")

Oh, I went into the water,
And I got my feet all wet.
I went into the water,
And I got my feet all wet.
I went into the water,
And I got my feet all wet.
But I didn't get my *(clap, clap)* wet—yet.

Oh, I went into the water,
And I got my ankles wet.
I went into the water,
And I got my ankles wet.
I went into the water,
And I got my ankles wet.
But I didn't get my *(clap, clap)* wet—yet.

(and so on, up to your head)

I went into the water, but I didn't get it wet.
I went into the water, but I didn't get it wet.
I went into the water, but I didn't get it wet.
I didn't get my camera wet.

Eddie Coocha Catcha Camma

(tell audience to say "WHO?" each time you say the boy's name in the song)

Eddie Coocha Catcha Camma Tosa Nara Tosa
Noka Samma Camma Wacky Brown,
(Who?)
Eddie Coocha Catcha Camma Tosa Nara Tosa
Noka Samma Camma Wacky Brown,
(Who?)
Fell into the well, fell into the well,
Fell into the deep dark well.

Susie Jones, was playing in her yard,
Saw him fall, and went inside to tell her ma that,
Eddie Coocha Catcha Camma Tosa Nara Tosa
Noka Samma Camma Wacky Brown,
(Who?)
Eddie Coocha Catcha Camma Tosa Nara Tosa
Noka Samma Camma Wacky Brown,
(Who?)
Fell into the well, fell into the well,
Fell into the deep dark well.

Susie's mom, was baking crackling bread,
Called old Joe,
And told old Joe what Susie said that,
Eddie Coocha Catcha Camma Tosa Nara Tosa
Noka Samma Camma Wacky Brown,
(Who?)
Eddie Coocha Catcha Camma Tosa Nara Tosa
Noka Samma Camma Wacky Brown,
(Who?)
Fell into the well, fell into the well,
Fell into the deep dark well.

Then old Joe, he set aside the phone,
Grabbed his cane,
And hobbled into town to tell them,
Eddie Coocha Catcha Camma Tosa Nara Tosa
Noka Samma Camma Wacky Brown,
(Who?)
Eddie Coocha Catcha Camma Tosa Nara Tosa
Noka Samma Camma Wacky Brown,
(Who?)
Fell into the well, fell into the well,
Fell into the deep dark well.

Then they came, the people from the town,
What a shame,
It took so long to say his name that,
Eddie Coocha Catcha Camma Tosa Nara Tosa
Noka Samma Camma Wacky Brown,
(Who?)
Eddie Coocha Catcha Camma Tosa Nara Tosa
Noka Samma Camma Wacky Brown,
(Who?)
Fell into the well, fell into the well,
Fell into the well and DROWNED!

Nobody Likes Me
(*traditional*)

Nobody likes me,
Everybody hates me,
I'm gonna eat some worms.

Long, slim, slimy ones, short, fat, fuzzy ones,
Ooey, gooey, gooey, gooey worms.

First you get a bucket,
Then you get a shovel,
Oh, how they wiggle and squirm.

Long, slim, slimy ones, short, fat, fuzzy ones,
Ooey, gooey, gooey, gooey worms.

Then you pull their heads off,
Then you suck their guts out,
Oh, how they wiggle and squirm.

Long, slim, slimy ones, short, fat, fuzzy ones,
Ooey, gooey, gooey, gooey worms.

Down goes the first one,
Then down goes the second one,
Oh, how they wiggle and squirm.

Long, slim, slimy ones, short, fat, fuzzy ones,
Ooey, gooey, gooey, gooey worms.

Up comes the first one,
Up comes the second one,
Oh, how they wiggle and squirm.

Long, slim, slimy ones, short, fat, fuzzy ones,
Ooey, gooey, gooey, gooey worms.

Everybody likes me,
Nobody hates me,
Why did I eat those worms?

Long, slim, slimy ones, short, fat, fuzzy ones,
Ooey, gooey, gooey, gooey worms.

(*final verse and refrain*)
Chop up their heads and
Squeeze out their juice,
And throw their tails away.

Nobody knows how I survive,
On worms three times a day!

CHAPTER SIXTEEN

Physical Activities and Games

Story programs for young children, of necessity, must include some types of physical activities, for neither the two-year-olds nor the eight-year-olds can hold still for very long periods of time. Their need for stretching and wiggling can be very distracting to you and to the other participants.

You can easily solve the problem, however, by structuring physical activities into your story program plan. Besides adding variety to the program, they can satisfy the children's need to contribute, introduce children to lesser known parts of the vast oral tradition, provide a vehicle for allowing immature muscles to stretch and move without interrupting the story program, and offer opportunities for children to share enjoyable experiences.

When introducing physical activities and games to your group, pay careful attention to keeping the directions as simple as possible. You don't want the explanation to last longer than the activity, so practice how and what you say before you do them "live." In addition, if you find that your planned routine falls flat, chalk it up to the weather and try it again another time. If, after several attempts, your best laid plans still run amuck, put that gem aside for a long while. Don't throw it out quite yet, for one day you may figure out why it failed for you.

Most importantly, don't take those little failures personally. Keep tying new material. Keep finding fresh approaches. Keep finding ways to recharge your creative batteries. Keep allowing yourself to have fun with your program. And if you are having fun, then you know everyone is too.

As much as possible, demonstrate the routine before you launch into the full version. This will give everyone a chance to keep up and feel involved. If you notice that some or most of your group hasn't yet caught on, it is perfectly appropriate to halt your forward motion and start again. Don't single anyone out for tutoring, however, just offer some additional group-wide instructions.

Use a great deal of eye contact in this portion of your program. Sometimes, you will find that you can actually lead your group through the routine by a simple nod of the head. For instance, if you notice an individual (adult or child) that looks puzzled but attempting the activity, a smile and a nodding "yes" will let them know they are on the right track, without you having to stop what you are doing to speak to them.

Included in this chapter on physical activities and games are dozens of full-body stretches and action rhymes for toddlers to primary level, as well as games for older children—knock knock jokes, tongue twisters, word games, and teasers. While the activities are divided by age group, you may discover that some things work better with older or younger children. The divisions in this chapter are meant as recommendations only, so feel free to mix and match as you go.

Don't forget to be exaggerated in gesture and

facial expression and diverse in your choice of sound effects. Feel free to make up tunes to tuneless action rhymes and change the names to incorporate those of the children in your program. Nothing, repeat, nothing here is carved in stone. It's *your* program, after all.

Physical Activities and Games for Toddlers

Teddy Bear, Teddy Bear
(*standing in place, do the motions as indicated*)

Teddy Bear, Teddy Bear, turn around;
Teddy Bear, Teddy Bear, touch the ground;
Teddy Bear, Teddy Bear, show your shoe;
Teddy Bear, Teddy Bear, that will do.

Teddy Bear, Teddy Bear, go upstairs;
Teddy Bear, Teddy Bear, say your prayers;
Teddy Bear, Teddy Bear, turn out the light;
Teddy Bear, Teddy Bear, say good night.

Mother and Father and Uncle John

Mother and Father and Uncle John,
    (*while seated, hold reins of horse
    and bounce*)
Went to town one by one.
Mother fell off.
    (*gently fall over to right side, then up*)
Father fell off.
    (*gently fall over to left side, then up*)
But Uncle John went on and on.
    (*back to holding reins and bouncing*)

Flying Man

Flying man, flying man, up in the sky,
    (*toddlers pretend to be airplanes*)
Where are you going to, flying so high?
Over the mountain, and over the seas,
    (*zoom around in small circles*)
Flying man, flying man, won't you take me?
    (*toddlers hug themselves*)

Clap Your Hands
(*follow motions as indicated*)

Clap your hands, clap your hands,
Clap them just like me.

Touch your shoulders, touch your shoulders,
Touch them just like me.

Tap your knees, tap your knees,
Tap them just like me.

Pat your tummy, pat your tummy,
Pat it just like me.

Shake your head, shake your head,
Shake it just like me.

Clap your hands, clap your hands,
Now let them silent be.

Elephant Goes Like This and That

An elephant goes like this and that.
    (*stamp feet*)
He's terribly big,
    (*raise arms high*)
And he's terribly fat.
    (*spread arms wide*)
He has no fingers,
    (*wiggle fingers on both hands*)
He has no toes,
    (*touch toes*)
But goodness gracious, what a nose!
    (*stretch arms out, hands clasped, to indicate
    long elephant nose*)

Jack Be Nimble

Jack be nimble, Jack be quick.
Jack jumped over the candlestick.
(*child should jump in place on word "over"*)

We Can
(*motions as indicated*)

We can jump, jump, jump, jump
We can wave, wave, wave, wave
We can clap, clap, clap, clap
We can hop, hop, hop
We can turn, turn, turn, turn
We can stretch, stretch, stretch, stretch,
We can bend and touch our toes
We can stand and touch our nose
We can sit, sit, sit, sit,
Sit down slow.

Monkey See, Monkey Do
(*motions as indicated*)

When you clap, clap, clap your hands,
The monkey claps, claps, claps his hands.
Monkey see and monkey do,
Monkey does the same as you.

When you stamp, stamp, stamp your feet,
The monkey stamps, stamps, stamps his feet.
Monkey see and monkey do,
Monkey does the same as you.

When you turn, turn, turn around,
The monkey turns, turns, turns around.
Monkey see and monkey do,
Monkey does the same as you.

When you jump, jump, jump up high,
The monkey jumps, jumps, jumps up high.
Monkey see and monkey do,
Monkey does the same as you.

Hands on Shoulders
(*motions as indicated*)

Hands on shoulders, hands on knees,
Hands behind you, if you please.
Touch your hair,
Now your toes,
Hands up high in the air.
Down at your sides, now touch your hair.
Hands up high, as before.
Now clap your hands, one, two, three, four!

Here We Go Up

Here we go up, up, up,
  (*raise arms high above head*)
Here we go down, down, down.
  (*lower arms to the floor*)
Here we go up, up, up,
  (*raise arms high above head*)
Here we go down, down, down.
  (*lower arms to the floor*)

Look At What I Can Do
(*motions as indicated*)

Look at all the things I can do:
I can reach above my head,
And bend and touch my shoe.
I can sway from side to side,
And march my feet in place.
I can wiggle all my fingers,
And touch my nose upon my face.
I can make a circle with my hand,
And point to the clouds way up,
I can clap my hands real loud,
And waddle like a duck.
So many things that I can do,
So many things I know,
And now its time to sit right down,
And observe the story show.

Physical Activities and Games for Preschoolers

Head and Shoulders, Baby

Head and shoulders, baby—one, two, three.
  (*hands to head and shoulders, then clap three times*)
Head and shoulders, baby—one, two, three.
Head and shoulders, head and shoulders,
Head and shoulders, baby—one, two, three.

Shoulders, hips, baby—one, two, three.
  (*motion as indicated, then clap three times*)
Shoulders, hips, baby—one, two, three.
Shoulders, hip, shoulders, hips,
Shoulders, hips, baby—one, two, three.

Hips, knees, baby—one, two, three.
  (*motion as indicated, then clap three times*)
Hips, knees, baby—one, two, three.
Hips, knees, hips, knees,
Hips, knees, baby—one, two, three.

Knees, toes, baby—one, two, three.
  (*motion as indicated, then clap three times*)
Knees, toes, baby—one, two, three.
Knees, toes, knees, toes,
Knees, toes, baby—one, two, three.

Touch the ground, baby—one, two, there.
  (*motion as indicated, then clap three times*)
Touch the ground, baby—one, two, there.
Touch the ground, touch the ground,
Touch the ground, baby—one, two, there.

Sit down, baby—one, two, three.
  (*sit down slowly, clap three times*)
Sit down, baby—one, two, three.
Sit down, sit down, sit down,
Sit down, baby—one, two, three.

Peanut Butter and Jelly
(*use as chant, motions as indicated*)

First you take the peanuts
And your crush 'em, you crush 'em.
First you take the peanuts
And your crush 'em, you crush 'em.

(*refrain*)
For your peanut,
Peanut butter, and jelly.
Peanut, peanut butter, and jelly.

Then you take the grapes
And you squish 'em, you squish 'em.
Then you take the grapes
And you squish 'em, you squish 'em.

Then you take the bread
And you spread it, you spread it.
Then you take the bread
And you spread it, you spread it.

Then you take your sandwich
And you eat it, you eat it.
Then you take your sandwich
And you eat it, you eat it.

'Cause it's good, peanut butter and jelly.
Good peanut butter, and jelly!

First you take the peanuts and you crush 'em,
Then you take the grapes and you squish 'em,
Then you take the bread and you spread it,
Then you take the sandwich and you eat it.

'Cause it's good, peanut butter and jelly.
Good peanut butter, and jelly!

Pepper

Pepper was a small black kitten. Each day as he awakened, he would arch his back and stretch (*stretch as though waking up*). Then he would stretch his legs: first the front left leg (*stretch front left leg*), then the front right leg (*stretch front right leg*), next the back left leg (*stretch back left leg*), and last the back right leg (*stretch back right leg*). Then he would lap up some milk for breakfast (*pretend to lap up milk*).

Pepper liked to play. Sometimes he would play Chase-My-Tail (*run in a circle*). Sometimes he would play Bat-the-Ball (*juggle ball with hands*). And sometimes he would play See-How-High-I-Can-Jump (*jump up several times*).

When Pepper grew tired, he would carefully give himself a bath (*lick paws and wash*). Then he would curl up in a furry, purry heap and go to sleep (*curl up and pretend to sleep*).

Open, Shut Them
(*Perform as game and instruct the group that they must "do as you say, and not as you do" or you will trick them. Then, as you do the game, put your hands on any other part of your body than the one you say.*)

Open, shut them, open, shut them,
    (*open and close both hands held in front*)
Give a little clap, clap, clap,
    (*clap three times*)
Open shut them, open shut them,
    (*as before*)
Put them on your knees.
    (*put your hands somewhere else, say on your head, in order to trick the group*)

    (*continue with various parts of the body until they are told to "fold them in your lap"*)

Hi, My Name Is Joe
(*perform as chant, follow commas for beat*)

Hi! My name is Joe, and I work, in a button factory, I've got a wife, three kids, and a dog.
One day, my boss came by, to see me,
And he said, "Joe, are you busy?"
And I said, "No."
And he said, "Turn this button with your right hand."
    (*turning motion with right hand*)

Hi! My name is Joe, and I work, in a button factory, I've got a wife, three kids, and a dog.
One day, my boss came by, to see me,
And he said, "Joe, are you busy?"
And I said, "No."
And he said, "Turn this button with your left hand."
    (*continue from above, plus begin turning motion with left hand*)

Hi! My name is Joe, and I work, in a button factory, I've got a wife, three kids, and a dog.
One day, my boss came by, to see me,
And he said, "Joe, are you busy?"
And I said, "No."
And he said, "Turn this button with your left foot."
    (*continue from above, plus begin turning motion with left foot*)

    (*continue chant, until group is turning buttons with right and left hands, right and left feet, and mouth, until the final verse*)

Hi! My name is Joe, and I work, in a button factory, I've got a wife, three kids, and a dog.
One day, my boss came by, to see me,
And he said, "Joe, are you busy?"
And I said, "YES."

Five Little Monkeys

Five little monkeys jumping on the bed,
   (*left hand palm up, five fingers of right hand
   jumping on the left palm*)
One fell off and bumped his head.
   (*one finger pointed, jumps off palm and down*)
Mama called the doctor and the doctor said,
   (*indicate phone to the ear*)
"NO more monkeys jumping on the bed!"
   (*wag finger as if tsk, tsk, tsk*)

Four little monkeys jumping on the bed, etc.

Three little monkeys jumping on the bed, etc.

Two little monkeys jumping on the bed, etc.

One little monkey jumping on the bed,
He fell off and bumped his head.
Mama called the doctor and the doctor said,
"That's what you get for jumping on the bed!"

Just Like Me

(*this game requires that your group repeat the
phrase "just like me" following every line you say*)

I walked upon the porch,   (*just like me*)
I opened the front door,
I climbed up the stairs,
I walked down a hallway,
I went into a big room,
I walked over to the dresser,
I looked into the mirror,
I saw a monkey,
Just like you?

Pete and Repeat

(*repeat this one and drive them crazy*)

Pete and Repeat were sitting on the fence.
Pete fell off. Who was left?

The Old Dead Horse

(*tell the group to repeat what you say, but say
one number higher each time*)

I saw an old dead horse. I one it.
I saw an old dead horse. I two it.
I saw an old dead horse. I three it.
I saw an old dead horse. I four it.
I saw an old dead horse. I five it.
I saw an old dead horse. I six it.
I saw an old dead horse. I seven it.
I saw an old dead horse. I eight it.
You ate it? Yuck!

Mary Mack

(*perform as clap rhyme*)

Miss Mary Mack, Mack, Mack,
All dressed in black, black, black
With silver button, buttons, buttons
All down her back, back, back

She asked her mother, mother, mother
For fifty cents, cents, cents
To see the elephants, elephants, elephants
Jump the fence, fence, fence

They jumped so high, high, high
They touched the sky, sky, sky
And never came back, back, back
Til the fourth of July, ly, ly.

Bear Hunt

(instruct your group to do what you do and say, after you say and do it)

We're going on a bear hunt! Ready? Let's go!

(slap legs to make the sound of walking)

Leader:	Oh, look!
Group:	(Oh, look!)
Leader:	I see a bridge!
	(right hand to forehead)
Group:	(I see a bridge!)
	(mimic)
Leader:	Can't go under it.
	(make under motion with hand)
Group:	(Can't go under it.)
	(mimic)
Leader:	Can't go around it.
	(make a motion as if to go around)
Group:	(Can't go around it.)
	(mimic)
Leader:	Gotta go over it!
	(mimic)
Group:	(Gotta go over it!)
	(mimic)

(make clicking noises with mouth as you pantomime your hands walking up an inclined bridge and down the other side)

(slap legs again to simulate walking)
Oh, look! I see a river.
Can't go over it. Can't go around it.
Gotta swim through it.
(make swimming motions with both arms and some sort of sound effect for swimming in the river, then back to slapping legs to simulate walking)
Oh, look! I see a swamp.
Can't go over it.
Can't go around it. Gotta go through it!

(frown and move your hands as if trudging through a sticky swamp, make raspberry sound at each footfall, then back to slapping legs)

Oh, look! I see a fence.
Can't go under it.
Can't go around it. Gotta climb over it!
(climb over fence with both hands, making some sort of sound effect, then back down the other side, return to slapping legs)

Oh, look! I see a wheat field.
Can't go under it. Can't go around it.
Gotta go through it!
(wave both hands back and forth, side to side, making a swishing sound with your mouth, then return to slapping legs)

Oh, look! I see a cave.
Oh, it's cold in here.
    (hug your body tight and shiver)
Oh, it's dark in here.
    (cover your eyes with one hand)
But I feel something warm.
    (reach out with one hand to feel this)
And I feel something big.
    (reach up with one hand to feel this)
And I feel something furry!
    (reach out and pat furry thing)
Oh, IT'S A BEAR!!!
    (yell and start slapping legs very fast to
    simulate running)

(repeat the entire hunt backwards, very fast, including sound effects, until . . .)
Whew! That was a close call! Safe and sound!
    (wipe your brow of imaginary sweat)

Physical Activities and Games for Primary Level

Little Elf's Adventure

Little Elf sat up in her rose petal bed (*sit hunched up with head on arms, then sit up straight*). She rubbed her eyes sleepily, yawned, and stretched (*rub eyes, yawn, and stretch*). Then she climbed out of bed. She carefully washed her face and her pointed ears and then she brushed her hair (*pretend to wash face and brush hair*). She put on her tiny elfin shirt and pants and pulled on her slippers with the curled-up toes (*pretend to dress self*). She ate her breakfast and brushed her teeth (*pretend to eat and to brush teeth*).

Little Elf looked at herself very carefully in the mirror. "Yes," she said, "I look like a fine, brave elf. Today's my day for an adventure." And with that she walked outside (*slap legs in walking rhythm*) closing the door behind her (*clap hands*). She walked (*slap legs*) through the grass on her own little elfin path, stopping now and then to peer (*place hand above eyes as if looking into the distance*) through the tall grass as she looked for her adventure. Once she saw a mouse asleep under a toadstool, but that was no adventure. Then she saw a squirrel burying nuts in a hole, but that was

no adventure. Then she saw a huge brown shoe, and that was no adventure, until——she saw that a human child was wearing that shoe!

She stood stock still staring with wide eyes and open mouth (*look surprised*). Never had she dreamed that a human child would be so large. She stood there ever so still and looked at that human child from brown shoes to brown eyes. Never had she dreamed that a human child would stand so very tall!

Suddenly, she tiptoed (*tap legs lightly*) backward through the grass until she reached her path. She turned and ran, (*slap legs very fast*) faster and faster until she arrived at her own home. She went inside and closed the door (*clap hands*). She pulled off her slippers with the curled up toes (*pretend to remove shoes*). She took off her tiny elfin shirt and pants (*pretend to undress*). She climbed back into her rose petal bed and closed her eyes (*sit hunched up with head on arms*). "I'm going to start this day all over," she said, "I'm not in the mood for an adventure after all!"

—C. S. Peterson

Tongue Twisters
(*practice these many times before you do them live*)

How Much Wood?

How much wood would a woodchuck chuck
If a woodchuck could chuck wood?
A woodchuck would chuck
All the wood he could chuck,
If a woodchuck could chuck wood.

Peter Piper

Peter Piper picked a peck of pickled peppers.
A peck of pickled peppers, Peter Piper picked.
If Peter Piper picked a peck of pickled peppers,
Where's the peck of pickled peppers that Peter Piper picked?

Knott and Shott

Knott and Shott fought a duel.
Knott was shot and Shott was not.
It was better to be Shott than Knott.

A Fly and a Flea

A fly and a flea flew up in a flue.
Said the fly to the flea, "What shall we do?"
"Let's fly," said the flea. "Let's flee," said the fly.
So they flew up a flaw in the flue to the sky.

Tree Toad

A tree toad loved a she-toad
Who lived up in a tree,
He was two-toed tree toad
But a three-toed toad was she.
The two-toed tree toad tried to win
The three-toed she-toad's heart,
For the two-toed tree toad loved the ground
That the three-toed tree toad trod.
But the two-toed tree toad tried in vain,
He couldn't please her whim.
From her tree toad bower,
With her three-toed power,
The she-toad vetoed him.

Betty Botter

Betty Botter bought some butter but, she said,
"This butter's bitter. If I put it in my batter, it will
make my batter bitter. But a bit of better butter
will make my batter better." So she bought a bit of
better butter, better than her bitter butter, and she
put it in her batter and the batter was not bitter. So
twas better Betty Botter bought a bit of better
butter.

Night Light

You've no need to light a night light
On a light night like tonight,
For a night light's light's a slight light,
and tonight's a night that's light.

When a night's light, like tonight's light,
It's really not quite right
To light night lights with their slight lights,
On a light night like tonight.

The Tutor

A tutor who tooted a flute, tried to teach two
tooters to toot.
Said the two to the tutor, "Is it harder to toot, or
tutor two tooters to toot?"

Single Lines

Fluffy finches flying fast.

Unique New York.

Lucy loosened Suzi's shoes and Suzi's shoes
stayed loose while Suzi snoozed.

Fruit float. (*repeat three times, quickly*)

Martin met a mob of marching munching monkeys.

Toy boat. (*say three times quickly*)

The bootblack brought the black book back.

Sally sells seashells by the seashore.

Round and round the rough and ragged rock the
ragged rascal ran.

Seven silly sheep slowly shuffled south.

The sixth sheik's sixth sheep's sick.

Shallow ships show some signs of sinking.

Three tree toads tied together tried to trot to town.

A big black bug bled black blood.

Six thick thistle sticks.

Frank threw Fred three free throws.

Old oily Ollie oils old oily autos.

A noise annoys an oyster, but a noisy noise annoys an oyster more.

Whether the Weather

Whether the weather be fine, or whether the weather be not, whether the weather be cold, or whether the weather be hot, we'll weather the weather, whatever the weather, whether we like or not.

"KNOCK KNOCK." "WHO'S THERE?":

Ima.
Ima tired of knocking. Let me in!

Ida.
If Ida known you were coming, Ida baked a cake.

Oswald.
Oswald my bubble gum.

Duane.
Duane the tub. I dwowning!

Atish.
Bless you.

Japan.
Japan was full of brownies. Who ate them all?

Little old lady.
I didn't know that you could yodel.

Tick.
Tick em up. I'm a tongue tied towboy.

Alaska.
Alaska one more time. Let me in!

Pencil.
Pencil fall down if you don't wear a belt.

Who.
Is there an echo in here?

sssssss.
Make up your mind, are you a snake or an owl?

Rude interrupting cow.
(*interrupting*) MOOOO!

Zsa Zsa.
Zsa Zsa last knock knock I every want to hear!

Think of a Number

(This is more of a trick than a game, but it works every time! Address these instructions to your entire group.)

Think of a number. Any number at all. Got it?
Now add eight. Got it?
Now subtract two. Okay?
Now close your eyes.
Dark, isn't it?

Herman, the Magic Flea

(ask for a volunteer for this one)

Do you believe in Herman, the Magic Flea?
(hold out palm of hand to show "Herman")

No? Well, you just watch.
(pretend to set Herman down on table or chair, then extend your right index finger and set it near where you have put Herman)

Jump over my finger Herman! Come on! Oh, he didn't make it. Must be too heavy with his coat on. Here, will you hold Herman's coat?
(pass Herman's imaginary coat to your volunteer, who will probably take it)

Jump over my finger Herman! Come on! Oh, he didn't make it. Must still be too heavy with those jeans on. Here, will you hold Herman's jeans?
(pass Herman's imaginary jeans to your volunteer)

Jump over my finger Herman! Come on! Alight! He did it! He did it!
Now do you believe in Herman, the Magic Flea?
(volunteer will still say no)
Then why are you holding his coat and pants????

My Aunt Came Back

(to the tune of "How Dry I Am")

Leader:	My aunt came back
Group:	(My aunt came back)
Leader:	From old Japan
Group:	(From old Japan)
Leader:	And brought with her
Group:	(And brought with her)
Leader:	A paper fan
Group:	(A paper fan)

(wave right hand as if using a paper fan)

My aunt came back from County Claire
And brought with her a rocking chair.
　　　(add motion of rocking body back and forth)

My aunt came back from old Juneau
And brought with her a fine yo-yo
　　　(add motion of left hand moving up and down)
or
My aunt came back from London piers
And brought with her some pinking sheers
　　　(add movement of left hand using scissors)

My aunt came back from old Nepal
And brought with her a ping-pong ball
　　　(add motion of head bouncing side to side)

My aunt came back from South Pole loop
And brought with her a hula-hoop
　　　(add motion of hip rotation)

My aunt came back from old Hong Kong
And brought with her some chewing gum
　　　(add motion of exaggerated chewing)

My aunt came back from the New York zoo
And brought with her some nuts like you!!
　　　(point to audience)

PART FIVE

APPRAISAL AND PROBLEM SOLVING

CHAPTER SEVENTEEN

Judging Your Success

While you most certainly can determine for yourself how you are doing in your programs based on immediate audience response—whether they seem happy and involved or disinterested and restless—it is still extremely important to reach beyond your own subjective experience into more objective avenues of program evaluation. In this way, you will be supplementing your knowledge with statistics and commentary culled from sources outside of yourself, and therefore considered as reliable, if not more so, than your insight alone can afford.

One of the simplest ways to obtain comments from your audiences is to permanently install or temporarily set up a comment box somewhere in your program room or children's department. Provide preformatted cards and pencils so that no one will have to search for writing tools and paper in order to participate. Try not to hover anywhere near the box as this might intimidate those who wish to anonymously share their views and suggestions. A sample comment card is included on the following page.

Comment cards work well if you are interested in short personal statements regarding your audience's satisfaction level. They can additionally be used as the basis of a mailing list, if you provide space for the adult to volunteer this information. Don't be surprised if you receive some fake cards that appear to be filled out by children who are having fun. Keep these completed cards as well,

for they may offer you insight into the success or failure of this form of solicitation. The cards filled out by children will also make a humorous addition to your program diary log, detailed in chapter one.

In addition to comment cards, you might consider taking surveys of your audience on a periodic basis. Surveys are like extended comment cards that ask various questions relating to audience satisfaction and ideas for further enhancement of the story program experience, such as preferred times, dates, and length of programs, plus issues relating to program content. Surveys may be the only way you have to obtain such detailed opinions regarding audience satisfaction.

Surveys can be tricky things, and careful thought must be given to not only the questions you ask but the way in which you ask them. The last thing you want is a manipulated result which would negate the value of the outcome. You should consult several sources regarding survey construction techniques before you attempt to create one for use in your programs. Contact other librarians or professional storytellers for advice regarding their use of surveys if you want the straight scoop. Most will also be happy to share their own versions with you which could greatly reduce the time and effort involved with starting from scratch.

Of course, it goes without saying, that you should be keeping attendance statistics for every program you offer. If you do a great deal of programming, consider designing a simple attendance log that can be kept either near the program materials or in the program room for ease of use. Include columns for date and time of program (including beginning and ending times), type of program presented, attendance broken down by developmental level, storyteller initials, and information relating to formal group attendance. A sample attendance form is included on the last page of this chapter.

You may need to total your figures on a monthly basis for reporting purposes, so make this form large enough for at least thirty days of events. Don't ever rely on your memory to re-create attendance figures or you will be short-changing both yourself and your program.

Your coworkers represent another avenue of feedback that you may not have considered. If you ask for their opinions, however, you must be open to their comments, both constructive and otherwise. Sometimes, this type of feedback is the most valuable of all, for who else but your coworkers can evaluate your program from the position of knowing what you do and why you do it.

You should also regularly self-evaluate your program. A handy check sheet of areas to consider should include all of the following questions:

1. Did the audience listen well?
2. Did you convey the sequence of events?
3. Did you speak clearly and distinctly?
4. Did you maintain eye contact throughout?
5. Did your gestures feel natural to you?
6. Were there many interruptions?
7. If so, how did you handle them?
8. Did your stories feel age appropriate?
9. Was your audience able to "keep up"?
10. Did you remember all that you wanted?
11. Would you change anything for next time?
12. If so, what specifically would you change?
13. How was your pacing?
14. How was your voice control?
15. Were you nervous? How much? Why?

Consider program evaluation as a tool for ensuring that you are offering the best story program possible. Think of the process of feedback as an opportunity to learn and improve you skills, instead of a threat to your professional sense and talents. Sometimes, as storytellers, we are so close to our programs that we lose sight of our impact or fail to notice important details. Allow yourself the luxury of not going it alone. Lastly, don't be afraid to discover that *you are* making a difference!

STORY PROGRAM COMMENT CARD

Which type of program did you attend (circle one)? Infant Toddler Preschooler
School Age   Family

How would you rate your overall impression (circle one)? EXCELLENT GOOD
FINE   NEEDS WORK   TERRIBLE

What additional comments do you have regarding your visit to this story program?

_____

_____

_____

Feel free to use the back of this card for additional comments.   Thank You!

STORY PROGRAM ATTENDANCE LOG										
Date	start time end time	prog type	baby	tod	ch	YA	Adu	ind.	grps	st

GROUP NAMES/DATE OF ATTENDANCE	

CHAPTER EIGHTEEN

Tricky Questions and Crowd Control

Unexpected things are going to happen to you in your story programs, things for which you could never have prepared or predicted. From interruptions to wacky questions posed by audience members, your safest route is to take it all in stride. Try not to be discouraged by the unbelievably bad behavior of some adults and don't let heckling youth get your goat. If you can at least get to the place in you own mind where you are undaunted by what is thrown at you, figuratively and literally, you will have won this battle of control.

Interruptions may come from many differing sources, some preventable, some inevitable, some inadvertent. In the preventable category of interruptions we find: ringing cellular phones, beeping wrist watches and pagers, squeaky doors, broken chairs, unsteady book displays, uncomfortable room temperatures, dirty story spaces, and damaged story materials.

These interruptions are preventable with a little preparation and a lot of foresight. It goes without saying that you should conduct a walk-through of the program space well before each program. This affords you the opportunity to catch any problems and get them fixed, removed, or adjusted before the public is invited to enter. Interruptions caused by cellular phones, pagers, and watches can be circumvented with signage or pre-show announcements regarding their prohibition. If you don't make an effort to remind your audience that they should turn these noisemakers off, you have

no excuse for being disturbed by them. Once they are set off, it is really too late to do anything about it; the damage has been done.

In the inevitable column of interruptions you will find emergency bathroom breaks, cranky children, smelly diapers, nursing mothers, crying babies, and disinterested children in programs either below or above their level of development. While these events are labeled inevitable, there are still a couple of things you can do to try to prevent them from happening, although they do not always work—the phrase "the best laid plans of mice and men oft go awry" is a cliche for a very good reason!

Include in your preshow announcements a word or two about these "whatifs" in order to provide the adults in your programs with some guidelines in case they find themselves so burdened. Each adult's sense of what is too much and what may disrupt is different, so setting some across-the-board levels of expectation is not at all inappropriate and, in fact, may be welcomed.

Then there are those interruptions that will startle you by their rudeness. These include discourteous adults, paper shuffling teachers, gossiping parents, unruly or fighting children, picture-taking teachers, sarcastic youth, inattentive caregivers, flirting fathers, and snoring parents. These interruptions fall in the inadvertent category because you must trust that these people don't mean you any harm or intend to stop your program cold in its tracks, even though they still have that effect. In fact, these are the types of incidents that you probably feel warrant you actually halting the forward movement of your story time and address the problem with immediacy. You know in your heart that you can't go on with that going on, yet you are puzzled and frustrated by not knowing the "right way" to handle this disruption.

Unfortunately, there is no one right response to these pesky problems. These are the types of interruptions you are going to have to learn how to handle as you encounter them, by making mistakes and finding your own way through them.

A few suggestions regarding general approach may assist you in this area.

1. Don't provoke the person by copping an attitude of complete disgust. It will only make you look bad and them look victimized, even when the truth of it is the exact opposite. Stay calm, take a deep breath, and internally adjust your focus so that this problem magically doesn't bother you any more.

2. Fighting children is a reason to stop your program, especially if it has gone beyond the "he's touching me" stage to the slapping, hitting, pushing stage. Find the parent or caregiver of these children and immediately request that they be removed from your program. They are not only disrupting the program for others but creating a hazardous environment for all of the children.

3. A paper-shuffling adult is an annoyance, as is the mother who chooses your program to clean out her purse or balance her checkbook. Try to block these events out of your reality instead of saying anything to them or attempting to get their attention to show your displeasure. It is a lost cause

from the beginning.

4. Inattentive adults, however, are another problem entirely and could lead to more dire circumstances if left without attending to it. Try switching gears when this happens, and offer your entire group a participatory activity or story that begs their involvement without you having to directly request it.

5. Snoring adults, really loudly snoring adults, can easily throw you off. They can make you lose your place in your story precisely because you are not expecting to hear this sound in your purposely involving and entertaining program. Never take a sleeping adult personally. Chances are this is the one moment during their busy day when they don't have to be on and their system just turns off. While adult caregivers should never sleep on the job, let this one go and do the best you can to avoid thinking about the rudeness of it all.

If your carefully planned, age-specific story program contains children of either older or younger ages, you might encounter some disruptions while you are doing your best to focus on either those infants, toddlers, preschoolers, or primary level children. When this happens, it is best not to panic or become discouraged by what has quickly become a less-than-rewarding experience.

A recommended and logical way to avoid such problems is to make some sort of friendly announcement at the beginning of your program regarding behavior. Perhaps you might reiterate the age-specific nature of the program and ask those older children in the room to act as "helpers" for the smaller ones, thereby entrusting each older brother and sister with a task to occupy their attentions. Also consider inviting all of the people in the story program, children and adults alike, to assist you in making the space safe and comfortable for those around them by observing some "soft rules" such as no loud noises, no keys given to distract small children, no reading while the program is in progress, and no food or drink (which might make that child or parent the most popular one in the room and turn attention away from the program).

You might ask parents of younger children in programs structured for older ones to also consider the needs of those around them. A nice way of putting this is to gently let them know that you understand that their children or infants might have "changed their minds" about staying for the whole program, and if this occurs the parent should consider taking the child out of the room and browse at books instead, opting to try the program again another time. Offer the time-honored encouragement that there is no such thing as failure in story programs, only opportunities for further development.

Sometimes, however, the problem may not be with noisy or crying, running, jumping, screaming children, but with those who should know better—the grown-ups. If this is your situation, you must remember to handle the adults with aplomb, humor, and courtesy. Make a special announcement before the program, perhaps humorously, asking the adults to participate with their children to maximize both their enjoyment and experience. Remind the adults that their children mimic them in word and deed and stress the importance of setting a good example.

Often, the disruptive adults turn out to be those who have walked in late to the program and not heard your perfectly planned and politically correct announcement regarding appropriate behavior. You are not out of luck. Pick a moment in the program, perhaps at a break between a story and a transition activity, to reiterate your intentions regarding everyone having a good time by participating and listening. Even when it may be against your first inclination, make sure that you

direct these comments *to the entire group*, thereby avoiding embarrassing the offending adult by pointing your finger at them.

Generally speaking, adults who act inappropriately are not very happy about getting caught red-handed. They also detest having the attention turned toward them in group situations. Not only might you create a greater disturbance by singling out the adult offender, but you also might turn someone off to the library and the entire story program experience. In addition, you might inadvertently undermine that adult's authority with their child by making papa or mama the bad guy. Use your sense of humor to bring them back.

When all else fails, and no matter how frustrated you might become, or how much they ask for it, always remember a single rule of thumb: smile and be sweet.

Just when you thought you had done a fantastic job and everyone liked your program, parents took the time to come up to you and give you a lot of positive feedback and the children were leaving the room whistling your songs, a question will be posed to you, out of the blue, that makes you really stop and wonder if you were completely misunderstood after all.

Also, sometimes questions pop up during your program, right in the middle of your story, and you are unsure how to handle them so you simply ignore them. Questions such as "was that a true story?", "how much money do you make?", "are you married?", and the ever popular, "how old are you?" As long as these questions are posed by children, you don't have much to worry about. In fact, questions such as these offer you the opportunity to flex your quick wit and exercise your teasing skills. In most cases, and unless you are offended by the question, honesty is still the best policy.

There are quite literally dozens of responses to the question as to whether the story you just shared was true or not. Often the question is posed by the child who merely wants the reassurance that the tale was definitely invented so they won't have to worry about it happening to them. This is especially true after a scary story. Even young adults will want to know your opinion as to the veracity of the story, even as they scoff at the possibility that it could have happened.

You may approach the truth issue with humor, with a shoulder shrug, or with a serious discussion concerning possibilities. Whichever way you choose, try not to make your response sound too pat or rehearsed. Consider the answer as coming from your storytelling persona, not from the serious adult in you that feels like they must apologize for somehow misleading children into believing a far-fetched tale.

Try some of these answers on for size or invent your own. Either way, have fun with it!

- ✧ All stories have a thread of truth in them. The trick is to find the thread.
- ✧ Take care, if you do not believe this story, your ears will fall off.
- ✧ Truth and falsehood live in the same house, use the same door, and wipe their feet on the same rug.
- ✧ What, you don't believe me?
- ✧ It is the storyteller's job to tell the story. It is the listener's job to decide what is true and what is not.
- ✧ Yes, it's true. But I don't know if it actually happened.
- ✧ Some believe it to be true.

- ✧ The truth is for you to decide.
- ✧ That's the way I heard it and it sounded true to me!
- ✧ It never happened to me, but some people believe it to be true.
- ✧ That's what they say!
- ✧ What do you think?
- ✧ Ask your mother.
- ✧ I hear tell it's true, but I can't be sure.
- ✧ In the words of the great Robert Ripley, believe it or not!
- ✧ From Alice Kane in *The Dreamer Awakes*: "The dreamer awakes, The shadow goes by; When I tell you a tale, The tale is a lie. But ponder it well, Fair maiden, good youth: The tale is a lie, What it tells is the truth.

Take care yourself not to be the one who puts others on the spot by asking inappropriate questions of the children in your programs. Questions of a personal nature that involve information about their family or their feeling regarding their siblings, etc., are off limits, as are questions which might embarrass.

If you keep your questioning in your programs to a minimum you can't go wrong. Remember that asking questions, even simple ones like "what is your favorite food?" may be considered inappropriate to some of the cultures in the room. Always respect a child's wish not to answer and, to cover all bases, always offer the option of "passing" to a question in lieu of participating.

PART SIX

STORY PROGRAM SOURCES

CHAPTER NINETEEN

Program Planning Resources

The following professional bibliographies do not pretend to be exhaustive. They are selective and of necessity subjective. For information regarding primary level programming, please refer to individual storytelling sources and collections in chapter twenty. Likewise, most of the programming materials for preschoolers will be located in the flannel board section in the same chapter.

General Program Planning

Carlson, Ann D. *Early Childhood Literature Sharing Programs in Libraries*. Shoe String, 1985.

DeSalvo, Nancy N. *Beginning with Books: Library Programming for Infants, Toddlers, and Preschoolers*. Library Professional Publications, 1993.

DeWit, Dorothy. *Children's Faces Looking Up: Program Building for the Storyteller*. ALA, 1979.

Fiore, Carol. *Programming for Young Children: Birth through Age Five*. ALA, 1996.

First Steps to Literacy: Library Programs for Parents, Teachers, and Caregivers. ALA, 1990.

Greene, Ellin. *Books, Babies, and Libraries: Serving Infants, Toddlers, Their Parents and Caregivers*. ALA, 1991.

Harrington, Janice N. *Multiculturalism in Library Programs for Children*. ALA, 1994.

Jeffrey, Debby Ann. *Literate Beginnings: Programs for Babies and Toddlers*. ALA, 1995.

Johnson, Ferne, ed. *Start Early for an Early Start*. ALA, 1976.

Polkingharn, Anne T., and Catherine Toohey. *More Creative Encounters: Activities to Expand Children's Responses to Literature*. Libraries Unlimited, 1998.

Infant Programming

Ernst, Linda. *Lapsit Services for the Very Young Child: A How-to-do-it Manual*. Neal-Schuman, 1995.

Lamont, Priscilla. *Ring-a-Round-a-Rosy: Nursery Rhymes, Action Rhymes, and Lullabies*. Joy Street, 1990.

Marino, Jane. *Mother Goose Time: Library Programs for Babies and Their Caregivers*. H. W. Wilson, 1992.

Scott, Ann. *The Laughing Baby: Remembering Nursery Rhymes and Reasons*. Bergin & Garvey, 1987.

Story-Hoffman, Ru. *Nursery Rhyme Time*. Alleyside, 1996.

Williams, Jerry. *Here's a Ball for Baby: Finger Rhymes for Young Children*. Dial, 1987.

Williams, Sarah. *Round and Round the Garden*. Oxford University Press, 1983.

Wood, Jenny. *First Songs and Action Rhymes*. Maxwell Macmillan, 1990.

Toddler Programming

Brennan, Jan. *Treasured Time with Your Toddler: A Monthly Guide to Activities*. August House, 1991.

Briggs, Diane. *Toddler Storytime Programs*. Scarecrow, 1993.

Davis, Robin Works. *Toddle on Over: Developing Infant & Toddler Literature Programs*. Alleyside, 1998.

Nichols, Judy. *Storytimes for Two-Year-Olds*. 2nd ed. ALA, 1998.

Sierra, Judy. *Mother Goose's Playhouse: Toddler Tales and Nursery Rhymes with Patterns for Puppets and Feltboards*. Bob Kaminski Media Arts, 1994.

Warren, Jean. *Toddler Theme-a-Saurus: The Great Big Book of Toddler Teaching Themes*. Totline, 1991.

Preschooler Programming

Briggs, Diane. *52 Programs for Preschoolers: The Librarian's Year-Round Planner*. ALA, 1997.

Kladder, Jeri. *Story Hour: 55 Preschool Programs for Public Libraries*. McFarland, 1995.

MacDonald, Margaret Read. *Booksharing: 101 Programs to Use with Preschoolers*. Library Professional Publications, 1988.

Moore, Vardine. *Preschool Story Hour*. Scarecrow, 1972.

Family Programming

Pellowiski, Anne. *The Family Storytelling Handbook*. Macmillan, 1987.

Reid, Rob. *Family Storytime: Twenty-Four Creative Programs for All Ages*. ALA, 1999.

CHAPTER TWENTY

Storytelling and Storysharing Resources

Storytelling Resources

General Storytelling Guides

Bauer, Caroline Feller. *The New Handbook for Storytellers*. ALA, 1995.

Bone, Woutrina Agatha. *Children's Stories and How to Tell Them*. Gale, 1971.

Breneman, Lucille N. *Once Upon a Time: A Storytelling Handbook*. Nelson-Hall, 1983.

Bruchac, Joseph. *Tell Me a Tale: A Book about Storytelling*. Harcourt Brace, 1997.

Cabral, Len. *Len Cabral's Storytelling Book*. Neal-Schuman, 1997.

Carlson, Bernice Wells. *Listen! And Help Tell the Story*. Abingdon, 1965.

Colwell, Eileen. *Storytelling*. Bodley Head, 1980.

Cooper, Cathie. *Storyteller's Cornucopia*. 2nd ed. Alleyside, 1998.

Cullum, Carolyn. *The Storytime Sourcebook*. Neal-Schuman, 1990.

Dailey, Sheila. *Putting the World in a Nutshell: The Art of the Formula Tale*. H. W. Wilson, 1994.

Davis, Donald. *Telling Your Own Stories: For Family and Classroom, Storytelling, Public Speaking, and Personal Journaling*. August House, 1993.

deVos, Gail. *Storytelling for Young Adults: Techniques and Treasury*. Libraries Unlimited, 1991.

DeWit, Dorothy. *Children's Faces Looking Up: Program Building for the Storyteller*. ALA, 1979.

Farrell, Catharine. *Word Weaving: A Guide to Storytelling*. Zellerbach, 1983.

Garrity, Linda K. *The Gingerbread Guide: Using Folktales with Young Children*. Scott, Foresman and Company, 1987.

Gillard, Marni. *Storyteller, Storyteacher: Discovering the Power of Storytelling for Teaching and Living*. Stenhouse, 1996.

Greene, Ellin. *Storytelling: Art and Technique*. 3rd ed. Bowker, 1996.

Lerach, Helen. *Creative Storytimes: A Resource Book for Childcare Workers*. Regina Public Library (Canada), 1993.

Lipman, Doug. *The Storytelling Coach*. August House, 1995.

Livo, Norma. *Storytelling Folklore Sourcebook*. Libraries Unlimited, 1988.

Livo, Norma, and Sandra A. Rietz. *Storytelling Activities*. Libraries Unlimited, 1987.

———. *Storytelling Process and Practice*. Libraries Unlimited, 1986.

MacDonald, Margaret Read. *The Parent's Guide to Storytelling*. HarperCollins, 1995.

———. *The Storyteller's Start-Up Book: Finding, Learning, Performing, and Using Folktales*. August House, 1993.

———. *The Storyteller's Sourcebook: A Subject, Title and Motif Index to Folklore Collections for Children*. Gale, 1993.

Maguire, Jack. *Creative Storytelling: Choosing, Inventing, and Sharing Tales for Children*. Yellow Moon Press, 1992.

Mooney, Bill, and David Holt. *The Storyteller's Guide: Storytellers Share Advice for the Classroom, Boardroom, Showroom, Podium, Pulpit, and Center Stage*. August House, 1996.

Moore, Robin. *Awakening the Hidden Storyteller: How to Build a Storytelling Tradition in Your Family*. Shambhala, 1991.

Painter, William M. *Storytelling with Music, Puppets, and Arts for Libraries and Classrooms*. Library Professional Publications, 1994.

Pellowski, Anne. *The Storytelling Handbook: A Young People's Collection of Unusual Tales and Helpful Hints on How to Tell Them*. Simon & Schuster, 1995.

———. *The World of Storytelling*. H. W. Wilson, 1990.

Ross, Ramon Royal. *Storyteller*. August House, 1996.

Sawyer, Ruth. *The Way of the Storyteller*. Viking, 1962.

Schimmel, Nancy. *Just Enough to Make a Story: A Sourcebook for Storytelling*. Sisters Choice Press, 1992.

Sierra, Judy. *Storytellers' Research Guide: Folktales, Myths, Legends*. Folkprint, 1996.

Zipes, Jack. *Creative Storytelling: Building Community, Changing Lives*. Routledge, 1995.

Ziskind, S. *Telling Stories to Children*. H. W. Wilson, 1976.

Story Collections

Allison, Christine. *I'll Tell You a Story, I'll Sing You a Song: A Parent's Guide to the Fairy Tales, Fables, Songs, and Rhymes of Childhood*. Delacorte, 1987.

Ausubel, Nathan. *A Treasury of Jewish Folklore*. Crown, 1975.

Baltuck, Naomi. *Apples from Heaven: Multicultural Folktales about Stories and Storytelling*. Linnet, 1995.

Barchers, Suzanne. *Wise Women Folk and Fairy Tales from Around the World*. Libraries Unlimited, 1990.

Best-Loved Stories Told at the National Storytelling Festival. National Storytelling Press, 1991.

Brenner, Anita. *The Boy Who Could Do Anything and Other Mexican Folktales*. Shoe String, 1992.

Chase, Richard. *Grandfather Tales*. Houghton, 1948.

———. *The Jack Tales*. Houghton, 1943.

Cole, Joanna. *Best-Loved Folktales of the World*. Doubleday, 1982.

DeSpain, Pleasant. *Eleven Nature Tales: A Multicultural Journey*. August House, 1996.

———. *Thirty-Three Multicultural Tales to Tell*. August House, 1993.

———. *Twenty-Two Splendid Tales to Tell from Around the World, Volume 1*. August House, 1994.

———. *Twenty-Two Splendid Tales to Tell from Around the World, Volume 2*. August House, 1994.

Fogey, William W. *Campfire Tales: Ghoulies, Ghosties, and Long-Leggety Beasties*. ICS, 1989.

Forest, Heather. *Wonder Tales from Around the World*. August House, 1995.

Hamilton, Martha. *Stories in My Pocket: Tales Kids Can Tell*. Fulcrum, 1996.

Hamilton, Virginia. *The People Could Fly: American Black Folktales*. Knopf, 1985.

Holt, David, and Bill Mooney. *Ready-To-Tell Tales: Sure-Fire Stories from America's Favorite Storytellers*. August House, 1994.

Irving, Jan, and Robin Currie. *Glad Rags: Stories and Activities Featuring Clothes for Children*. Libraries Unlimited, 1987.

———. *Mudluscious: Stories and Activities Featuring Food for Preschool Children*. Libraries Unlimited, 1986.

Kronberg, Ruthhilde. *Clever Folk: Tales of Wisdom, Wit, and Wonder*. Libraries Unlimited, 1993.

Leach, Maria. *The Thing At the Foot of the Bed and Other Scary Tales*. Collins World, 1959.

Lester, Julius. *How Many Spots Does a Leopard Have? and Other Tales*. Scholastic, 1989.

Lyon, Mary E. *Raw Head, Bloody Bones: African-American Tales of the Supernatural*. Scribners, 1991.

MacDonald, Margaret Read. *Look Back and See: Twenty Lively Tales for Gentle Tellers*. H. W. Wilson, 1991.

———. *Twenty Tellable Tales: A Collection of Audience Participation Folktales for the Beginning Storyteller*. H. W. Wilson, 1986.

———. *When the Lights Go Out: Twenty Scary Tales to Tell*. H. W. Wilson, 1990.

Marsh, Valerie. *Terrific Tales to Tell: From the Storytelling Tradition*. Alleyside, 1997.

———. *A Treasury of Trickster Tales*. Alleyside, 1997.

McKinnon, Elizabeth. *Teeny-Tiny Folktales*. Warren Publishing House, 1987.

McKissack. *A Piece of the Wind: And Other Stories to Tell*. Harper & Row, 1990.

Pellowksi, Anne. *The Story Vine: A Source Book of Unusual and Easy-to-Tell Stories from Around the World*. Collier MacMillan, 1984.

Reaver, J. Russell. *Florida Folktales*. University of Florida Press, 1987.

Roberts, P. *Multicultural Friendship Stories and Activities for Children Ages 5-15*. Scarecrow, 1997.

Schram, Peninnah. *Jewish Stories One Generation Tells Another*. Jason Aronson, 1987.

Schwartz, Alvin. *All of Our Noses Are Here and Other Noodle Tales*. Harper & Row, 1985.

———. *Tales of Trickery from the Land of Spoof*. Farrar, Straus & Girioux, 1985.

———. *Whoppers: Tall Tales and Other Lies*. Lippincott, 1975.

Scott, D. *Campfire Stories: More Things That Go Bump in the Night*. ICS, 1995.

Sierra, Judy. *Twice Upon a Time: Stories to Tell, Retell, Act Out, and Write About*. H. W. Wilson, 1989.

Sierra, Judy, and Robert Kaminski. *Multicultural Folktales: Stories to Tell Young Children*. Oryx, 1991.

Smith, Jimmy Neil, ed. *Homespun: Tales from America's Favorite Storytellers*. Crown, 1988.

Spagnoli, Cathy. *A Treasury of Asian Stories and Activities: A Guide for Schools and Libraries*. Alleyside, 1998.

Wolkstein, Diane, and Elsa Henriquez. *The Magic Orange Tree: And Other Haitian Folktales*. Schocken Books, 1997 (reprint).

Yolen, Jane. *Favorite Folktales from Around the World*. Pantheon, 1986.

Young, Richard, and Judy Dockrey Young. *African-American Folktales for Young Readers: Including Familiar Stories from Africa and African-American Storytellers*. August House, 1993.

———. *Favorite Scary Stories of American Children*. August House, 1990.

———. *Race with Buffalo and Other Native American Stories for Young Readers*. August House, 1994.

Zipes, Jack. *The Complete Fairy Tales of the Brothers Grimm*. Bantam, 1987.

Flannel Board Storysharing

Anderson, Paul S. *Storytelling with the Flannelboard*. Part I. Denison, 1963.

———. *Storytelling with the Flannelboard*. Part II. Denison, 1970.

Bay, Jeanette Graham. *A Treasury of Flannelboard Stories*. Alleyside, 1995.

Briggs, Diane. *Flannel Board Fun: A Collection of Stories, Songs, and Poems*. Scarecrow, 1992.

Carlson, Ann D. *Flannelboard Stories for Infants and Toddlers*. ALA, 1999.

Chadwick, Roxanne. *Felt Board Story Times*. Alleyside, 1997.

Hartwig, Vicki. *Science Flannel Board Stories for Primary Grades*. Denison, 1974.

Hicks, Doris. *Flannelboard Classic Tales*. ALA, 1997.

Krepelin, Elizabeth, and Bonnie Mae Smith. *Ready-to-Use Flannel Board Stories, Figures, and Activities for ESL Children*. Center for Applied Research in Education, 1995.

Noel, Karen. *Cut and Color Flannel Board Stories: Books 1 and 2*. Denison, 1985.

Peterson, Carolyn Sue, and Ann D. Fenton. *Christmas Story Programs*. Moonlight Press, 1981.

Peterson, Carolyn S., and Christina Sterchele. *Story Program Activities for Older Children*. Moonlight Press, 1987.

Scott, Louise Binder, and J. J. Thompson. *Rhymes for Fingers and Flannel Boards*. Denison, 1984.

Sierra, Judy. *The Flannel Board Storytelling Book*. H. W. Wilson, 1987.

———. *Multicultural Folktales for the Feltboard and Reader's Theater*. Oryx Press, 1996.

Taylor, Frances S., and Gloria G. Vaughn. *Flannel Board Storybook*. Humanities, 1986.

Wilmes, Liz and Dick. *2's Experience Felt Board Fun*. Building Blocks, 1994.

Puppetry

Anderson, Dee. *Amazingly Easy Puppet Plays*. ALA, 1997.

Astell-Burt, Caroline. *Puppetry for Mentally Handicapped People*. Souvenir Press, 1981.

Bauer, Caroline Feller. *Leading Kids into Books Through Puppets*. ALA, 1997.

Briggs, Diane. *101 Fingerplays, Stories, and Songs to Use with Finger Puppets*. ALA, 1999.

Champlin, Connie. *Puppetry and Creative Dramatics in Storytelling*. Nancy Renfro Studios, 1980.

———. *Storytelling with Puppets*, 2nd ed. ALA, 1998.

Gates, Frieda. *Easy-to-Make Puppets*. Prentice-Hall, 1981

———. *Glove, Mitten and Sock Puppets*. Walker, 1978.

Hunt, Tamara, and Nancy Renfro. *Puppetry in Early Childhood Education*. Nancy Renfro Studios, 1982.

Marsh, Valerie. *Puppet Tales*. Alleyside, 1998.

Painter, William M. *Story Hours with Puppets and Other Props*. Shoe String, 1990.

Renfro, Nancy. *A Puppet Corner in Every Library*. Renfro Studios, 1978.

Roberts, Lynda. *Mitt Magic: Fingerplays for Finger Puppets*. Gryphon, 1987.

Ross, Laura. *Finger Puppets: Easy to Make and Fun to Use*. Lothrop, Lee & Shepard, 1971.

———. *Hand Puppets: How to Make and Use Them*. Lothrop, Lee & Shepard, 1969.

Sims, Judy. *Puppets for Dreaming and Scheming: A Puppet Source Book*. Learning Works, 1988.

VanSchuyver, Jan. *Storytelling Made Easy with Puppets*. Oryx, 1993.

Warren, Jean. *1, 2, 3 Puppets*. Warren, 1989.

Wright, Denise Anton. *One-Person Puppet Plays*. Libraries Unlimited, 1990.

Reading Aloud

Barton, Bob. *Tell Me Another: Storytelling and Reading Aloud at Home, at School, and in the Community*. Pembroke, 1986.

Bauer, Caroline Feller. *Celebrations: Read-Aloud Holiday and Theme Book Programs*. H. W. Wilson, 1985.

———. *Read for the Fun of It: Active Programming with Books for Children*. H. W. Wilson, 1992.

Cole, Joanna et al., eds. *The Read-Aloud Treasury*. Doubleday, 1988.

Kimmel, Margaret Mary. *For Reading Out Loud! A Guide to Sharing Books with Children*. Delacorte, 1988.

Lima, Carolyn W. *A to Zoo: Subject Access to Children's Picture Books*. 4th ed. Bowker, 1993.

Polette, Nancy. *E is for Everybody: A Manual for Bringing Fine Picture Books into the Hands and Hearts of Children*. Scarecrow, 1976.

Read-Aloud Rhymes for the Very Young. Knopf, 1986.

Richey, Virginia H., and Katharyn E. Puckett. *Wordless/Almost Wordless Picture Books: A Guide*. Libraries Unlimited, 1992.

Sitarz, Paula Gaj. *More Picture Book Story Hours: From Parties to Pets*. Libraries Unlimited, 1990.

———. *Picture Book Story Hours: From Birthdays to Bears*. Libraries Unlimited, 1987.

———. *Story Time Sampler: Read Alouds, Booktalks, and Activities for Children*. Libraries Unlimited, 1997.

Trelease, Jim. *The Read-Aloud Handbook*. Rev. ed. of *The New Read-Aloud Handbook*. Penguin, 1995.

Other Ways to Tell Stories

Albright, Nancy. *Do Tell: Holiday Draw-n-Tell Stories*. Moonlight Press, 1989.

Bauer, Caroline Feller. *Leading Kids to Books through Magic*. ALA, 1996.

Druce, Arden. *Chalk Talk Stories*. Scarecrow, 1993.

———. *Paper Bag Puppets*. Scarecrow, 1998.

Kipnis, Lois, and Marilyn Gilbat. *Have You Ever . . .: Bringing Literature to Life through Creative Dramatics*. Alleyside, 1993.

Liptak, Karen. *North American Indian Sign Language*. Watts, 1990.

Mallett, Jerry, and Marion R. Bartch. *Stories to Draw*. Freline, 1982.

Mallett, Jerry J., and Timothy S. Ervin. *More Stories to Draw*. Alleyside, 1990.

Marsh, Valerie. *Beyond Words: Great Stories for Hand and Voice*. Alleyside, 1995.

———. *Mystery-Fold: Stories to Tell, Draw, and Fold*. Alleyside, 1993.

———. *Paper-Cutting from A to Z*. Alleyside, 1992.

———. *Paper-Cutting Stories for Holidays and Special Events*. Alleyside, 1994.

———. *Story Puzzles: Tales in the Tangram Tradition*. Alleyside, 1996.

———. *A Storyteller's Sampler*. Alleyside, 1996.

———. *Storytelling with Shapes and Numbers*. Alleyside, 1999.

———. *Terrific Tales to Tell: From the Storyknifing Tradition*. Alleyside, 1997.

Newman, Frederick R. *Zounds! The Kid's Guide to Sound Making*. Random House, 1983.

Nursery Rhymes from Mother Goose in Signed English. Gallaudet College Press, 1972.

Olson, Margaret. *Tell and Draw Stories*. Arts and Crafts, 1963.

Pflomm, Phyllis Noe. *Chalk in Hand: The Draw and Tell Book*. Scarecrow, 1986.

Warren, Jean. *Cut and Tell Stories for Fall (Winter and Spring)*. Totline, 1984.

CHAPTER TWENTY-ONE

Participation and Wigglebreak Resources

Fingerplays

Brown, Marc. *Hand Rhymes*. Dutton, 1985.

——. *Play Rhymes*. Dutton, 1987.

Cole, Joanna, and Stephanie Calmenson. *The Eentsy, Weentsy Spider: Fingerplays and Action Rhymes*. Morrow Junior Books, 1991.

Defty, Jeff. *Creative Fingerplays & Action Rhymes: An Index and Guide to Their Use*. Oryx, 1992.

Delamar, Gloria T. *Children's Counting-Out Rhymes, Fingerplays, Jump-Rope, and Bounce Ball Chants and Other Rhythms*. McFarland, 1983.

Dowell, Ruth I. *Move over Mother Goose: Fingerplays, Activity Verses, and Funny Rhymes*. Gryphon, 1994.

Gawron, Marlene. *Busy Bodies: Finger Plays and Action Rhymes*. Moonlight Press, 1985.

Graham, Terry Lynne. *Fingerplays and Rhymes for Always and Sometimes*. Humanities, 1984.

Grayson, Marion F. *Let's Do Fingerplays*. Luce, 1962.

Lohnes, Marilyn. *Finger Folk*. Alleyside, 1999.

Matterson, Elizabeth. *Games for the Very Young: Finger Plays and Nursery Rhymes*. American Heritage Press, 1971.

Ring a Ring O'Roses: Finger Plays for Preschool Children. 10th ed. Flint Public Library (Michigan), 1996.

Roberts, Lynda. *Mitt Magic: Finger Plays for Finger Puppets*. Gryphon, 1985.

Schiller, Pam, and Thomas Moore. *Where Is Thumbkin? 500 Activities to Use with Songs You Already Know*. Gryphon, 1993.

Wilmes, Liz, and Dick Wilmes. *2's Experience Fingerplays*. Building Blocks, 1994.

Wirth, Marian, et al. *Musical Games, Fingerplays, and Rhythmic Activities for Early Childhood*. Parker, 1983.

Songs and Singing Activities

Delacre, Lulu, ed. *Arroz Con Leche: Popular Songs and Rhymes from Latin America*. Scholastic, 1989.

Fink, Cathy. *Grandma Slid Down the Mountain.* Rounder Records, 1984 (audio cassette).

———. *When the Rain Comes Down.* Rounder Records, 1988 (audio cassette).

Glazer, Tom. *Do Your Ears Hang Low? Fifty More Musical Fingerplays with Piano Arrangements and Guitar Chords.* Doubleday, 1980.

———. *Eye Winker, Tom Tinker, Chin Chopper: Fifty Musical Fingerplays with Piano Arrangements and Guitar Chords.* Doubleday, 1973.

———. *Music for Ones and Twos: Songs and Games for the Very Young Child.* Doubleday, 1983.

Guthrie, Woody. *Songs to Grow on for Mother and Child.* Smithsonian Folkways, 1991 (audio cassette).

Hammett, Carol. *Toddlers on Parade: Musical Exercises for Infants and Toddlers.* Kimbo Educational, 1985 (audio cassette).

Hart, Jane. *Singing Bee! A Collection of Favorite Children's Songs.* Lothrop, 1982.

Jenkins, Ella. *African-American Folk Rhythms.* Smithsonian Folkways, 1995 (audio cassette).

———. *Call and Response.* Smithsonian Folkways, 1990 (audio cassette).

———. *Counting Games and Rhythms for the Little Ones.* Smithsonian Folkways, 1990 (audio cassette).

———. *Ella Jenkins Song Book for Children.* Oak, 1966.

———. *Growing Up with Ella Jenkins: Rhythms, Songs, and Rhymes.* Smithsonian Folkways, 1990 (audio cassette).

———. *Jambo and Other Call and Response Songs and Chants.* Smithsonian Folkways, 1990 (audio cassette).

———. *Multicultural Children's Songs.* Smithsonian Folkways, 1995 (audio cassette).

———. *My Street Begins At My House: And Other Songs and Rhythms from the "Me Too" Show.* Smithsonian Folkways, 1989 (audio cassette).

——— *Nursery Rhymes: Rhyming and Remembering for Young Children and for Older Girls and Boys with Special Language Needs.* Smithsonian Folkways, 1974 (audio cassette).

———. *Play Your Instruments and Make a Pretty Sound.* Smithsonian Folkways, 1990 (audio cassette).

———. *Rhythm and Game Songs for the Little Ones.* Smithsonian Folkways, 1990 (audio cassette).

———. *Rhythms of Childhood.* Smithsonian Folkways, 1989 (audio cassette).

———. *Songs and Rhythms from Near and Far.* Smithsonian Folkways, 1992 (audio cassette).

———. *Songs, Rhythms & Chants for the Dance.* Smithsonian Folkways, 1992 (audio cassette).

———. *This-a-Way, That-a-Way.* Smithsonian Folkways, 1989 (audio cassette).

———. *Travelin' with Ella Jenkins: A Bilingual Journey.* Smithsonian Folkways, 1989 (audio cassette).

————. *You'll Sing a Song and I'll Sing a Song*. Smithsonian Folkways, 1989 (audio cassette).

Krull, Kathleen. *Gonna Sing My Head Off: American Folk Songs for Children*. Knopf, 1992.

Marino, Jane. *Sing Us a Story: Using Music in Preschool and Family Storytimes*. H. W. Wilson, 1994.

McGrath, Bob, and Katharine Smithrim. *Songs and Games for Toddlers*. Kids' Records, 1985 (audio cassette).

Nelson, Esther L. *Singing and Dancing Games for the Very Young*. Sterling, 1977.

Painter, William M. *Musical Story Hours: Using Music with Storytelling and Puppetry*. Library Professional Publications, 1989.

Raffi. *Corner Grocery Store and Other Singable Songs*. Troubadour Records, 1979 (audio cassette).

————. *Everything Grows*. A & M, 1987 (audio cassette).

————. *One Light, One Sun*. MCA Records, 1985 (audio cassette).

————. *The Raffi Everything Grows Songbook*. Crown, 1989.

————. *The Raffi Singable Songbook*. Crown, 1980.

————. *Rise and Shine*. Troubadour Records, 1982 (audio cassette).

————. *The 2nd Raffi Songbook*. Crown, 1986.

Seeger, Pete. *Birds, Beasts, Bugs, and Little Fishes*. Smithsonian Folkways, 1991 (audio cassette).

Sherman, Josepha, and T.K.F. Weisskopf. *Greasy Grimy Gopher Guts*. August House, 1995.

Simon, Willima L., ed. *The Reader's Digest Children's Songbook*. Reader's Digest, 1985.

Stewart, Georgiana Liccione. *My Teddy Bear and Me: Musical Play Activities for Infants and Toddlers*. Kimbo Educational, 1984 (audio cassette).

Warren, Jean. *Piggyback Songs for Infants and Toddlers*. Warren, 1985.

Yolen, Jane. *The Lap-Time Song and Play Book*. Harcourt, 1989.

Physical Activities, Games, and Word Play

Arnold, Arnold. *The Big Book of Tongue Twisters and Double Talk*. Random, 1964.

Baltuck, Naomi. *Crazy Gibberish*. Linnet, 1993.

Cole, Joanna. *Anna Banana: 101 Jump-Rope Rhymes*. Morrow Junior Books, 1989.

Colgin, Mary Lou. *One Potato, Two Potato, Three Potato, Four: 165 Chants for Children*. Gryphon, 1988.

Hall, Katy, and Lisa Eisenberg. *Spacy Riddles*. Dial, 1992.

Hays, Sarah. *Stamp Your Feet*. Lothrop, 1988.

Johnstone, Michael. *1,000 Crazy Jokes for Kids.* Ballantine, 1987.

Keller, Charles. *Tongue Twisters.* Simon & Schuster, 1989.

Kessler, Leonard. *Old Turtle's 90 Knock-Knocks, Jokes, and Riddles.* Greenwillow, 1991.

Lee, Carol K. *57 Games to Play in the Library or Classroom.* Alleyside, 1997.

Lee, Carol K., and Janet Langford. *Storytime Companion: Learning Games for Schools and Libraries.* Alleyside, 1998.

Lipman, Doug. *Storytelling Games: Creative Activities for Language, Communication, and Composition Across the Curriculum.* Oryx, 1995.

Potts, Cheryl. *Poetry Fun by the Ton by Jack Prelutsky.* Alleyside, 1995.

———. *Poetry Galore and More with Shel Silverstein.* Alleyside, 1993.

———. *Poetry Play Any Day with Jane Yolen.* Alleyside, 1999.

———. *Poetry Time with Dr. Seuss Rhyme.* Alleyside, 1997.

Rosenbloom, Joseph. *World's Toughest Tongue Twisters.* Sterling, 1986.

Schwartz, Alvin. *Cross Your Fingers, Spit in Your Hat: Superstitions and Other Beliefs.* Lippincott, 1974.

———. *Tomfoolery: Trickery and Foolery with Words.* Lippincott, 1973.

———. *Wisecracks: Jokes and Jests from American Folklore.* Lippincott, 1973.

Sierra, Judy. *Children's Traditional Games: Games from 137 Countries and Cultures.* Oryx, 1995.

Silberg, Jackie. *Games to Play with Toddlers.* Gryphon, 1993.

———. *Games to Play with Two Year Olds.* Gryphon, 1994.

———. *More Games to Play with Toddlers.* Gryphon, 1996.

Sloane, Paul. *Lateral Thinking Puzzlers.* Sterling, 1992.

Smith, William Jay, and Carol Ra, eds. *Behind the King's Kitchen: A Roster of Rhyming Riddles.* Wordsong, 1992.

Tashijian, Virginia A. *Juba This and Juba That: Story Hour Stretches for Large or Small Groups.* Little, Brown, 1969.

———. *With a Deep Sea Smile: Story Hour Stretches for Large and Small Groups.* Little, Brown, 1974.

Wirth, Marian, et al., eds. *Musical Games, Fingerplays and Rhythmic Activities for Early Childhood.* Parker, 1983.

INDEX

INDEX

319

ABOUT THE AUTHORS

Carolyn S. Peterson, retired head of the children's department at the Orange County Library System in Florida, holds an M.A. in librarianship from the University of Denver and an M.A. in counseling psychology from Goddard College in Vermont. She is the recipient of the American Library Association's Grolier Award and has published numerous books on children's programming as well as several seminal reference works. She is the author of *Story Program Activities for Older Children* (1987) and *Story Programs: A Source Book of Materials* (1980), and the co-author of *Reference Books for Children*, 4th ed. (1992), *Index to Children's Songs: A Title, First Line, and Subject Index* (1979), and *Christmas Story Programs* (1981), all with Ann Fenton.

Ann D. Fenton has been a children's librarian for twenty-five years and holds an M.L.S. from Florida State University. She is the co-author (with Carolyn S. Peterson) of several significant reference works and children's programming guides, including *Reference Books for Children*, 4th ed. (1992), *Index to Children's Songs: A Title, First Line, and Subject Index* (1979), and *Christmas Story Programs* (1981). Currently, she is the branch manager of the South Orange Library in the Orange County Library System in Florida.

ABOUT THE EDITOR

Dr. Stefani Koorey worked for eight years as a children's librarian, professional storyteller, and booktalker at the Orange County Library System in Florida. In these capacities she performed story-telling programs for infants, toddlers, preschoolers, and primary level children as well as assembly-type booktalks to all Orange County middle school students. She holds an M.A. in theatre, an M.F.A. in theatre management, and earned a doctorate in theatre history and dramatic criticism from Penn State University in 1997. She is a regular contributing reviewer for *VOYA* (Voice of Youth Advocates) and is currently teaching theatre and writing non-fiction.